THE

MW00477559

The White Devil

THE WEREWOLF IN EUROPEAN CULTURE

MATTHEW BERESFORD

REAKTION BOOKS

Published by Reaktion Books Ltd
33 Great Sutton Street
London EC1V 0DX, UK
www.reaktionbooks.co.uk

First published 2013

Copyright © Matthew Beresford 2013

All rights reserved
No part of this publication may be reproduced, stored in a retrieval
system, or transmitted, in any form or by any means, electronic,
mechanical, photocopying, recording or otherwise, without the prior
permission of the publishers.

Printed and bound in Great Britain
by Bell & Bain, Glasgow

A catalogue record for this book is available from the British Library.

ISBN 978 1 78023 188 4

Contents

Illustration from Guillaume de Palerne.

Introduction

Once upon a time wolves and men lived alongside one another,
each respecting and benefiting from the other's way of life.
Those days are gone, and ... we are poorer for that.
Shaun Ellis, *The Man Who Lives with Wolves*

This book is not just about werewolves, it is about wolves and it is about Man. A long time ago, men sought to become wolves, and when they succeeded, they became cursed and wished they were wolves no longer. In popular lore, it is said that a man is transformed into a werewolf on the night of a full moon. As he undergoes the physical change into beast, he is beset by murderous urges. A silver bullet would be the only way to stop the man-beast from killing.

Contemporary preconceptions of the werewolf are predominantly formed by film productions. Indeed, werewolves remain a prolific and marketable theme in popular culture, arguably prompted by Stephanie Meyer's recent *Twilight Saga* which has undoubtedly reignited literary and filmic interest.

This book, however, is more concerned with the origins of the werewolf myth. It also investigates why the man-wolf has featured in almost every period of human history and prehistory. As we shall see, Romans and Greeks were cursed by the man-wolf, Vikings revered him, medieval peasants feared him and witches tried to control him. Before considering the extensive European evidence available on the werewolf , we must first consider what exactly this 'werewolf' is. In her 2006 book on werewolves, Chantal Bourgault du Coudray suggests that a werewolf is 'a human being who changes into a wolf',[1] but here we will examine whether this 'change' is physical or merely metaphorical.

Although it is claimed that 'No rational human being today believes that it is physically possible for a human being to be metamorphosed into a wolf, into any animal, for that matter',[2] throughout history, the very opposite has been true. The Sufic scholar Idries Shah suggested that

> most of what is taught and written about esotericism is actually the broken fossilized remains of once-living schools. We study the bones of the ancient esoteric philosophies; the oral traditions, and especially the practical, experiential traditions, have been lost, or nearly so.[3]

The deep-rooted beliefs, fears, superstitions and religious ideas of the past can guide us to an understanding of the werewolf as a modern myth. In *The Universal Kinship,* John Howard Moore suggested that we should 'label beings by what they are, by the souls that are in them and the deeds they do'.[4] My Part One adopts Moore's framework to investigate the 'guises' of the werewolf and considers examples of man emulating the wolf to try to acquire a version of his power, cunning and strength. Part Two explores links with the devil and the dark arts – an angle observed by Ralph Waldo Emerson's study *Demonology* (published in 1877): 'these fables are our own thoughts carried out. What keeps these wild tales in circulation for thousands of years? What but the wild fact to which they suggest some approximation of theory.'[5] It was the devil who conjured up such 'wild facts', Emerson and many others argued.

The reasons for the apparent perpetuation of the werewolf myth in the popular psyche are considered in Part Three. These are viewed in tandem with the notion that contemporary culture continues to expand its fascination with the supernatural through the werewolf myth, despite the abundance of scientific facts disproving the existence of werewolves:

> we must speak here of lycanthropy, or the nocturnal transformation of men into wolves, histories so well substantiated that sceptical science has had to recourse to furious mania

Woodcut by
Lucas Cranach
the Elder, 1512.

and to masquerading as animals for explanations. But such
hypotheses are puerile and explain nothing.[6]

If the werewolf is a 'primitive psychological mechanism to escape the
real violence in contemporary society',[7] we have an early indicator
of why our interest and willingness to believe in a man-beast pre-
vails. But why is it a wolf, and not, say, a monkey, that should be the
animal through which human transformative fantasies are chanelled
and fetishized? Part One will address the role of the wolf as 'totem'.

According to folklore and superstition and as defined lexically
then, a 'werewolf' is variously:

Someone who, in stories, changes into a wolf at the time of
the full moon.[8]

In folklore a person who changes for periods of time into a
wolf, typically when there is a full moon.[9]

In folklore and superstition a human being who has changed into a wolf, or is capable of assuming the form of a wolf, while retaining human intelligence.[10]

Each of these dictionary definitions pinpoints a 'werewolf' as a human being who has undergone a *physical* transformation into a wolf, whilst two entries attribute this to lunar workings. The appearance of a full moon, according to more contemporary folklore, turns men into werewolves. Yet historically, human transformation into canine form is exacted by the corporeal application of a magic ointment:

> the *were-wolves* are certaine sorcerers, who having annoynted their bodyes, with an ointment which they make by the instinct of the devil; and putting on a certaine inchanted girdel, do not only unto the view of others seeme as wolves, but to their own thinking have both the shape and nature of wolves, so long as they weare the said girdel. And they do dispose themselves as very wolves; in worrying and killing moste of humane creatures.[11]

In *A Restitution of Decayed Intelligence* (1605), Richard Rowlands advances that the man who has 'become' a werewolf has undergone a mental transformation only; others merely perceive his actions to be *wolflike*. Thus the 'transformed' man remains human but is made delirious by the stupefying ointment.

The eighth-century apostle St Boniface, patron saint of Germany and Church reformer, wrote of a '*fictos lupos*' (a fear of wolves) within society. Whether this is a fear of actual wolves or werewolves, we cannot be sure, but the occultist Montague Summers claimed that from '*fictos lupos*', and thus 'fear-wolf' or perhaps 'beware-wolf', stems the term 'werewolf'.[12] Summers also related that he had heard the term 'werewolf' as a description of a man using sorcery who had attacked sheep and torn out their throats in a human-canine transformation. The technical term for a werewolf is a 'lycanthrope', from the Greek *lykos* (wolf) and *anthropos* (human), which combine to form 'wolf-man'. In medical parlance, 'lycanthropy' today

Anglo-Saxon silver
sceat, *c.* 710, showing
a coiled wolf design.

defines a condition whereby the patient believes him- or herself to
be a wolf. The Norse term for the werewolf beast is *vargr* (echoed
in the Anglo-Saxon term *earg*), meaning 'restless'. Its meaning is
retained in *var-ulf* in Danish, and *garou* in French (the full term is
loup-garou or werewolf). From the Norse and Danish terms, we
could suggest 'restless-wolf', whilst the French evidently considered
the *loup-garou* as a devil, and the Anglo-Saxon meaning referred to an
'evil man' or 'scoundrel' (*wearg*) and sometimes an 'outlaw'. In Norman
times, criminals were often damned to be *wargus esto*, – or 'an outlaw'. However, none of these explanations comes particularly close
to the concept of the modern werewolf. The English word *were* (that
is, were-wolf), however, seems closest to the original meaning.

The English antiquarian Algernon Herbert (1792–1855) wrote
at length on this matter in his *Letter to Lord Cawdor* of 1831. He
argued that *were* is actually a Low Dutch word (*werre*) meaning
'war' and it is from this that the French word *guerre* (war) derives.
Chaucer uses the word in his poem *Hypermnestra* when he writes
how 'The drede of death doith her so much woe, That thrice doune
she fell, in soche a were, She rist her up, and stakereth here and
there'.[13] Here Chaucer uses it to mean 'a confusion of the mind'.
In *Romaunt of the Rose* the word is employed to mean 'trouble', which
is a more or less direct translation of the French term *guerre*.[14] In

the the following year, Herbert continued his theory on the word by linking it to Anglo-Saxon society. Here he argued that the Anglo-Saxon word *waer* generally means 'man' (as absorbed by the word 'werewolf'), but sometimes refers to 'war', hence *waer-boda* (war-maker), *waered* (army) and *waerig* (to weary or overpower). Herbert then argues that 'war' in the modern sense really means to 'defend against', as in the original purpose of a warrior to defend his settlement, property or villagers against attack. So, the Anglo-Saxon *waeran*, *waerdian* and *waren* mean 'to defend'. Later, the words 'ward', 'guard', 'garer', 'ware' and 'beware', for example, meant to 'wear away' or 'ward off', that is, 'to defend yourself'. Finally, Herbert linked the word *waer* to the Latin *vir* (pronounced 'whir'), attributing the quality *virtus*, with the original meaning of 'warlike' or 'excellence'. The modern 'virtuous' has developed from this root. From *waer*, the alternatives *herus*, *harra* or *herr* (lord), *here* (an army) and *here-man* (a warrior) also develop. Indeed, the *Anglo-Saxon Chronicle* describes the Viking army that conquered York in 866 as *micel here* (great army). Herbert's suggestion that the term 'were' in werewolf should mean war (that is, war-wolf) is fully intelligible in relation to the warriors deemed to be 'werewolves' in the Roman, Greek, Anglo-Saxon and Viking periods, and may well explain how our modern understanding of the term originates. The tradition persists in Norman times, with the Norman Lord Hugh d'Avranches (1047–1101) being known as 'Hugh Lupus' (Hugh the Wolf). Hugh Lupus was one of William the Conqueror's most powerful lords, and eventually became the first Earl of Chester in 1071. Clearly the wolf moniker was something to revere.

So why is the wolf 'elevated' and favoured above other animals? Perhaps it had something to do with man's domestication of the 'wolf' as dog. Is this an example of man's ability to train the fierce wolf to be an equally fierce but loyal ally? Paul Ewald, a biologist at Amherst College, Massachusetts, studies parasites and diseases and looks at how humans can combat them. One theory he advanced suggested that although wolves have been a threat to humans for much of our evolutionary history, man has lived with a species of the wolf, that is, the increasingly domesticated dog, for centuries.

The Court of
Hugh Lupus.

Man and wolf were 'enemies' for thousands of years. With the
Neolithic period and the gradual development of farming techniques
(*c.* 4500 BC for Britain), more permanent settlements took shape. Up
to this point, wolves attacked early nomadic sites, but with the creation of settlements (the early villages), the slow 'refinement' of a
variety of the wolf species, and their desired company in camps,
started to become more commonplace.

Nevertheless, the wolf itself remained a threat to man, and wolf
persecution and systematic destruction was finally enforced by legis-
lation in the early sixteenth century in England by Henry VII. In
Scotland, however, it proved difficult because of the vast wooded areas,
and the simple solution was the systematic destruction of forests.
The last wolves eventually died out around 1684 in Britain, and by
around 1770 in Ireland. As Herbert put it, 'it suffices to observe at
present, that where there is no natural wolf there is no werewolf'.[15]

Wolf extinction in wider Europe, however, was confirmed in 1975 by the International Union for the Conservation of Nature and Natural Resources. Its study proved their extinction in France, Belgium, the Netherlands, Denmark, Germany, Switzerland, Austria and Hungary, and their virtual elimination in Finland, Norway and Sweden. They were also endangered species in Portugal, Spain, Italy, Bulgaria, the Czech Republic, Poland and Russia.[16]

Yet, the call for extinction may have been unwarranted, as typical wolf behaviour opposes the general belief that wolves attack humans. If this is so, the medieval (and beyond) tales of wolves attacking and killing people cannot be accurate. As Charlotte Otten in her *Lycanthropy Reader* explains,

> wolves (except in case of injury or hunger) do not kill, attack, or mutilate. According to recent research, wolves live in packs and establish congenial, bonding relationships and a society founded on trust. If one of their number develops killer-instincts, that criminal wolf is destroyed for the good of the community.[17]

These are words echoed by the British wolf expert Shaun Ellis, who has spent years studying and living with wolves both in Britain and America.

For now, our story of the evolution of the werewolf myth begins with the early 'wolf cults', and looks at prehistory and how religious groups focused on the wolf. Some of those critics who discredit werewolves argue that the 'anomaly originates in the impression made on man in early times by the great elemental powers of nature',[18] such as the sun, moon, stars and elements (for example, thunder). This might in turn have led to a belief in gods, or spiritual beings, particularly in early history, and then to a relationship between hunting practices seen in the wolf that were then adapted by man. How these early traditions grew into religious beliefs in Classical Europe (that is, in Rome and Greece), will be our next point of focus as we examine some of the literary evidence relating to werewolves. The final chapter of Part One then looks at the Germanic and Scandinavian wolf-warriors such as the Viking berserkers, the Germanic tribes, together with Anglo-Saxon crime and punishment.

Our study then focuses on the links in the Middle Ages between the werewolf, the devil and witchcraft, and looks at medieval beliefs pertaining to the werewolf myth. Such myths reveal that while werewolf legends were common in the early Christian period, over the next thousand years, frequent accounts appear in patristic writings that turn these legends on their head, attacking them and viewing them as pagan superstitions. From the twelfth century onwards, literary accounts then began to reappear – the Breton *lais*, for example (a *lai* is a short medieval popular romance narrative in Middle English or French) – but at that point, the 'werewolf' was very different from its ancestor, 'the one we're supposed to fear'.[19] Folkloric accounts of werewolves will then be examined including those of the so-called 'actual' werewolves.

The final part of this work discusses the various medical explanations of the werewolf myth including madness, depression, porphyria and other illnesses. Moving from a medical to a cultural perspective, we will see the transformation of the creature in popular imagination over the last century, as provided by filmic examples, more recent medical studies, as well as alleged sightings of the man-beast. As such, we will see how and why the werewolf maintains its place in European culture and popular imagination.

My previous book *From Demons to Dracula* (2008) analysed the vampire myth in Europe and concluded that the vampire was a metaphor for death – for the darkness in humanity – and acted as a talisman for society's fear and fascination with death. For the werewolf, however, I do not believe this to be the case. Where there is darkness in the vampire, a Black Devil, if you will, the werewolf is an object or myth of light. This was particularly so for the first few thousand years of the myth's history, when the creature was revered and emulated. *The White Devil*, borrowed from John Webster's play of the same name, is thus a fitting title for the book and our starting point.

While this book is a study of mankind's fascination with the wolf, it is also an attempt to explore the neglected areas of European culture that the wolf has penetrated in history. It will look at the werewolf's 'interaction' with religion, as well as the werewolf as a symbol, and the occult activities and tales that surround the werewolf, the 'white devil'.

PART ONE
The Cult of the Wolf

one

Of Man and Beast:
The Prehistoric Cults
of Europe

*Traditional or esoteric philosophy is perennial. It recurs at different
periods of time, always to create a cultural renaissance that will begin
a cycle of culture, a cycle of civilisation.*
John Mitchell, *The Ancient Temple and Modern Cosmology*

To understand contemporary thought and beliefs pertaining to
the werewolf myth, the roots of the myth have to be explored.
For such myths to still exist and regenerate in modern popular culture, man must at some point have either believed he could become
a wolf, or indeed *did* become a wolf, however untenable that notion
might be to modern minds. Is this a purely metaphorical transformation from man to beast? And why the wolf, above all other
creatures? In *The Werewolf* (1933), Montague Summers discusses
were-tigers, were-jaguars, were-lions and were-leopards, and Frank
Hamel (*Human Animals*, 1915) dedicates a whole chapter to the
Wer-Fox and Wer-Vixen. To gauge why the wolf became dominant
in our catalogue of were-beasts, we will unpack the earliest werewolf
beliefs and attempt to reach a conclusive hypothesis why 'the belief
that men can change into animals and animals into men is as old as
life itself'.[1]

Evidence for this assertion can be traced at least back to the
European Palaeolithic, or Old Stone Age, and certainly to the Upper
Palaeolithic (*c.* 45,000 BP for Europe). Woolly mammoth, rhinoceros, lions, hyenas, bisons, horses, wolves, arctic foxes and reindeer
were all present at this time and can be grouped into two distinct,
and important, categories: the hunter and the hunted. If the notion
of human to animal transformation is considered against this division of hunter and hunted, it is said that the creature chosen for such
a metamorphosis 'can take many forms but. . . will often include

those most feared by a given society'.[2] Thus different societies select different animals, and habitually one that is locally present.

Prehistoric man (that is, the hunter–gatherer) was surrounded by physically powerful and threatening animals, with 'greater bulk, physical make-up that included weapons such as horns, hooves, large curved teeth or tusks, greater speed, infinitely more ferocity and much more strength'.[3] It follows that man would try to imitate wild animals in order to survive and to find food. In this chapter we analyse man's attempts to look and feel like the wolf by wearing its pelt or its teeth, for example, and also his involvement of the wolf in ritualistic ceremonies, and magic to contact animal spirits. John Campbell has noted that within the period of modern human occupation in Europe, we see a split of hyena, lion, wolf and fox dominant in the period 45,000–20,000 BP and northern lynx, wolf common and arctic fox and bear in the period 15,000–10,000 BP.[4] This split clarifies our understanding of early animal worship cultures. The wolf, fox and bear are apparent in both periods and archaeological evidence from potential animal worship sites confirms the importance of these animals in society as early animal worshippers would have used 'ceremonial dances and festivals . . . in which animal masks and skins are used [and these] are closely connected with the idea of ancestor worship and with transformation'.[5] Hamel also remarks that that rhythmic and imitative sounds and narcotics or pungent perfumes would also have been created and used in such ceremonies. Evidence of these ritualistic dances can be seen on an engraved rhinoceros bone discovered in 1928 at the Pin Hole Cave, Creswell Crags, Derbyshire, that appears to show a 'masked human figure in the act of dancing a ceremonial dance'.[6] A bullroarer (a ceremonial instrument that resonates when it is whirled around the head) was also recovered from the cave. The Creswell engraving has similarities with continental examples found in Altamira (Spain) and Chancelade (France) and therefore suggests a widespread European practice.[7] The engraved animal masks also closely resemble the head and pelt of a wolf, meaning that if they are indeed wolf pelts, then this would be the earliest artistic representation of 'werewolves' within Europe.

Armstrong's
illustration of
the Pin Hole Man
engraving found
at Creswell Crags,
Derbyshire.

Such ceremonial practices could have been carried out to invoke the spirits of the animals (or perhaps the gods) to draw the spirit into the human body. Thus transformation may not have been physical so much as spiritual. As Prentice Mulford in *The Gift of the Spirit* (1904) points out, the

> size and shape of the spirit of a horse need not be like the horse materialised in flesh and blood. Spirit takes hold of a mass of matter and holds that matter in accordance with its ruling desire and the amount of its intelligence.[8]

Here, the horse could be substituted for the wolf, or indeed the bear, or any other animal. Besides the spiritual predilection for the wolf as man's animal for his human–beast transformation is a semi-physical transformation where the human does not become the wolf per se, but disguises himself as one:

from a useful and necessary disguise for purposes of obtaining food, the wolf-robe and mask became, in unscrupulous hands, an instrument for personal aggrandisement and gain through intimidation.[9]

While such a disguise was perhaps at first a hunting aid or costume for ceremonial purposes, it probably became a symbol of authority or a tool that could be exploited to strike fear.

Scholar and cave art specialist David Lewis-Williams has pointed out that

> we should note the ancient universal human neurological inheritance that includes the capacity of the nervous system to enter altered states and the need to make sense of the resultant dreams and hallucinations within a foraging way of life.[10]

Moreover, in *Human Evolution*, Roger Lewin comments that

> during trance-induced hallucination the subject experiences a small set of so-called entoptic images, such as grids, zig-zags, dots, spirals and curves. In deeper stages of trance these images may be manipulated into recognisable objects, and subjects may eventually come to see therianthropes, or chimeras of animal and human forms.[11]

There may be a link here between 'visions' derived from trance-like states or conditions of mind altered by narcotics and man's attempts to take on the personality of an animal. Given that the wolf, fox and bear were the dominant predatory animals, it corresponds that in a mind-altered state, early man could have convinced himself that he could become one of these beasts. How, though, could he convince others that he was that beast? It is of course feasible that he did not try to do this and that the concept of wolf-men or bear-men was a much later invention. However, the so-called *Löwenmensch*, or Lion-man, from Hohlenstein-Stadel, which dates to *c.* 32,000 BP, suggests quite the opposite. Carved from mammoth ivory and approximately 30 cm (12 inches) in height, it represents an entity that it is half-man, half-lion.

In the Apse in Lascaux, southwest France, the site of Palaeolithic cave paintings, horse, bison, aurochs, ibex and deer all figure. Similar animals are represented on the cave walls at sites in Altamira, Spain, and Creswell in Britain. Generally, the depicted animals are the hunted, whilst the 'hunter', the wolf or bear, is what early man apparently wants to become or to copy. Man then considered himself as another hunter and not as prey. To an extent, the wolf's 'clothing' allowed man to abandon his human form by hiding it, thereby securing some of the wolf's power over certain less ferocious

Lowenmensch from Hohlenstein-Stadel in the Swabian Alps.

animals while he hunted. Man, it seems, considered himself an animal, which brings us closer to understanding the evolution of the early werewolf myth.

Although, as Brenda Lewis makes clear, 'Once thought to simply be pictorial representations of hunting-magic, painted to ensure a good kill, prehistoric art carried an extra message – the attachment, despite the rivalry, of humans and animals'.[12] This 'bonding' of animals and humans makes it more explicit why the relationship between man and domesticated wolves took a sideways step, as it were, after this time of hunting magic, when it mutated into a healthy 'bonding' relationship on the one hand, and a werewolf fantasy on the other. Humans did not manage, or probably even try, to domesticate the bear, lion or fox, and so there can be no 'were-lion' or 'were-bear' myth.

This theory of 'hunting magic' is supported by evidence from human burials from the period that reveal a shamanistic status, where links to wolves are again apparent. Grave goods including necklaces, bracelets and hats (although the material has long since disappeared) decorated with wolf and fox teeth have been unearthed from burials in many European countries, including Italy, Wales, France and Moravia, in the Czech Republic. Furthermore, at the Mesolithic (Middle Stone Age, *c.* 8,000–4500 BC) burial site in Oleneostrovski Mogilnik, Karelia, USSR, over 500 graves were discovered, nine of which contained carved representations of elks, snakes and humans. A further four were 'shaft' graves, where the dead were buried in a standing position. Steve Mithen argues that the occupants were of a special social status, perhaps shamans, which would suggest that the practice continued over thousands of years.[13] Although these carvings do not represent wolves, artefacts from other sites such as Cheddar Gorge in Somerset have revealed man and wolf connections. The burial site of the male known as Cheddar Man was discovered in 1903. He and his environment have recently been reconstructed at the site, with Cheddar Man wearing a wolf-pelt headdress, similar to the one depicted in the engraving from Creswell Crags.

The origins of the wolf cult and the role shamans played in it are key to understanding the evolution of the werewolf myth. Indeed, the wolf cult in prehistoric Europe was most probably reflective of society's spiritual beliefs and was, in essence, a cult of death. Here, Eastern Europe, the so-called homeland of the werewolf, arguably holds the roots of the wolf cult. In the Pavlov Hills in Moravia, Czech Republic, at least 36 skeletons in various stages of preservation were were recovered from a number of sites; twenty were partial skeletons and six near complete. Fox teeth pendants accompany all the Pavlovian burials. This practice was widespread throughout Europe during this period, which suggests that the Upper Palaeolithic peoples considered the wolf and the fox in a similar manner, if not identical, in terms of their predatory powers. This widespread and indeed generalized regional practice also extends to burials in Italy during the same period. Here, eight burials were discovered and all the interred had personal ornamentation on their heads – it seems they were buried with some sort of 'hat' adorned with perforated shells and animal teeth. Again, is this the burial of shamans? This is a widespread phenomenon – at Wilczyce in southwestern Poland a burial of a neonate was discovered with a necklace of around 89 perforated fox teeth; radiocarbon dating placed this burial just under 13,000 years' old.

At the excavation site Pavlov 1 in Moravia, a number of scorched wolf skeletons were found that appear to have had their legs bound together.[14] This could well be part of a ritual involving the sacrifice and burning of wolves. As archaeologist Paul Pettitt comments,

> for the Pavlovian, a complex mix of the processing, circulation and deposition of body parts, burial of partial skeletons and burial of complete individuals singularly, and, in one case, as a group of three, suggests the complex role of the dead in the cosmologies of the living that also occasioned the ritual burial of animals such as wolves.[15]

Clearly, some form of ritual practice was in operation, relating to a particular belief system. Indeed, remains from the archaeological site of Dolni Věstonice revealed traces of burning on both humans and wolves. Five individuals were buried here, including the famous triple burial, and all had fox or wolf teeth buried with them. One of the interred, a female, had been buried with five (unperforated) fox teeth clutched in her right hand, while a second exhumation was that of an elderly male who had three perforated fox teeth located near his legs.

The triple burial involves the arrangement of three side-by-side in the 'grave'. A covering of red ochre stained all three bodies, but particularly that of the head of the skeleton on the left, which, much like the Italian examples, suggests that a hat was worn at the time of burial. Both outer skeletons were male (the one in the middle was female) and were wearing pendants of fox and wolf teeth.

Archaeologists noted that the person buried on the right-hand side had suffered a blow to the head and that the corpse on the left had been staked to the ground – a thick wooden pole had been stabbed through his hip – suggesting they could well have been sacrifices, or perhaps killed by a rival tribe. Recent studies of the site have suggested that all three may have been family members, based on systematic kinship analysis such as impaction of the wisdom teeth and rare traits on both the mandible and the teeth.[16] However, as Paul Pettitt quite rightly argues, given the small-scale populations and nomadic lifestyles, it is highly likely that many members of a specific 'group' were related, so associating any kinship in a modern sense proves rather problematic.[17] What is striking though, is that the interred female had been lucky to survive to the age she did, given her deformities and abnormalities. However, the likelihood of the two males dying in quick succession to her appears very slim, thereby increasing the sacrifice theory. That all five burials from the site were buried with pendants or hats adorned with the teeth of wolves and foxes is significant and may offer a connection between shamans and hunting magic. It appears as if the people at Dolni Věstonice were seeking to resemble the wolf, or at least the power of the wolf, in a way that their society understood. They would have watched wolves hunting and seen them use their mouths and teeth to kill their prey – by taking the teeth and wearing them, they were in effect harnessing the wolves' power.

In many cultures 'eating human flesh was the cause of the transformation into a wolf, and thus abstaining was the key to reverting back'.[18] There does seem to be evidence of this in early prehistory and many sites throughout Europe have revealed human bones that have been smashed to extract the marrow, or have slash marks on them that point to the 'defleshing' of the body. Further evidence shows signs that the brain has been removed from the skull, which suggests that cannibalism was practised as part of the cult of the wolf. Herbert has argued

> that all pagan nations of antiquity, without any exception, used human sacrifice. And Pliny excellently well observes that 'immolating a man is removed but one step from eating him' (and that) to partake of the flesh of the victim was a part of the ceremony of sacrifice, and *anthropothysia* without *anthropophagia* was a maimed and imperfect rite.[19]

The Massageteans (Iranian nomadic tribes) were known to eat those who had died at an advanced age, as were many other cultures, and Herodotus, writing in the fifth century BC, tells us that

> human life does not come to its natural close with these people; but when a man grows very old, all his kinsfolk collect together and offer him up in sacrifice; offering at the same time some cattle also. After the sacrifice they boil the flesh and feast on it.[20]

In the Late Upper Palaeolithic Age in France nearly half of the known 232 corpses recovered carry cut and scrape marks, indicating the removal of flesh. Whether this flesh was then eaten is unknown, but numerous examples across Europe would seem to confirm this. At the Maszycka Cave in Poland, human remains of at least sixteen individuals bore evidence of having been killed, dismembered and, it appears, scalped and having had their brains removed, possibly for human consumption.[21] Further evidence from Gough's Cave at Cheddar Gorge, Somerset, shows cut marks on a human skull fragment that reflects a scalping and the removal of the lower jaw.[22] Herbert believes this apparent eating of the human flesh was part of a widespread pagan religious group and suggested that 'man turned into wolf [from eating the flesh] is the adept admitted to the cannibal banquet of Mars or of Appollo Lycius'.[23]

Several of the caves at Creswell Crags in Derbyshire harboured evidence of skull fragments from humans, and Robin Hood Cave at the site held three pieces that fitted together and a human mandible and tooth recovered separately but which were undoubtedly from the same person. In Mother Grundy's Parlour (also Creswell) a complete skull was discovered in 1877, and, as I have shown elsewhere,[24] from all the caves from which human remains have been recovered at Creswell, at least 50 per cent of these bodily parts have been from human heads. Clearly, some form of ritual practice involving human skulls was in operation, although dating has proved problematic, meaning tying this to a specific period is difficult. In the local area surrounding Creswell Crags a number of cave sites have revealed 'skull burials', for example Whaley II Rock Shelter and Langwith Bassett Cave. We have seen that animal teeth have frequently been used as decorations for pendants and hats in this period, but also, occasionally, so have human teeth. Bédeilhac Cave in the Ariège region in southwest France, the abri Pataud in the Dordogne, France, and Dolni Věstonice, Moravia, have all surrendered examples of perforated human teeth. Perhaps more disturbingly, pendants made from parts of human crania and mandibles have been excavated from certain French sites.

If humans sought to imitate wolves as well as sacrifice them, and involved them in ritualistic practices during this period, they also sought to control them, as is evidenced in the wolf's domestication into the modern dog. As Beauvois de Chauvincourt commented in his *Discours de la lycanthropie*,

> although wild beasts by their nature are enemies of mankind, nevertheless they revere man as their master and lord, and, from being untameable, change their savage and solitary style into a companionable one.[25]

For some time archaeologists have debated exactly when wolves became domesticated. In England evidence is scant: John Campbell discussed *canis* remains from the crags at Creswell but they appeared to be *canis lupus* (wolf). However,

> this is not to say that some sort of 'special relationship' was not already developing between wolf and man in the Late Upper Palaeolithic, a relationship which then evolved to the point where it became recognisable as *canis familiaris* in Zone IV at Star Carr [the Mesolithic site in Yorkshire].[26]

Indeed, evidence from the Mesolithic Age testifies that wolf had already become dog by then.

Until recently it was believed that the oldest domesticated wolf remains (that is, dog remains) were those found at Kesslerloch Cave in Switzerland, dating to *circa*. 14,000 BP. However, a wolf / dog tooth from Tübingen in Baden-Württemberg, Germany, has recently been dated to between 14,600–14,000 BP, pushing the date to a few hundred years earlier. Whilst these dates easily coincide with the final stages of the Ice Age, scholars have argued that contemporary hunting practices probably did not utilize dogs.[27] It could be that dogs were originally used to guard the camps in much the same way that we use guard dogs today. Sites such as La Vache, in the Ariège region in France, and Creswell Crags used the natural bottle-neck of the gorge to drive prey into waiting ambushes. Cave art hunting depictions bear no representations of hunting with dogs. It seems that it was only when the ice had melted and forests had taken root in the Mesolithic period that dogs would have been useful hunting aids, with the hunter using bows and arrows to kill his prey. However, an engraving of a horse on a horse rib-bone that was discovered at Robin Hood Cave in Creswell may be proof of dogs being used for hunting:

> If we look carefully at the engraving it is possible to note a series of vertical lines drawn over the top of the horse itself. Jill Cook of the British Museum discussed her ideas that these lines may represent 'guide posts' placed in the ground to lure the galloping horse into a waiting ambush.

She commented how modern reindeer hunters use similar methods as the animals see the wooden posts out of the corner of their eye as they are running and believe it to be a solid fence, so instead of simply running through the gaps between the guide posts and escaping they continue to follow the marked out path. Could this be what the lines on the horse engraving represent, as the engraved horse is almost certainly galloping at speed in the artwork?[28]

Dogs would have been particularly suited to chasing the horse and would obviously have been much faster than humans. If dogs were not used for hunting, though, the question of why wolves were domesticated remains. One possibility is their use as protection. If wolves, scavenging 'kill sites' and searching for leftover animal carcasses, began to approach human campsites as their interest or bravery was peaked, they might feasibly and gradually have started to enter the camp itself. It is at this point that a 'mutual respect' between man and wolf, each knowing the other's ability and prowess as a hunter, may well have started. In addition, the physical mutations of canines reflect their occupational uses: Labunsky, for example, has shown that early dogs had a skull shape very similar to that of the Central Asian Shepherd Dog, which was originally used for protection against animals such as bears, wolves and hyenas.[29]

Further work by Mietje Germonpre and team has revealed that the oldest known record of a domesticated wolf – from Goyet Cave, Belgium (c. 31,700 BP) – is much older than originally thought. This would indicate that domestication had begun as early as the Aurignacian period. Germonpre's study used mtDNA studies to compare known skeletal assemblages from both ancient and modern wolves and dogs. It compared the datable remains from Goyet and suggested a date of around 40,000 BP with an 'ancient genetic bottleneck' around 27,000 BP.[30] The research findings outline that when it was underway, domestication occurred rapidly but when it was established, skull shape remained unchanged for thousands of years. Until the recent 'breeding boom' of the last two hundred years or so, diversity levels (in terms of mtDNA) would have been relatively low,

Engraving of a horse on a horse rib-bone from Robin Hood Cave,
Creswell Crags.

thus reflecting a close lineage pattern between dogs and wolves. The
first dogs, therefore, would have had a wolf-like genetic sequence very
similar to the modern grey wolf.

The findings of Mietje Germonpré and her colleagues showed
that the known wolf / dog remains from the sites of Goyet (Belgium),
Mezhirich (Ukraine), Mézin (France) and Eliseevich 1 (Russia) are
all Palaeolithic dogs, and not wolves.[31] They further reported that
'compared to wolves, ancient dogs exhibit a shorter and broader
snout'[32] and that all the Palaeolithic dogs in their study conformed
to this pattern. These snout characteristics suggest that early dogs
had powerful jaws and well-developed carnassials, with skull size
suggesting they were large animals, similar to modern large dog
breeds such as the Irish Wolfhound.

Although fascination with the wolf may have started as early as
40,000 BP, evidence suggests that at this time and over the next 10,000
years or so the wolf was seen as a powerful ally and not quite man's
servant. By 14,000 BP, domestication had certainly occurred and by
12,000 BP man's longstanding friendship with the dog had finally
begun, evidenced in the burial at Bonn-Oberkassel in Germany of
a man and a woman and their dog. Furthermore, at Skateholm in
Sweden, a number of dogs were buried with grave goods in the
Late Mesolithic period. Two cemetery sites were excavated here,
with the earliest containing dogs buried with their owners and the
later housing them in their own graves accompanied by grave goods
including a reindeer antler, three flint blades and an antler hammer,
covered with red ochre.[33] With the domestication of the wolf and a

corresponding demonstrable bond between man and dog by the time of the Neolithic period (*c.* 4500 BC for Britain), we might expect to see a decline, if not a disappearance, of the cult of the wolf, but this is far from true.

In order to understand the early links between man copying or imitating the wolf, the use of hunting magic and wider social beliefs must be explored. In short, this is devotion to Mother Earth. Evidence of this can be found in the Upper Palaeolithic's Venus figurines, *circa* 27,000 BP, and again in cave art of the Late Upper Palaeolithic. However, I want to focus on later examples, which, I believe, are directly linked to our werewolf myth. During the 1960s, at the Neolithic site of Çatalhöyük in Anatolia, Turkey, the archaeologist James Mellaart discovered a number of small, female figurines and evidence of another animal cult. He believed they represented a female goddess and that they 'far outnumber those of the male deity, who moreover, does not appear to be represented at all after Level VI'.[34] In all, eighteen separate 'levels' were identified. Many examples of wall paintings were also discovered. One of these figurines, a female seated on a throne with what seem to be two lions, was discovered inside a grain bin, perhaps evidence of a harvest goddess? However, Ian Hodder and his team carried out further excavations in 2004–5 and from these new excavations argued that the theories put forward by Mellaart relating to the figurines were inaccurate, and that generally they were *not* statues of a female goddess.[35] This makes the figurine found in the 'grain bin' even more intriguing. Nevertheless, Mellaart argued that they were female 'deity' figurines and that they were found in 'shrines'. Later work by Bulliet identified over 40 of these shrines, with depictions of horned bulls, leopards, female breasts and goddesses adorning the walls.[36]

Corpses were discovered under a number of the houses that were excavated just 30 centimetres under the living surfaces. No grave goods were buried with the dead except for a few personal items – necklaces or bone tools for women and a knife or a belt for men. Of more interest is the fact that they were wrapped in a cloth or burial shroud and placed in the ground in the foetal position. Much like our burials discussed earlier, this seems to reflect an idea of rebirth and may be linked to devotion to the Mother Earth goddess. Furthermore, a number of horns of bulls or bisons were noted at the site – some were physical versions such as those set into pillars, others were representations such as those painted onto the walls. Again, there may be a link here with the Earth Mother goddess as the horns were always paired with symbols of the goddess. William Carl Eichman has argued that this is 'arguably the source of the Great Mother Goddess religion'.[37] However, this is probably inaccurate as it undoubtedly dates to a much earlier time. Another sticking point in the theories surrounding the Çatalhöyük site goes back to Mellaart's figurines. In the 1960s he found around 200 of these, but to date, excavation has revealed over 2999 of them, and yet only 5 per cent of them represent the female form, whilst the rest are of animals. The art also may represent less the Earth Mother goddess than hunting:

Female deity
from Çatalhöyük,
flanked by lions.

the representational art at Çatal Hüyük makes it clear that hunting retained a powerful hold on people's minds. Wall paintings of hunting scenes closely resemble earlier cave paintings. Many depict men and women adorned with leopard skins.[38]

Here we seem to have evidence of Montague Summers's 'were-leopards'. Strecker and Bahn also relate a hunting scene from the cave site at Cueva de las Manos, Rio Pinturas, Argentina, that is very similar to that at Çatalhöyük and dates from around 7300 BC.[39] Casamiquela believes it is 'surely associated with hunting magic'.[40] So we may have been wrong in thinking that 'hunting magic' disappeared along with the ice – it just might be harder to find.

Stephanie Meece has argued that the paintings at Çatalhöyük almost certainly reflect the hunters wearing leopard skins:

> in several later paintings, notably the large so-called hunting scenes, human figures are depicted wearing stiff 'skirts' and head coverings that are painted with simple dots. The skirts are conventionally depicted as two wide triangles connected at their base, with two sharp points. They are twice as long as they are wide, and are filled in with dark-coloured dots, similar to the appearance of a stretched, prepared leopard skin. Incised dots are used in three-dimensional sculpture to represent leopard skins as well.[41]

Certain hallucinogenic states affect the mind in such a way that various shapes and animals are perceived. In Mellaart's 1967 report he mentioned that the mound at Çatalhöyük was covered with the Syrian rue plant – the seeds of which contain both harmine and harmaline. Harmine is known to cause hallucinations and often the person who has ingested it will experience visions of panthers and leopards. Furthermore, Çatalhöyük is located in a region where the pscyhoactive plants of Europe – Amanita mushrooms, ergotized grains, the aforementioned Syrian rue and cannabis – are all commonly found.[42] Combined with the fact that the economy at Çatalhöyük appears to have been based on agriculture, and in particular barley

Hunting scene from Çatalhöyük, depicting hunters wearing leopard-skins engaged in a ceremonial dance.

Hunting scene from Cueva de las Manos, Rio Pinturas, Argentina, dated to c. 7,300 BC (after Aschero).

and emmer wheat, and that the rituals involved burning dishes of grains (and remember the goddess figurine in the grain pit), devotion to the Earth Mother goddess becomes a more viable theory.

In Denmark, the megalithic burial tombs built in the landscape are from the same era as a type of pottery known as 'funnel-necked beakers', which were probably used in some form of drinking ceremony. Further evidence for this comes from the Neolithic site of Skara Brae in the Orkney Islands in Scotland, where a drink consisting of barley grain, meadowsweet (for flavour), deadly nightshade and henbane was consumed. The resulting mixture would have been a hallucinogenic 'beer' drink with a porridge-like consistency. In the Bronze Age, the Corded Ware people, living in Germanic areas, used a type of pottery that was incised with patterns created using hemp cords. These Corded Ware pots were drinking vessels, and some archaeologists believe they held a hemp or cannabis-based brew for use in rituals.[43]

In later prehistory, for example, in the British Iron Age (*c.* 700 BC–AD 43), we see further evidence of this hallucinogenic drink being used, in what appears to be ritual sacrifices, from excavated Iron Age bog corpses found throughout Europe. The body of Clonycavan Man was discovered partially preserved in a bog in Ireland in 2003. He was aged between 25 and 40 years old and had an elaborate hairstyle, shaved from ear to ear, and a high hairline, with the hair at the neck cut to around 1 cm in length. The rest was left quite long (around 17–20 cm) and then swept upwards and partly folded back, held in place with a 'gel' made from conifer resin mixed with lipid (probably a vegetable oil). Chemical analysis showed the resin was from the *Pinus pinaster* (maritime pine), a tree that grows in southwest France and northern Spain. Moreover, 'This gel was undoubtedly a highly exclusive and luxurious commodity, clearly not available to all strata in society'.[44] Clonycavan Man had been killed by a series of blows to the head and chest, most likely with an axe. A 49-cm long incision in his abdomen suggests he was disembowelled. Dating showed he died somewhere between 392–201 BC.

In the same year, a second bog body was discovered – Old Croghan Man – who had died somewhere in the same period, 362–175 BC.

Again, he was aged around 25–40 years at the time of his death, and also appeared to have been murdered. He had a stab wound to his chest and a deep cut to his left arm, suggesting he might have tried to ward off the blow to his chest. Strangely, he also had circular cuts around his nipples and both his upper arms had been pierced with a sharp implement, after which hazel rods were inserted through the holes. This treatment would suggest torture, or at the very least, a painful form of ritualistic ceremony. Finally, his head had been cut off and he had been partially dismembered.[45] Old Croghan Man was found naked except for a leather armband with copper alloy fittings on his upper left arm. This immediately drew parallels to another bog body, that of Lindow Man, who had been found in a peat bog near Manchester in the UK in 1984. He, too, was found naked except for an armband on his upper left arm, this time of fox fur. It has been suggested that this might be symbolic of Lindow Man's lycan-thropic status, his delusional belief in his transformation into a wolf, a condition known from medieval times.[46] Also, it was noted that Old Croghan Man's 'manicured fingernails, minimal scarring to the fingers and absence of wear to the fingertips seem to denote an individual from the upper echelons of society'.[47] Lindow Man, who also was approximately 25 years old at time of death, had manicured finger-nails and his hair had been cut 2–3 days prior to his death. More importantly, Old Croghan Man's last meal had been a ground cere-al mixed with buttermilk, even though subsequent analysis showed that he had generally enjoyed a protein-rich diet, and that he was killed in winter when traditionally (in the Iron Age) meat consumption was at its highest. It is my belief that this was a ceremonial barley-drug meal, consumed before he was sacrificed.

Melanie Giles discusses the fact that many of the bog bodies that have been discovered were naked except for a specific item: Old Croghan Man's leather armband, Lindow Man's fox-fur armband and Tollund Man's hat. Giles believes that 'these are meant to endear us to the deceased, by revealing intimate traces of stitching, wear and repair . . . such objects prompt us to think of the life behind the moment of death'.[48] I would opt for a much less personal view and suggest they mirror the body adornments of the burials discussed earlier – the Italian shaman hats or the Pavlovian fox and wolf teeth pendants. Eamonn Kelly of the National Museum of Ireland in Dublin has pointed out that other objects – headdresses, cauldrons and weapons – are found in similar locations to the bog bodies in Ireland and are on tribal boundaries.[49] Perhaps they are offerings to a fertility god, as Kelly suggests. This aspect will be considered in more detail in Chapter Three when we follow the progression of the fertility / Earth Mother cult. Now, though, we must turn to the many examples of werewolves in the literary records of the classical world in order to shed light on the widespread beliefs of this period.

two
The Wolves of Rome: Classical Accounts of the Werewolf Myth

A wolf ther stood berforn hym at his feet,
With eyen rede, and of a man he eet,
With soutil pencel depeynted was this storie,
In redoutiyngeng of mars and of his glorie.
Geoffrey Chaucer, 'The Knight's Tale', lines 2049–52

Early ideas on religion, and religious practices including 'shaman magic', rituals, sacrifices and imitating beasts, created a foundation for the possibility of werewolves, or at least the founding of a werewolf myth. Bears were probably the first animal to be idolized, possibly because they represented strength and power and had the ability to resurrect themselves from the dead (hibernation). As such, the cyclical doctrine of nature began. From this, it is easy to see how and why early religions focused on the cycles of nature: the seasons were witnessed by all and plant life 'died' in winter only to be 'reborn' in spring. It made sense that this was the work of an unseen and almighty entity. Exactly why this entity was chosen as a female we will never know, but I would suggest that it must be linked to pregnancy and birth – after all, society would have witnessed females 'magically' creating life.

The main difference between 'Prehistory' and 'History' (widely accepted as beginning with the advent of the Roman Period in Europe) is literature, and the ability to document the world. Whilst we have to rely solely on the archaeological evidence for the period of prehistory, we have a plethora of documentary evidence to support that of an archaeological nature for the historical period. And that early documentary evidence from the classical world of Rome and Greece is filled with tales of men being turned into wolves, sometimes in a positive light (that is, of their own accord), and sometimes in a negative way (transformed as a punishment). In essence, here are our first contemporary accounts of werewolves, not just in the classical world, but perhaps crucially amongst the 'barbarian' hordes elsewhere. These accounts can help our understanding of archaeological discoveries of bog bodies and the many curious early representations of artwork.

The Greek historian Herodotus, writing in the fifth century BC, compiled a detailed set of *Histories* in which he documented the various beliefs and practices of the period. For example, in Egypt, he said they sacrificed animals as part of their religious rituals. Only the purest animals would be chosen, and during the ritual its head was cut off as it was believed to be the fount of evil and was cursed by priests. The animal was then sold off to the Greek merchants or, if no buyer was found, dumped in the river. Pausanias, the Greek traveller and writer, told of Greece's practice of animal sacrifice in his second-century AD account, *Description of Greece*. He wrote how, at the festival of the goddess Artemis Laphria at Patras,

> they throw game-birds alive onto the altar and all the other victims in the same way, even wild boars and deer and gazelles, and some of them throw on wolf-cubs and bear-cubs and others fully grown beasts.[1]

Some sacrifices went further than just offering up animals to the gods, however, and two examples reflect a continuation of an Earth Mother cult. The first relates to the many oracle sites that existed in Greece, believed to be 'portals' to the gods and places where the future could be predicted. When animals were sacrificed, a strict procedure had to be followed. Firstly, water had to be sprinkled over the beast's head and then barley was thrown over it. This symbolized the violence that was to come.[2] The fact that barley was again involved most likely attests to a link with fertility and the Earth Mother. The second example also involves barley, at the festival of Ino. Ino, also known as 'Leucothea', was a Greek sea goddess. She is also known in the Roman world as 'Mater Matuta', the goddess of ripening grain:

about two stades to the right is the water of Ino, as it is called, in extent like a small lake, but going deeper into the earth. Into this water they throw cakes of barley meal at the festival of Ino. If good luck is portended to the thrower, the water keeps them under. But if it brings them to the surface, it is judged a bad sign.[3]

Similarly, sacrifices of pigs were made to the Greek corn god, Demeter.

There were many 'cults' or religions in the classical world, particularly in the Roman empire. The so-called mystery religions (from the Latin *mysterium* meaning 'hidden' or 'secret') included those of Bacchus (the god of wine), Apollo (the sun god) and Mithras (an early Roman bull cult) – the last of which was hugely popular in the army. Ironically, all the mystery cults were tolerated in the early Empire except that of Christianity, which would eventually triumph

Stone carving depicting Mithras slaying the bull from Osterburken, Germany.

above all others and become the adopted religion of Rome. It is this notion of a bull cult that is most important to our werewolf myth, as it seems that bulls were the main sacrifice in both Rome and Greece. Bulls were deemed to be the most noble of creatures, a fitting sacrifice to the all-powerful gods, and were offered up to Zeus and Dionysius in Greece and Cybele, another Mother goddess, in Rome. None, however, was as popular as that of Mithras. An early Mithraic stone carving found in Rome and believed to date to around AD 199 shows Mithras slaughtering a bull, and this is the main feature of the Mithraic religion.[4] The Mithraic legend is that Mithras killed the bull in a cave, and indeed temples to Mithras are always found underground or in a cave. In total, 429 temples have been discovered so far.[5] There are similarities here with the earlier religion, where caves played a prominent role particularly in the burial (or containment) of the dead. I would argue that caves symbolize a route into the Mother Earth, and may even depict the womb. Burying the dead in caves is a way, therefore, of ensuring that the dead regain Mother Earth. The seeing of bears 'reincarnated' and emerge from caves after hibernation most probably added weight to this theory. Later, prehistoric peoples constructed huge burial mounds, particularly Neolithic long mounds or chambered tombs, to house the dead. Here an entrance passage (the birth canal?) leads to an inner chamber (or chambers) in which the dead are placed, in a womb-like environment. The whole structure is then covered with earth, generally to the extent that the actual burial chamber is dwarfed. Burial mounds are distinctively long (hence the long mound), with the burial chamber at one end. Arguably, this was designed to represent the female form, perhaps the goddess, with a swollen stomach (the earthen mound), and a womb containing the dead in preparation for rebirth.

Among the early animal / man legends is the 'Leontocephaline', a naked creature that is half man, half lion. Parallels are drawn between this and the Lowenmensch. It is believed that the Leonto-cephaline is a Mithraic god dedicated to time and seasonal change.[6] This creature is only a step removed from the undoubtedly more well-known creature, the Minotaur, the half-man, half-bull creature from Greek mythology. The word 'Minotaur' translates as 'bull of Minos', relating to the legend that King Minos of Crete had a labyrinthine maze constructed at his palace to house the beast. The Minotaur was more commonly known as 'Asterion' in Crete.[7] The beast was created when Minos decided to keep the white bull he was planning to sacrifice for the god Poseidon, and in punishment, Aphrodite made Minos' wife fall in love with the Cretan bull. They had intercourse and she gave birth to the Minotaur. To contain the Minotaur, Minos hired Daedalus and his son Icarus to build a labyrinth. This is a moral tale concerning the creation of a half-man, half-beast entity, and of how upsetting the gods can result in punishment. Moreover, it is very similar to much later werewolf beliefs that involve the Church, in which becoming a werewolf was said to be a curse for not being a good Christian. This may come as no surprise when we consider that the Roman poet Ovid's account of the Minotaur was widely available during the medieval period, when werewolf beliefs were widespread.

In 1900 the archaeologist Sir Arthur Evans bought the Cretan site of Knossos, where in 1878 remains of a palace had been discovered. He excavated the site and found evidence to suggest that it was not a palace at all (that is, not in the modern terms) but probably a religious and administrative centre with over one thousand interlocking rooms, and certainly maze-like in structure. Evidence of human sacrifice has been discovered at Knossos, in a building known as the 'North House', and goddess figurines have also been recovered, indicating again that an Earth Mother goddess was worshipped. Whether the human sacrifices are related to this is unknown, as is any sacrifice relating to the Minotaur myth. Whilst certainly not a real creature, it is possible that the Minotaur was a metaphorical or spiritual being that religious worshippers idolized, which means that sacrifices could be connected in this way. As historian Rodney Castleden argues,

> the idea of human sacrifice and ritual cannibalism adds a
> new and unpleasant dimension to the picture of Minoan reli-
> gious practices but – given the mythic horror-story of the

tribute-children and the all-devouring Minotaur – perhaps we should have been prepared for this.[8]

At the core of the classical world are myths of half-man, half-beast creatures, evidence of human sacrifice and a continuation of an early Earth Mother goddess cult. How though does this all fit into the developing werewolf myth? Sabine Baring-Gould, in what remains one of the classic texts on the werewolf myth, *The Book of Werewolves* (1865), points out that changing into wolves, or into any other beast for that matter, in the classical period should not come as a shock as classical accounts are full of such transformations – Actaeon, for example, was turned into a stag, Hecuba into a dog, the daughters of Proteus became cows and Jupiter himself a bull. The difference here is that these mutations tend to be god-aided, often meted out as punishments, rather than being purposeful transformations, as is often the case with the werewolf. Indeed, the Egyptian god Anubis is depicted with the head of a jackal,[9] which clearly points to a godly link in these early accounts. In Isaiah, speaking of the desolation of Babylon, we learn how 'their houses shall be full of dolleful creatures, and owles shall dwell there, and Satyres shall daunce there'.[10] As Elliot O'Donnell argues, 'are not satyrs every whit as grotesque and out-rageous as werewolves?'[11] Later in Isaiah, we hear of the land of the Idumeans, where dragons live and devils and monsters meet. Here also live the creatures the Greeks knew as 'Pans' and the Latins as 'Incubi', and St Isidore of Seville (*c.* 560–636) in his *Eighth Book* recounts how they lust 'lecherously after women' and copulate with them: 'O Faunus, love of fleeing nymphs, go gently over my lands and smiling fields.'[12]

Faunus was a Roman horned god of the forest but is sometimes known as Lupercus ('he who wards off the wolf') and St Valentine's Day probably has its origins in the Faunus / Lupercus festival, the 'Lupercalia' (or wolf festival), originally celebrated on 15 February. In the Lupercalia festival, young males dressed in wolf and goat costumes chased women through the streets playfully 'whipping' them with leather thongs in a fertility ritual.[13] To understand this festival, it is important to recognize the role of the aforementioned

The Lupercalia festival.

god Pan. The Greek version of the god, and the more well known
'version', was the son of Hermes and was half-man, half-goat (think
of Bottom in Shakespeare's *A Midsummer Night's Dream*). He was
also known as 'Pan Leaks' (wolf-Pan), and the origins of the Roman
festival perhaps explain the wolf costume of the Lupercalia revellers.
In his work *The City of God* (*c.* 426), St Augustine relates that Pan
was so named because he held the key to the mystery of men becoming wolves: 'the epithet Lycæus was applied in Arcadia to Pan and
Jupiter for no other reason than this metamorphosis of men into
wolves, because it was thought it could not be wrought except by a
divine power'.[14] Furthermore, A. K. Michels in *The Topography and
Interpretation of the Lupercalia*, has argued that in ancient Italy wolves
would have mated only in February, hence the date of the Lupercalia
and St Valentine's Day (the day of love).[15]

In modern-day Romania (and indeed throughout wider Europe,
although the symbolism is in most cases lost), the festival of Candlemas
(also 15 February) involves people eating pancakes that symbolize
the consumption of the old moon and its disappearance from the sky

during the festival. In Romania, the *vârcolac* is a mythological creature with wolf-like characteristics that are very similar to the werewolf. The *vârcolac* eats the moon and sun, causing eclipses, or bites the moon until it is covered in blood, again causing a partial eclipse.[16] Again, does this stem from early pagan religious beliefs from the Roman and Greek myths? Marcellus Sidetes, who lived in the second century AD, wrote in his poem *De Lycanthropia* that men are afflicted with a type of madness at the beginning of the year that becomes much worse in February. Whilst this madness could be an illness, it could equally be interpreted as a madness based on euphoria as the Lupercalia festival dawns, hence the running of citizens through the streets chasing young women.

The Greek poet Homer mentions a race of people known as the 'Lycians' and their god 'Lycegenean Apollo' ('born of wolf'). It was believed Apollo's Mother, Leto, disguised herself as a she-wolf when she came from the land of the Hyperboreans. Her region, Lycia, meaning 'wolfish' or 'belonging to a wolf' is named in honour of this. Apollo himself, it is said, visited Lycia in the form of a wolf and slaughtered the Telchines.[17] Apollo and his mother are not the only gods to be associated with the wolf: Mars, the Roman god of war, also had the wolf as his symbol, and Jupiter, god of the sky and thunder and king of the Roman gods, turned King Lycaon into a wolf as a punishment. The story recounts how Lycaon was known to practise human sacrifice and cannibalistic rituals, and this angered the gods. Jupiter, disguised as a traveller, journeyed to Lycaon's palace and was invited by Lycaon's sons to join in their banquet that contained human remains. Outraged, he turned the king into a werewolf:

> News of these evil times had reached my ears. Hoping it false I left Olympus's heights, and travelled the earth, a god in human form. It would take too long to tell what wickedness I found everywhere. Those rumours were even milder than the truth. I had crossed Maenala, those mountains bristling with wild beasts' lairs, Cyllene, and the pinewoods of chill Lycaeus. Then, as the last shadows gave way to night,

Lycaon in wolf form. A 16th-century engraving by Agostino de Musi.

I entered the inhospitable house of the Arcadian king. I gave them signs that a god had come, and the people began to worship me. At first Lycaon ridiculed their piety, then exclaimed 'I will prove by a straightforward test whether he is a god or a mortal. The truth will not be in doubt.' He planned to destroy me in the depths of sleep, unexpectedly, by night. That is how he resolved to prove the truth. Not satisfied with this he took a hostage sent by the Molossi, opened his throat with a knife, and made some of the still warm limbs tender in seething water, roasting others in the fire. No sooner were these placed on the table than I brought the roof down on the household gods, with my avenging flames, those gods worthy of such a master. He himself ran in terror, and reaching the silent fields howled aloud, frustrated of speech. Foaming at the mouth, and greedy as ever for killing, he turned against the sheep, still delighting in blood. His clothes became bristling hair, his arms became legs. He was a wolf, but kept some vestige of his former shape. There were the same grey hairs, the same violent face, the same glittering eyes, the same savage image.[18]

There are several other accounts like this, where a man is turned into what we would recognize as a werewolf, and it is worth considering these now. Apollas, otherwise known as 'Agriopas', was the Greek writer of an account of Olympic victors mentioned by Pliny in his book *Naturalis Historia* (*Natural History*). In his account, the *Olympionics*, Apollas recounts a certain Daemenetus of Parrhasia who was turned into a wolf after eating the entrails of a boy that had been sacrificed to Zeus Lycaeus. His punishment lasted ten years, after which he turned back into a man. He then entered the Olympic games as a boxer and won. Pliny was deeply suspicious of the notion that men could be turned to wolves, and comments on the transformation:

> that men have been turned into wolves, and again restored to their original form, we must confidently look upon as

48

untrue, unless, indeed, we are ready to believe all the tales, which, for so many ages, have been found to be fabulous.[19]

Pliny says that this notion of changing into a wolf is quite common, and that it is known as *versipellis*, that is, 'skin changer' or 'turn skin'. In the classical world the word seems to have referred to a form of madness that men could suffer from, whereby they believed themselves changed into a wolf. This is our earliest reference to what became known as the condition 'lycanthropy', a disease which was obviously known to the Romans, and seems to have been applied to a person who had undergone a noticeable change in his character or habits.[20] Pliny further explains where this initial belief comes from, and quotes the Greek author Euanthes, when he says that

the Arcadians assert that a member of the family of one Anthus is chosen by lot, and then taken to a certain lake in that district, where, after suspending his clothes on an oak,

Lycaon is transformed by Zeus, an engraving by Johann Ulrich Krauss, 1690.

he swims across the water and goes away into the desert, where he is changed into a wolf and associates with other animals of the same species for a space of nine years. If he has kept himself from beholding a man during the whole of that time, he returns to the same lake, and, after swimming across it, resumes his original form, only with the addition of nine years in age to his former appearance.[21]

In Plautus' play *Amphitryon* we hear the line 'now I see it was all true, which I have heard in old tales, that the Anthican men in Arcadia were changed, and remained savage brutes, and were never recognised again even by their own parents'.[22] Widespread knowledge of the werewolf myth in society at this time is therefore made clear. Other than by the wrath of the gods or some strange curse, how could men be turned into werewolves at this time, and how does this transformation compare to the more traditional view from the Middle Ages onwards? The Roman poet Virgil, in his eighth *Eclogue* (37 BC), told of a powerful magician named Moeris who had a great knowledge of herbs and potions, and used a mixture of these to become a werewolf, although the transformation was only temporary. This use of 'magic' or of a special formula is very similar to later medieval traditions, particularly surrounding the idea of witchcraft. Plato also mentions how mixing certain human remains also does the trick: 'the tale is that he who has tasted the entrails of a single human victim minced up with the entrails of other victims is destined to become a wolf. Have you never heard it?'.[23] Although this links back to the myths surrounding the gods, we have seen that human remains may have been consumed at sites such as Knossos. However, the Greek archaeologist Konstantinos Kourouniotis, who excavated the Temple of Zeus on Mount Lykaion in the early 1900s, found no human bones whatsoever, perhaps relegating the story to myth.[24] Yet, as the historian Richard Buxton quite rightly points out in quoting Walter Burkert, 'only a very few people are going to know exactly what is in the casserole – the rest is suggestion'.[25]

One of the more prevalent werewolf cases from the period is that depicted in *The Satyricon of Petronius Arbiter*. The *Satyricon* is a

work of prose and poetry in Latin, believed to have been written by
Gaius Petronius (*c.* 27–66), a Roman courtier to Emperor Nero. In the
chapter entitled 'Trimalchio's Dinner', Niceros regales the guests with
a story of an event that befell him while he was still a slave. He fell
in love with a girl named Melissa who was the tavern-keeper's wife.
Lo and behold, the husband died, so Niceros decided to visit Melissa
when his master was away in Capua on business, and he persuaded
his master's lodger to accompany him.

It so happened my master had gone to Capua, to attend to
various trifles of business. So seizing the opportunity, I
persuade our lodger to accompany me as far as the fifth mile-
stone. He was a soldier, as bold as Hell. We got under way
about first cockcrow, with the moon shining as bright as
day. We arrive at the tombs; my man lingers behind among
the gravestones, whilst I sit down singing, and start counting the gravestones. Presently I looked back for my comrade;
he had stripped off all his clothes and laid them down by
the wayside. My heart was in my mouth; and there I stood
feeling like a dead man. Then he made water all round the
clothes, and in an instant changed into a wolf. Don't imagine
I'm joking; I would not tell a lie for the finest fortune ever
man had.

However, as I was telling you, directly he was turned into
a wolf, he set up a howl, and away to the woods. At first I
didn't know where I was, but presently I went forward to
gather up his clothes; but lo and behold! they were turned
into stone. If ever a man was like to die of terror, I was that
man! Still I drew my sword and let out at every shadow on
the road till I arrived at my sweetheart's house. I rushed in
looking like a ghost, soul and body barely sticking together.
The sweat was pouring down between my legs, my eyes
were set, my wits gone almost past recovery. Melissa was
astounded at my plight, wondering why ever I was abroad
so late. 'Had you come a little sooner', she said, 'you might
have given us a hand; a wolf broke into the farm and has

slaughtered all the cattle, just as if a butcher had bled them.
Still he didn't altogether have the laugh on us, though he did
escape; for one of the laborers ran him through the neck
with a pike.'

After hearing this, I could not close an eye, but directly
it was broad daylight, I started off for our good Gaius's house,
like a peddler whose pack's been stolen; and coming to the
spot where the clothes had been turned into stone, I found
nothing whatever but a pool of blood. When eventually I got
home, there lay my soldier a-bed like a great ox, while a
surgeon was dressing his neck. I saw at once he was a werewolf and I could never afterwards eat bread with him, no! not
if you'd killed me. Other people may think what they please;
but as for me, if I'm telling you a lie, may your guardian
spirits confound me!.[26]

Another classical account of a werewolf comes from the Mesopo-
tamian poem *The Epic of Gilgamesh*, one of the earliest surviving
pieces of literature. Today there are twelve clay tablets bearing
cuneiforms that once belonged to the seventh-century BC king,
Ashurbanipal of Assyria. The tablets were written sometime between 1300–1000 BC, but the subject-matter was possibly influenced by earlier works dating from as early as 2000 BC. The part
that relates to our werewolf myth is Tablet VI, which includes the
following lines:

> You loved a shepherd, a herdsman, who endlessly put up
> cakes for you, and everyday slaughtered kids for you. You
> struck him, turned him into a wolf. His own boys drove
> him away, and his dogs tore his hide to bits.[27]

This event has parallels with the Greek legend of Actaeon who
stumbled upon the goddess Artemis who was bathing naked in the
forest. She turned Actaeon into a stag in punishment for looking
at her, and his raging hounds, struck with a 'wolf's frenzy', tore him
apart as they would a stag.[28]

Wolf statue thought to date from the 5th century BC. The Romulus and Remus figures were added later.

Finally, in terms of the classical accounts, it is worth noting those relating to the Neurians, who were said to transform themselves into wolves. Herodotus wrote an account of the Neurians in his *Histories*, and relates that Neuris was divided from Scythia by the river Tyres but maintained the Scythian laws. Herod mentions that 'these people are very little better than conjurors. For the Scythae, as well as the Greeks who are settled in Scythia, say of them that every Neurian is turned into a wolf for a few days each year, after which he returns to his former state'.[29] Pomponius Mela, an early Roman geographer, also mentions this: 'there is a fixed time for each Neurian, at which time they change, if they like, into wolves, and back again into their former condition'.[30]

From the accounts of the period it seems that werewolves were thought to be quite prevalent, particularly in terms of religion and mythology surrounding their gods. Also, it seems there were particular tribes or groups of people for whom the werewolf myth held more importance than most, for whatever reason. Certainly, these

Roman mosaic depicting the Romulus and Remus story from
Aldborough, Yorkshire, *c.* 4th century.

peoples could not be *physical* werewolves, so what other reasons were
there for believing they could undergo an actual transformation?
Pliny's thoughts against 'werewolfery' can be viewed against those of
early Christian author Quintus Septimius Florens (*c.* 155–229). In
his work *On the Soul,* he argued against the possibility of men becoming animals, as it was 'impossible for the human soul to pass into
beasts, even though the philosophers may hold that both are made
up of the same substantial elements'.[31] Homer may shed some light
on the matter:

> from his head they took the weasel-skin helmet, and the
> wolf-skin, with the bent bow and spear [and] immediately
> he threw around his shoulders his crooked bow, and put on
> above the hide of grey wolf.[32]

Here we do not see a literal werewolf but a man dressed to look
like one, which is infinitely easier to comprehend than the so-called

man-beast. Perhaps this is where the myths and legends came from. If the Arcadians, or the Neuri or the Lycians *dressed* as wolves for battle, then we may be able to make sense of some of the accounts discussed. Ultimately, they may have played on the notion of being able to transform themselves into wolves to strike fear into their enemies. Also, in the *Iliad*, Homer describes the Myrmidons, the warrior elite of Achilles, who are

> like carnivorous wolves, in whose hearts is immense strength, and which, having slain a great horned stag in the mountains, tearing devour it; but the jaws of all are red with blood; and then they rush in a pack, lapping with slender tongues the surface of the dark water from a black-water fountain, vomiting forth clots of blood.[33]

Here, again, the Myrmidons are not wolves; they are wolf-like. The adjective is used to describe their stealth, their cunning and their ferocity. This suggestion of 'warrior wolves' becomes increasingly prevalent, particularly among the Germanic tribes.

The link between wolves and the Mother Earth goddess is clear in Plutarch's *Natural Questions*, in which he discusses the work *On Animals* by Antipater:

> Antipater in his book 'On Animals' asserts that wolves give birth at the time when trees that bear nuts or acorns shed their flowers: when they eat these, their wombs are opened. But if there is no supply of these flowers, their offspring die within them and cannot see the light. Moreover these parts of the world that are not fertile in nut-trees or oak-trees are not troubled by wolves.[34]

Here, Plutarch argues, is a link between those people who eat acorns (that is, the Arcadians) and wolves. Of more poignancy, however, is the notion that a supply of nuts and acorns is necessary for the wolves to thrive, so peoples for whom the wolf, or the werewolf myth, is important would be reliant on this – a fact which could then explain the apparent link between werewolves (in the ancient sense so far described) and the provider of such supplies, the Earth Mother. Towards the Early Middle Ages, and particularly within the final throes of paganism, the werewolf myth flourished and became more and more apparent before Christianity changed the fundamental basis of the werewolf cult forever.

three
Fits of Fury: The Wolves
of Germania

He met a hound that came from Hel.
That one had blood upon his breast,
and long did he bark at Baldr's father.
Baldr's Dreams from the *Poetic Edda*.

A round 445, Rome was under attack by barbarian hordes that posed such a threat to the Empire that Britain was abandoned. Although the Roman garrisons based in Britain withdrew to Rome, it ultimately proved too late; Rome was sacked. Whether the Romans left behind any tales or believers in werewolves is not known, but what they did leave behind was a number of Germanic mercenaries who had been fighting in the Roman army. These were the Angles, Saxons, Frisians and Jutes. According to popular belief, these groups invaded Britain in the mid-fifth century. However, this is inaccurate as they were already there. Word was most probably sent back that Britain was ripe for the taking and over several decades an influx of Germanic peoples filtered into Britain to eventually create England, or 'Angle-land', land of the Anglo-Saxons.

Through the *Anglo-Saxon Chronicle*, a contemporary document which narrates the main events of Britain year by year, we hear how King Vortigern invited some of the Germanic tribes to Britain and gave them land in the southeast on condition that they help him fight the Picts, who were rallying themselves after the Romans had left. The Picts were an indigenous Iron Age tribe living in northern Britain (now Scotland) that had continually opposed Roman forces attempting to seize their lands. This is the period when the famous warlords Hengist and Horsa arrived; they destroyed the king's enemies before turning on the king himself and ravaged Britain through 'fire and sword's edge'. This influx of Germanic peoples coincided with rising sea levels and warring tribes in their homelands, probably making the 'easy picking' of Britain's lands rather appealing. It was in this period that the British war leader Ambrosius Aurelianus achieved a great victory over the marauding Anglo-Saxons at Mount Badon, near Bath, and this historical figure is now thought to be the inspiration behind the mythic King Arthur legend.

The Roman writer Tacitus (56–117) described the roots of these invading Anglo-Saxons when he documented the Germanic tribes in *Germania* towards the very end of the first century. He writes that the term 'Germanic' did not represent a specific ethnic people but rather a group of people who shared a common language and culture (perhaps similar to the Iron Age Picts or Celts that existed in Britain). These Germanic peoples were split into three tribes: the Herminones (who lived in the central areas), the Ingaevones (who lived on the coast) and the Istaevones (who occupied other areas). Tacitus says that they were named after the three sons of Mannus, the earth god Tuisto's son. Does this suggest that these tribes, too, worshipped an earth god like many of the other cultures we have discussed? Tacitus further recounts how kings or leaders were elected and that the people agreed on matters of importance within special assemblies. From these, matters of law were decided and upheld and a strict 'penal code' seems to have been in place: traitors and deserters were hanged, cowards, shirkers and sodomites were drowned in bogs, and 'death payments' were used, all of which is very similar to the later Anglo-Saxon 'wer-gild' (man-price).[1] These payments were made to a victim or victim's family in cases of injury or death.[2]

The werewolf myth seems to have come with the arriving tribes to Britain, particularly the concept of wanting to pass the power of the wolf to man (again, this is not necessarily a belief in a physical transformation into a wolf, but rather a metaphorical one). For example, when the Anglo-Saxon chronicler Asser wrote his biography of King Alfred, the *De Rebus Gestis Aelfredi*, he spoke of a Mercian priest called Werwulfhum, allegedly a friend of Bishop Werfrith of Worcester. Here are two, unusually Christian, examples of people attaching the moniker of the wolf or werewolf to themselves.[3]

However, the most striking example of the myth (and indeed the religious beliefs behind the myth) comes to us from the epic Anglo-Saxon poem *Beowulf,* composed possibly in the eighth century. The poem narrates the hero Beowulf's fight against two mythological creatures – the Grendel, a fearsome half-man, half-beast monster, and a dragon – and is a tale of bravery, heroism and honour. The first half of the poem is dedicated to his plight against the Grendel and Grendel's mother and sees him journey to the great hall at Heorot, which is being plagued by the Grendel. When the hero Beowulf goes to kill Grendel's mother, he says she may try to hide in 'gyfenes grund', which the historian John Grigsby has argued should be translated as 'Gefion's ground' and relates to the Norse goddess Gefion mentioned in the Icelandic historian Snorri Sturluson's (1179–1241) collection known as the *Prose Edda.* Sturluson was writing in the late twelfth / early thirteenth century and documented the Viking Sagas, and wrote how Gefion lived on an island with Skjold, the son of the Viking god Odin. Grigsby believes that Gefion is the same goddess known to the Germanic tribes as 'Northies' and that the writer of *Beowulf* (and therefore presumably the audience) created a relationship between the legends of Gefion / Nerthus and the lake in which the Grendel's mother dwelt.[4]

Furthermore, is it a coincidence that in Norse legend Skjold was the same person as Scyld Scefing (Shield Sheafson), the young boy who appears at the beginning of *Beowulf* and the great-grandfather of Hrothgar, the lord of Heorot? Grigsby's argument is that whilst *Beowulf* can be read as a poem to entertain, it is in fact an extremely rare example of religious pagan beliefs in a period when old gods were being abandoned in favour of new ones.

Other parts of *Beowulf* also attest to this myth – even the name of the poem and its hero seem to reflect some similarities with the wolf. The historian Michael Wood tells us that 'the England of Beowulf was a wild and under-populated land, there were no real towns, the forests were full of wolves and the isolated farms and settlements and lonely monasteries were little centres of human life amidst a vast untamed nature – their mental life was surrounded by monsters'.[5] And Grendel was one of the worst: 'Grendel . . . the fiend's name.

Grim. Infamous. Wasteland stalker. Master of the moor and the fen-fortress. He is found in hell.'[6]

Tolkien gave a lecture on these monsters at the British Academy in the 1930s, when he was Professor of Anglo-Saxon at the University of Oxford, called 'Beowulf: the Monsters and the Critics'. He argued that whilst academia derided the sensationalist beasts of the poem, they should 'be regarded as central to the tale, rather than embarrassing additions'.[7] Was he suggesting that Anglo-Saxon society was familiar with these beasts and monsters, rather than merely entertained by their fanciful inclusion in the poem, not least by the wolf-man Grendel (his mother is referred to as the *brimwylf* or the 'lake-wolf')?

This idea of a 'lake-wolf', a supernatural being living in the murky depths of a bog, conjures up images of Iron Age bog bodies. Indeed, the Germanic region of Europe has given up numerous examples of these macabre remains. Studying these corpses can perhaps shed more light on those found in England and Ireland particularly the Celtic examples, as there is already strong documentary evidence for the Germanic ones. Let us return to Tacitus:

> they (the Germanic tribes) share a common worship of Nerthus, or Mother Earth. They believe she takes part in human affairs, riding in a chariot among her people ... [there follow] days of rejoicing and merrymaking ... no one goes to war, no one takes up arms; every iron object is locked away ... when she has had enough of the society of men ... the chariot, the vestments, and the goddess herself, are cleansed in a secluded lake. This service is performed by slaves who immediately afterwards are drowned in the lake. Thus mystery begets terror and a pious reluctance to ask what that sight can be which is seen only by men doomed to die.[8]

This passage apparently sheds light on why the bog bodies were slaughtered: they are ritual sacrifices to Nerthus, the Earth Mother. And yet, if they were slaves, as suggested by Tacitus, why did the bog bodies discussed in Chapter One seemingly issue from the upper echelons of society? Why did they have carefully manicured finger-nails, soft hands and freshly cut hair? From studying the hundreds of European bog corpses, we can see that only some of them appear to have been victims of 'ritual sacrifices', and that these are the ones who are found naked and bear the marks of 'multiple deaths'. These are also the ones that have smooth hands – they cannot be slaves, and arguably, they are priests or shamans in the early Earth Mother cult of Nerthus.

The discovery of bog bodies in the Germanic region is referred to in the German fairy tale known as 'Iron John' preserved in the collection made by the Brothers Grimm in the nineteenth century, in which, looking into a deep pool, huntsmen could see 'a wild man whose body was brown like rusty iron, and whose hair hung over his face down to his knees'. Interestingly, he was deemed to be still alive: 'they bound him with cords, and led him away to the castle'.[9]

Again, the victims of such Germanic bog sacrifices had eaten a final meal very similar to those eaten by victims from Britain and Ireland. Both the Tollund Man (found in 1959 near Silkeborg in Denmark) and Grauballe Man (discovered in 1952 in Jutland, Denmark) had eaten a meal of barley and ergot – a fungus that can cause hallucinations when ingested, owing to its 'properties' that include lysergic acid (LSD), which sometimes makes people believe that they are animals.[10]

John Grigsby further argues that the fungal ergot porridge detected in the bog bodies was known as 'wolf's tooth' and that those who ate it would feel as if they were being strangled and burned because of the side effects. However, when they 'came down', they would still be alive.[11]

Perhaps this gave them the sensation that they had been 'reborn'. What is puzzling, though, is that the bog bodies *were* killed, often by strangulation. Was this a ritual? Were the priests or shamans of Nerthus ritually killed in preparation for a rebirth? If so, it is further proof of the cyclical fertility cult that the early wolf-man myth seems to have a central role in, as discussed above.

The Iron Age hill fort at Danebury, Hampshire, which dates back to the sixth century BC, revealed that human sacrificial victims had been buried in the pits where grain was stored. Complete corpses, parts of corpses and especially the heads were all unearthed. One of the corpses had had a pile of rocks placed on top of it,[12] recalling methods of interment at an Iron Age burial site in Ehrenberg, Bavaria, where a man and a woman had been buried with large rocks on them.[13]

Do these practices again relate to the ritual sacrifices of the Nerthus cult? The Greek historian Strabo, in his *Histories*, explains exactly how these 'victims' were killed: '[they] stab him with a dagger in the region of the diaphragm and when he has fallen, they foretell

The Three Mothers statue from Cirencester, Gloucestershire.
Although dating to the Roman period, they are of Celtic belief.

the future from his fall and from the convulsions of his limbs and moreover, from the spurting of his blood'.[14]

The Roman poet Lucan added that the sacrifices were often conducted in 'supernatural groves' where the druids gathered:

> a grove there was untouched by men's hands from ancient times, whose interlacing boughs enclosed a space of darkness and cold shade, and banished the sunlight from above ... Gods were worshipped there with savage rites, the altars were heaped with hideous offerings and every tree was sprinkled with human gore ... the people never resorted thither to worship at close quarters, but left the place to the gods for, when the sun is in mid-heaven or dark night fills the sky, the priest himself dreads their approach and fears to surprise the lord of the grove.[15]

Adam of Bremen, writing in the eleventh century, told how every nine years sacrifices were carried out and that horses, dogs and men alike were hung in bloody groves. Strabo also explains that they would strike the victim

> in the back with a sword ... shoot them to death with arrows or impale them in the temples or having devised a colossus of straw and wood, thrown into the colossus cattle and wild animals of all sorts and humans, and then make a burnt offering of the whole thing.[16]

This sounds rather similar to the sacrifices practised by the Romans for the goddess Artemis.

Although it would appear that the tradition of making sacrifices to the Earth Mother goddess continued long after the old gods of *Beowulf* had disappeared, the cult of the gods might in fact have persisted under a different guise. If Nerthus, the early Germanic goddess, was translated into Old Norse to bring her into a more contemporaneous era with *Beowulf*, then we would be searching for a goddess called 'Njorthr'. In Norse mythology, such a deity does

Small statuette of the Norse god Freyr, depicted wearing a hat very similar to that of Tollund Man. The fertility power of the statue is clearly visible in the erect phallus.

exist but it is a *male* god and not a *female* one. Njorthr is the father of Freyr and Freyja, the brother and sister fertility gods, and is, intriguingly, depicted in Snorri Sturluson's *The Language of Poetry* as a god of wagons (which recalls the chariot tradition of Nerthus).[17]

Although the Nerthus-Njorthr transition collapses because of the change in sex of the god in Norse mythology, it is noteworthy that the religion seems to have continued with Njorthr's son, Freyr. Indeed, he owned a magical ship and a golden boar and is often depicted riding around the countryside on a wagon 'supplying' fertility. The evidence for this is the two 'Wagons of Nerthus', discovered in the region at Dejbjerg in Jutland, that date to around 200, whilst another was included in the ship burial at Oseberg in Norway. Here a female was buried with a wealth of grave goods including a wagon and nuts and apples. The nuts and apples may well represent the 'fruits' that the Mother Goddess provides, which perhaps supply proof of the worship of the Earth Mother. Further 'wagons' or 'chariots' were found at sites in Italy (two chariots were found at Sesto Calende near Lake Maggiore in northern Italy, with a bronze bucket-type object and dating to the sixth century BC) and in England. In total, there are 21 known 'chariot burials' in England, all of which were located in the East Riding of Yorkshire where the Parisii tribe lived. This includes the site at Wetwang in Yorkshire that was discovered with a female burial dating to *circa* 300 BC.

In the Viking saga known as the *Heimskringla*, Freyr embarked on a wagon tour through Sweden and the people there 'wondered how he would not receive living victims as before'. This is then a possible reference to the bog body sacrifices and a reflection on how the religion has shifted from the early Germanic religion into the later Norse religion. In this Norse religion the elves were linked with Freyr (who does not like weaponry), and in the earlier Nerthus religion, she too disliked this and had all 'iron objects' locked away. So, carrying or wearing an amulet of iron would keep the elves – the spirits of the landscape – away, so Norse mythology tells us. In Romanian folkloric customs, wearing an amulet of iron also keeps the *strigoi* at bay, and this may have been passed on to later vampire and werewolf customs, where wearing a cross or an amulet of silver defends against such creatures. In other early customs, elves or landscape spirits were believed to dance in circles and this is often linked to pagan stone circles – the Nine Ladies stone circle at Stanton Moor in the Peak District in Derbyshire in the UK has a legend that says its nine stones were once nine fairies or elves that danced in a circle but were turned to stone. Furthermore, the 'cup' marks mentioned in Chapter One and found carved into stones at some prehistoric sites might well have been 'sacrificial hollows' carved into the rock for pouring blood into during rituals, as opposed to merely rock art as is generally believed. Folkloric traditions later saw this blood being replaced by milk and some accounts describe porridge being left in them for the fairies.[18] Such an action would link to the similar rite of the wolf-tooth porridge discovered in the stomachs of the excavated bog bodies.

Grigsby argues that the poem *Beowulf* signifies the end of the Nerthus / Earth Mother cult and the adoption of the worshipping of Odin. This transition appears to have occurred in the late fifth / early sixth century, which is not long after the time when *Beowulf* is thought to have been first produced.[19]

However, a total end to these cults is unlikely, although a dramatic shift in religious allegiances did occur at some point in this period. The single most important piece of evidence that can help us understand this shift is arguably the Gundestrup Cauldron, found in a bog in Himmerland, Denmark. Dating to the first century BC, it is decorated with a number of 'plates' and each is adorned with specific images. Plausibly, it relates directly to the Earth Mother cult and bears important evidence as to how the religion changes in the period. Plate A depicts a horned figure believed to be Cernunnos, an Iron Age god, who wears reindeer antlers and is surrounded by a number of animals. This would confirm his position as a shaman. It also recalls earlier religious beliefs from prehistory (discussed in Chapter One). The figure is holding a torc, an item of Iron Age ornament worn around the neck. Cernunnos is usually depicted wearing a torc, believed to reflect his nobility. Plate B shows a female figure with two,

The Gundestrup Cauldron.

The horned god Cernunnos on the Gundestrup Cauldron.

six-spoked wheels, which is most probably Nerthus with her chariot. Plate c depicts a bearded man holding a broken, twelve-spoked wheel, and most of the chariot burials found in Europe have twelve-spoked wheels, so again this may be related and may represent a Freyr-type god. Plate D, meanwhile, shows three bulls being slain and this recalls the bull cult of Mithras, whilst Plate E is perhaps the most important to our wolf-myth exploration as it depicts a line of 'warriors' and a cauldron. The warriors all have spears and shields and seem to be waiting in line for what appears to be an initiation ceremony involving their being dunked in a cauldron by a female figure. This figure is conceivably Nerthus, and whether the figures are in effect 'baptized' or drowned by Nerthus is unclear. Nevertheless, a number of warriors on horseback are shown above them, going in the opposite direction, attesting to their 'rebirth'. The warriors on the bottom row are accompanied by carynx players. The carynx is played in a similar way to a trumpet, and dates from *c.* 300 BC to AD 200. The mouth of the carynx is often shaped like a boar, which would relate to the Freyr-god. Such instruments have been found as far apart as Scotland (at Deskford) and France (at Tintignac).

Whilst opinion is divided as to whether the figures outlined above are or are not reincarnated warriors, an examination of their helmets may assist in the matter. The first is adorned with some sort

Detail from inside the Gundestrup Cauldron showing warriors being
'reborn' after baptism by a female goddess.

of plume or crescent and its meaning is unknown, but probably
relates to a specific but unidentified god. The second is antler-crested
and represents Cernunnos; the boar-crested third relates to Freyr
and the fourth is bird-crested and represents Bran, a god who is also
depicted as having a magic cauldron. Similar helmets have been excavated, and two examples from Romania (Ciumeşti and Luncani) are
adorned with wolves.[20]

The carynx players are also led by a man wearing a boar-crested
helmet. Owing to its style, the cauldron probably originated from
the region covering Romania, Bulgaria and eastern Hungary.[21]

A similar cauldron depicting bull heads was found at Rynkeby
in Denmark. However, of all the helmet adornments it is the boar
feature that is important, as is the link to the Norse god Freyr. Arch-
aeologically, a decline of Nerthus worship and an increase in Freyr
worship seems quite clear here, and this shift is central to the growth
of the werewolf myth from the Viking period onwards.

It was suggested above that Odin worship also increased in the
period after *Beowulf* was composed, and at this point, the werewolf myth is at its most prevalent. Odin was a god for the wizards or
spellbinders (an orator whose words 'mesmerized' a captive audience)
of the period, and Swedish carvings often depict him alongside his
'spellbond' – a knot which is made up of three interlocking triangles.
Cremation urns from East Anglian cemeteries in the UK often depict

Detail showing the boar's head from the Sutton Hoo helmet.

Odin's spell-knots alongside images of wolves and are probably representations of the story in which Odin binds the great wolf Fenrir in Norse mythology. The story tells how the wolf was raised from a pup and grew into a dangerously powerful creature. To protect themselves, the gods tried to bind Fenrir, but the chains could not hold him and he broke free. After two failed attempts, the gods requested that the dwarfs, who were masters of magic, make a special binding chain. This was constructed from magical ingredients: the noise a cat makes when it moves; the beard of a woman; the growing roots of a mountain; the breath of a fish; the spittle of a bird and the sinews of a bear. Feeling he was being tricked, Fenrir agreed to be bound by it only if the god Tyr placed his hand inside his mouth, which he did. When the wolf could not break free of the dwarves' chain, he bit off Tyr's hand, but remained bound and trapped. A point of note is that in *Beowulf* the treasure that Beowulf wins is protected by magic, *galdre*, and the word used is *bewunden*, or 'wound round by'.[22]

The Icelandic writer Snorri Sturluson tells us that Odin turned his enemies into wild boars and this may be evidence of a forbidden religion after the *Beowulf* period. The Sagas often mention people being turned into boars, for example, in the *Vatnsdæla*, Ljot threatens to turn Þhorsteinn and Jökull into boars.[23]

However, in *Beowulf*, boars are said to be protective animals, which is why the warriors in the poem wear them on their helmets: 'the smith set the helmet with swine-figures so that neither sword nor battle blades should ever be able to bite it'.[24]

Boar helmets have been found in Britain at the sites of Sutton Hoo in Suffolk, where there were boars set in the decoration on the discovered objects, and at Benty Grange in Derbyshire, where a helmet had a boar on its peak. A 'stamping die' from a site in Sweden also demonstrates the use of boars as helmet decoration. In relation to the Sutton Hoo boar decoration, Sam Newton explains that 'the boars' heads with the tusks are exactly located as in the *Beowulf* description; "the boar-shape shone over the cheek guard", it protected the lives of the war-minded warriors'.[25]

The warriors who go to fight the Grendel in *Beowulf* all wear boar helmets (perhaps to protect them against the savage beast), and yet in the poem, we hear how Finn and his sons fight a great battle against the Danes at Friesland and many Danes are slaughtered, after which 'the pyre was heaped with boar-shaped helmets forged in gold'.[26] So the boar did not protect the soldiers, it seems. Gale Owen-Crocker has argued that the *Beowulf* poet 'does not explain that in those days people wore boar-figures on their helmets to protect them but simply describes the gilded boar that has survived its owner'.[27] Although *Beowulf* does suggest soldiers wear helmets for protection, their use is arguably more than this, and is particularly for religious purposes. Owen-Crocker also argues that the protection failed (consider, for example, the Friesland killings) but 'the boar as symbol seems to have had a much longer existence and wider currency than the boar-helmet. Tacitus mentioned the wearing of boar masks, probably in crop-fertility ceremonies, and as the familiar of the god Freyr the boar was well known in the North.'[28]

The use of the boar seems to have been limited exclusively to the sixth and seventh centuries. The Torslunda helmet die, the Benty Grange, the Wollaston (from Northamptonshire in the UK) and the Sutton Hoo helmets all date to this period. Further boar imagery is noted on the shoulder clasps and on the largest bowl, both of which were also found in Sutton Hoo. (Is it then possible that the bowl from Sutton Hoo may also be a 'cauldron'?) In fact, apart from hunting scenes, boars do not appear in any Anglo-Saxon artwork after the seventh century.[29]

In other 'barley god' cults, the Greek Adonis, Egyptian Osiris and Roman Attis were all attacked by a boar and gouged in the leg (symbolizing the cutting of the barley beneath the corn). The sickle associated with cutting this corn is also curved like the boar's tusk. In Germanic / Norse traditions boars would be sacrificed at certain times such as Midwinter solstice. The boar could arguably have represented the sun in such traditions, with Freyr's own boar called *Gullinbursti* (Golden Bristles) and possibly reflecting the rays of the sun. In the Old English text *The Life of St Christopher* there is a reference to a strange wolf-like creature that may be a werewolf who 'had the head of a hound . . . his locks were extremely long, and his eyes shone as bright as the morning star, and his teeth were as sharp as boar's tusks.'[30]

Both this text and the oldest surviving version of *Beowulf* were held in Cotton Vitellius A. xv of the collection of Sir John Cotton (*d.* 1792) located in Ashburnham House, Westminster, London, which also featured two other texts: *The Wonders of the East* and *The Letters of Alexander to Aristotle* (both of which also mention men with dog or wolf heads). Furthermore, as *Beowulf* featured the Grendel, the strange wolf-like creature, the collation of these four texts may point to an early collection of werewolf myths.

Werewolf links are also to be made in the Sutton Hoo burial, as the grave goods contained three potential 'cauldrons', two drinking horns, the helmet with birds with boar-head wings on it and a purse decorated with wolves. Also, the man believed to have been buried in the ship burial is King Raedwald of the Wuffinga dynasty, so named because of Raedwald's grandfather Wuffa ('Little Wolf').

Bronze plate from Oland, Sweden, showing a Berserker
wearing a wolf-pelt.

The family name 'Wuffinga' could also mean 'man or people of the
wolf'. Indeed, the Anglo-Saxon period provided many names with
'wolf' as in the prefix 'Wulfric' and 'Wulfstan', for example, which
again indicates society's profound links to the wolf.

However, it is the Viking age, from the ninth century onwards
for Britain, that provides the most significant evidence for the wolf
cult, as manifested in mythology, textual sources and archaeology.
In *Beowulf*, as we have seen, the 'boar shapes shone above the
cheek-guards [and] kept guard over life' but 'it was the wolf, above
all creatures, that typified the fury to the ancient north-west Euro-
peans'.[31] As such, these *ulfhednar* (wolf heads) are often mentioned.
This could be explained by the period's belief that ravens and wolves
were thought to take the souls of the dead after battles down to
the underworld. Also, the valkyries, female entities who took the
souls of dead warriors up to Valhalla, the Viking paradise, were

frequently depicted as riding through the skies on horses or wolves. The wolf-beast Fenrir, who in Norse mythology is depicted as eating the sun and moon, evokes the Romanian *varcolac*. Indeed, this can be seen on the Sutton Hoo purse. In Snorri Sturluson's *Ynglinga Saga 6*, '[Odin's] men went without their mailcoats and were mad as hounds or wolves, bit their shields and were as strong as bears or bulls', emphasizing the different qualities attributed to specific animals. These warriors, with the heads of bears and wolves, are depicted on helmets and sword scabbards from sites in Sweden.[32] Sabine Baring-Gould notes how in Iceland and Norway some men were known as *eigi einhamir*, 'not of one skin'.[33] As such, they could take on other forms, and were shapeshifters, thus endowed with improved strength and ferocity. These are the infamous 'berserkers' or 'bear skins', the fearless warriors of Odin and Thor, the Viking war gods. From an archaeological perspective, a number of graves have been excavated in Norway and Sweden, pre-dating the Viking era in many cases, in which bear skins have been apparently wrapped or laid over the dead, and bear claws have also been found in the graves.[34] It is also clear that some of the berserkers wore wolf-, and not bear skins, as the *Vatnsdœla Saga* attests: '[the berserkers] who were called *ulfheknir* had got wolf-skins over their mail coats'.[35] Saxo Grammaticus explained how the wolf or bear skins would appear in battle:

> Their eyes glared as though a flame burned in the sockets, they ground their teeth, and frothed at the mouth; they gnawed at their shield rims, and are said to have sometimes bitten them through, and as they rushed into conflict they yelped as dogs or howled as wolves.[36]

Initiation ceremonies are mentioned in many of the Sagas involving berserkers, and often twelve men have to fight a bear and cut off its paw or snout. Sturluson mentions a legend in the *Prose Edda* where Thor proves his strength by lifting twelve bear skins off the ground. These berserkers most likely used an intoxicating drink to prepare them for the 'battle frenzy'. Similarly, it is known that the

A 17th-century woodcut of a man in wolf – or possibly bear – form.

Celts used woad to the same ends. Perhaps this intoxicating drink was also similar to that used by the bog people. The Anglo-Saxons also used a comparable drink to 'become', at least in their minds, wild animals such as bears, boars and wolves. From using these mind-altering drinks, the wolf-man was mentally conjured: 'if he has taken the form of a wolf, or if he goes on a "wolf-ride", he is full of the rage and malignity of the creature'.[37]

In the *Volsunga Saga* two men, Sigmund and Sinfjötli, went into the woods to test their strength by attacking people for their possessions. They came to a woodland hut where two sleeping men lay with visible vestimentary links to sorcerers or witches. The two wolf skins that hung in the hut were taken and put on by Sigmund and Sinfjötli. The wolf persona was 'transferred' to them and they started to howl. As they could not remove the wolf skins, they knew they must kill seven men in order to be free. They parted and set off into the woods. Sinfjötli came across eleven men and killed them all. When Sigmund found out, he attacked Sinfjötli, tearing out his throat. Thus they were trapped in wolf form. Sigmund carried Sinfjötli back to the hall and cried out, 'Deuce, take the wolf-forms!' Later in the saga, Sigmund and nine men are set in stocks in the forest by his sister Signy, and at night an old she-wolf comes and eats one of the men. This consumption continues until all but Sigmund are dead. Signy has Sigmund's face smeared with honey in the hope that the wolf will kill him, but it merely licks off the honey. Whilst doing so, Sigmund rips out the she-wolf's tongue, thus killing it. Yet again, Sigmund survives.

The Scandinavian folklorist Nils Lid discusses the 'importance of the belt of wolf skin in shape-changing tales [in which] such a belt was put on by a man or woman who wanted to turn into a wolf'. In his 1937 work, , *Til varulvens historia*, Lid explains that this 'wolf-belt' is evident in a number of Norwegian witch trials.[38]

Interestingly, some Viking art from the period features images of what appear to be dancing warriors wearing horned helmets and naked except for a belt (possibly of wolf skin) and armed with a weapon. This image is very similar to the Pin Hole Man engraving from Creswell Crags discussed in Chapter One. The question of whether there is a difference between the Viking wolf skins and bear skins remains. In *Shape-changing in the Old Norse Sagas*, H. R. Ellis Davidson suggests that 'although highly dangerous and a formidable adversary, the bear was not thought to be an evil beast like the wolf'.[39]

For example, in the *Aigla Saga* we hear of a man named Ulf ('wolf') who was prone to turn from a placid, well-respected man by day to a savage beast by night. He was given the name 'evening-wolf' and was said to be a *hamrammr* (skin-changer or shape-shifter). Also in this Saga is an account of a man named 'Kveldulf' (which also means 'evening-wolf', and so is possibly the same person) who suffered from the 'berserker rage' and who slew a number of men with a cleaver before reaching his opponent Hallvard and cutting through both Hallvard's helmet and skull and flinging him overboard in one movement. With regard to this agitation, the Saga recounts that 'it is said of these men in the engagement who were were-wolves, or those on whom came the berserker rage, that as long as the fit was on them no one could oppose them, they were so strong'.[40]

The Black Shuck's claw marks burned into the door at
Blythburgh church.

It was probably believed that the difference between the bear and wolf was that by nature the bear is a lone fighter and relies on brute strength, whereas the wolf is more cunning and savage and fights as part of a pack. It also seems the Vikings esteemed the bear, and as Davidson points out, it is quite human in many respects. Unlike the wolf, the bear stands on two legs, hits with its paws, 'hugs' its victim and recalls a human when it is skinned. He also points out there were no bears in Iceland, so the stories must have originated in Norway.[41]

Again, names in Germanic areas where there were wolves and bears are particularly common, for example, 'Ulf' and 'Bjorn'. However, by the same token, the English city of Wolverhampton is a further example, as it translates as 'town of the wolves' from the Anglo-Saxon. Other examples from the Sagas include '*Ulfhekin*' (he of wolf skin) and '*Ulfhamr*' (wolf-shaped), and a certain 'Bjorn' (bear) was the son of '*Ulfhekin*', who was son of '*Ulfhamr*', who was son of '*Ulf*', who was son of '*Ulfhamr*', reflecting a family lineage closely associated with wolves and bears.[42]

It is interesting to note, though, that here there seems to be a difference between 'wolf skin' and 'wolf-shaped'. In certain areas these Old Norse werewolf myths still apparently continue. At Blythburgh close to the Suffolk coast in East Anglia, local legend says that on one fateful evening in August 1577 a huge thunderstorm occurred. East Anglians believed this to be a sign of Woden (or Odin) and his wild hunt. Indeed, his devil dog, the Black Shuck (from the Anglo-Saxon word *scucca* meaning 'demon' or 'hobgoblin'), was seen, black and shaggy with glowing red saucer-like eyes (echoing the description of the Grendel in *Beowulf*). Black Shuck attacked the north door of Holy Trinity church, which, in East Anglian folklore, belongs to the devil, and even today three claw marks can be seen burned into the wood. This idea of Odin's black dog relates to Norse mythology where Odin had two wolves called Geri and Freki. In the poem *Grímnismál*, Agnarr is told by a disguised Odin that: 'Freki and Geri does Heerfather feed, The far-famed fighter of old, But on wine alone does the weapon-decked god, Odin, forever live.'[43]

The Norse god Odin with his two wolves, Geri and Freki, and two ravens, Hugin and Munin.

Here Odin shows that he feeds his hounds whilst he survives only on wine. Evidence of Odin and his wolves comes from the Böksta runestone that bears the inscription 'Ingi . . . and Jógeraer, they had this stone raised in memory of Eistr, their son; Ernfastr and his brothers raised in memory of their brother'.[44]

The stone depicts a man on horseback deemed to be Odin on his four-legged horse Sleipnir (often depicted with eight legs) accompanied by his two wolves. There is also reference to his wolves in the story *Odin and his Companions*:

It was once told that Odin and his brothers created the world. In loneliness while travelling, Odin created the First Wolves, Geri and Freki, to accompany him in his travels and to be partners in the hunt. The wolves became Odin's special companions. Wherever Odin went, the wolves went with him.

Odin travelled all over the world with the wolves. This explains why there are wolves in so many places in the world. As they travelled with Odin, Geri and Freki left their grown offspring behind to enjoy the riches of the New World. Geri and Freki cured Odin's loneliness. The way the wolves celebrated life filled Odin with joy.

Odin also created two Ravens, Hugin and Munin, to help scout ahead as they travelled. Hugin and Munin were very good at finding game and were always hungry, giving meaning to the word 'ravenous'. Hugin and Munin were not able to take game by themselves, but teamed with Geri and Freki they were well fed. To this day, you will often find ravens in the company of their friends the wolves. The ravens still scout out the game for the wolves and the wolves leave a share of the meal for the ravens in thanks.

When Odin created the humans Embla and Ask (from whom all humans sprang), he instructed them to learn from the wolf. The wolf could teach them how to care for their family, how to cooperate with each other in the hunt for food, and how to protect and defend their families.

The wolf gave much wisdom and skill to the early humans. In the old times the wolf was respected. 'To be Wolf Clan (*Ulfhednar*) was a great honor. A Wolf Brother'.[45]

Throughout this period, and indeed much of history,

> wolves were feared because they hunted and ate the same food as the humans [and] they seemed to occupy a particularly ominous presence in the minds of humans. Humans inhabited settlements carved out of cleared areas of forest,

whereas wolves lived in the thick of the forest itself . . .
they seemed to be the essence of wildness pressing in on
the fragile civilisation. The threat posed by wolves pitched
them beyond simply material animals – they became
abstract forces, malevolent, magical beings'.[46]

With the Viking conversion to Christianity towards the end of the
tenth century and the end of paganism, the way wolves and indeed
wolf-men were viewed altered. No longer was it accepted practice
for a man to aspire to take the wolf's form. Nevertheless, this still
persisted in disparate areas, much as it seems to have done in the
Anglo-Saxon period when Christianity replaced paganism in a similar way: the East Anglian ruler Raedwald 'had in the same shrine
an altar for the holy Sacrifice of Christ side by side with a small altar
on which victims were offered to devils'.[47]

In his *Ecclesiastical Ordinances* XXVI, King Cnut (ruler of England
from 1016 to 1035) delivered a message containing a strong Christian emphasis in regard to the werewolf and its relationship with
the devil:

Therefore must the shepherds be very watchful and dili-
gently crying out, who have to shield the people against the
spoiler; such are bishops and mass-priests, who are to preserve
and defend their spiritual flocks with wise instructions, that
the madly audacious were-wolf do not too widely devastate,
nor bite too many of the spiritual flock.[48]

This passage even suggests that the werewolf is interchangeable
with the devil. Historian John Blair believes that the fears evident
in the Christian phases of the Anglo-Saxon and Viking eras relating to the dead and the possibility of a supernatural return to life
were 'deep-rooted fears going far back into pre-Christian English
culture'.[49] He points out that in sixth- and seventh-century cemeteries in England there is evidence of corpse mutilation, decapitation and a prone burial, and that some females were buried with
amulet objects which, he believes, suggests they had powers that

needed 'containing'. All of these elements could be early evidence of witchcraft.

Blair also suggests that many of these 'dangerous dead' were buried in boggy places. They include Cwoenthryth, who was 'thrown into some deep place' according to the *Vita* of St Kenelm; the sheriff who violated St Edmund's sanctuary and was 'taken from his grave, sewn in calf-skin and immersed in a pool'; Abbott Brihtwold of Malmesbury, who was 'dug up and plunged in a deep swamp', and the body of a Yorkshire rector from Byland that was 'dumped in an eerie, tree-encircled lake called Gormire'.[50]

All were accused of returning after death, in a manner perhaps more akin to the vampire myth than the werewolf myth. Nevertheless, there are clear parallels here with the evidence of the violent end of the earlier bog bodies. Could it be that the water is seen as a sort of cleanser perhaps? Let us consider the story surrounding St Edmund. The *Anglo-Saxon Chronicle* reports that: 'in that year (869) St Edmund the King fought against them [the Vikings] and the Danish took the victory, and killed the King'.[51]

In Manuscript (f) Canterbury, it is added that the Danes' leaders were Ingware (Ivar the Boneless) and Ubba (Ivar's brother), whilst the Abbott of Fleury claimed that Edmund was tied to a tree and arrows were shot at him:

> thus the heathens led the faithful King to a tree firmly rooted in earth, tightened him thereto with sturdy bonds, and again scourged him for a long time with straps ... they shot him with missiles, as if to amuse themselves, until he was all covered with their missiles as with bristles of a hedgehog ... then the heathens dragged the holy man to slaughter, and with a stroke struck the head from him.[52]

They then hid his body in a wood. When his followers found the head, it is alleged that it was being guarded by a wolf that allowed the head to be taken and followed the procession back to the town and then returned to the forest. When both head and body were recovered, the head miraculously reattached itself to the body, leaving a thin red scar. Edmund was temporarily buried until a church worthy of him could be built (which took several years), after which he was exhumed so as to be re-interred there, only for it to be discovered that all the arrow wounds had healed and that his skin was still soft and supple. This was a miracle. Most probably, his followers did not find his body at all, and instead came across a bog body. How ironic that the last of the 'wolf-kings' was lost and that in his place one of the sacrificial offerings to the Earth Mother was martyred as part of the barley-wolf faith. Furthermore, today it is argued that the name 'Beowulf' in fact translates to 'barley-wolf' and that the poem is dedicated to the Earth Mother and the barley-wolf cult.

Many of the Anglo-Saxon cemeteries that date to *circa* 550–700 contain further evidence of particular rites or beliefs that reflect the 'vampire-slaying' customs of Eastern European vampire lore. However, of more importance is the fact that later evidence of this practice (that is, post-700) is very rare. Nevertheless, examples of strange, vampire-like supernatural beings are found in documentary evidence, for example, William of Newburgh's accounts from the eleventh century. There is also a story of two peasants from Stapenhill village in Derbyshire, who, according to the writings of Geoffrey of Burton, had plagued the nearby village of Drakelow after their deaths. In *The River Trent*, Richard Stone explains that Drakelow derives from the Saxon *Dracan Hlaw* meaning 'Dragon Low', but in fact the word *hlaw* actually meant hill in Anglo-Saxon times, and it is often mistranslated. Also in Derbyshire are sites such as Arbor Low, Minninglow and Wigber Low that all have Prehistoric burial mounds on them. This geographical feature could suggest that Drakelow was once similarly shaped. Indeed, at Wigber Low, the bodies of at least seven individuals and an Anglo-Saxon spearhead were recovered that may indicate that the site was once another Anglo-Saxon cemetery. Further examples include a copper-alloy mount with gilded interlace and several spearheads found near Minninglow that also suggests Anglo-Saxon occupation of earlier prehistoric sites, whilst at Drakelow, a small sixth-century earthenware bowl of a type often associated with early Anglo-Saxon burials was found. This latter example would link to the site's use for housing the dead in the period.[53]

The dead Drakelow peasants mentioned above were seen 'wandering' through the village with their coffins on their backs, banging on doors and bringing sickness and death with them. To combat this, they were exhumed, decapitated and their hearts were removed, which were then 'carried across the running water of the Trent to a place of the kind favoured by late Anglo-Saxon authorities for executing felons: a hilltop beacon above Burton at a junction of parish boundaries'.[54]

Whilst there are clear similarities with the vampire myth here, these dead peasants were treated as outlaws, or indeed, werewolves. In some hunter-gatherer societies such as the Lapp of Finland, certain measures were deemed necessary for 'dangerous' members of society, and stronger measures were needed to keep them in their graves, for example being staked to the ground, decapitated, having rocks placed on them, and buried prone.

All the examples of these early stories from England notably occur in the north. Indeed, as early as 1914, Ernst Havekost, in his thesis *Die Vampirsage*, pointed out the definite northern bias of the evidence can be no coincidence since all examples are drawn from the Viking Danelaw which was the region of Britain ruled over by the Vikings. Havekost believed that the ideas originated in Scandinavian countries and found their way to Britain sometime in the ninth–eleventh centuries. Whilst the vampire myth did not originate in these countries, a werewolf myth could well have done, and from this period onwards the two creatures are irrevocably linked.[55]

Moreover, the werewolf myth is not 'missing' from traditional vampire 'works', and rather is often an integral part of these. Writing in the seventh century, Paul of Aegina suggested that the notion of 'werewolfism', or lycanthropy, was not self-induced, gratified or welcome, but rather a result of a disease of the mind caused by 'brain malfunction, humoral pathology and hallucinogenic drugs' and this mirrors some of the Roman texts on the subject. As the Viking era ended and the Norman Conquest of England signalled the beginning of the Middle Ages, the werewolf myth appears to have evolved rapidly, not least due to the Church's stand. The cult of the wolf, it seems, was no more and in place of the cunning and fearful ally was a savage and destructive beast; a beast that has remained in human consciousness for the past thousand years.

PART TWO

Magic and Mayhem

four
The Medieval Werewolf

Fair is foul, and foul is fair,
Hover through the fog and filthy air
William Shakespeare, *Macbeth*

The werewolf myth underwent a 'mirrored-transformation' in the Middle Ages following the advent of Christianity. Key examples of the desperation felt by a person cursed into being a werewolf are found in the werewolf tales from the twelfth century onwards, such as *Mélion* or *Guillaume de Palerne*, which will be discussed later in this chapter. Drawing on the *Macbeth* quotation above and applying its transitional emphasis to the werewolf myth, why was the shift from 'fair', that is, welcoming the form or power of the beast from earlier periods, to that of 'foul' and the curse that the werewolf becomes? Richard Buxton argues that the difference between Classical examples of werewolves and later medieval instances is that

> in both cultures to be a wolf signifies that one has forfeited humanity and is obliged to lead an 'outside' existence . . . but the Medieval werewolf . . . is typically represented as having that power [to change his shape] thanks to demonic assistance. The conceptual background to Medieval werewolfism is Christianity'.[1]

The complexity of the issue is thus: the main contemporary documentary evidence of the period is largely penned from a Christian point of view, as the literate of the Middle Ages in Western Europe were, on the whole, members of the clergy and the only 'authorized' voice.

Hence there is an inescapable link between werewolves and the devil (that is, through demonic possession and / or witchcraft). To make our way through 'the fog and filthy air' that hinders the continuation of a pagan belief in werewolves, the Christian doctrine surrounding the mythical being must be unpicked. According to the medieval specialist Claude Lecouteux,

> it is possible to discover an important belief in the history of our ancestors only if we shed the weight of clerical inter-pretation obscuring the pagan substratum – that is, the interpretation representing the Church's true dictatorship and facilitated by the monopoly over fact that the Church exerts on the world of writing'.[2]

Much of the continued pagan ideology surrounding the werewolf myth can be found within the Germanic sagas which will be examined further. For now, the use of the werewolf as a religious scapegoat by the Church throughout the Middle Ages is intrinsic to the develop-ment of the myth of the modern beast. What was once, as we have seen, a highly revered and worshipped beast, emerges in the medieval period as a savage creature, poisonous, destructive and wholly evil; a beast to be feared not imitated.

Even before the medieval era following the Norman conquest, evidence of a Christian response to the widespread belief in the werewolf was apparent in England. Early thought relating to the existence of a werewolf creature was posited on the notion that 'if nature reflects God's law and thus provides a standard through which humans might approach God, how could nature and possible perver-sions of it, such as werewolves, be understood?'[3]

Christianity had been introduced in Britain during the Roman period, and reinvigorated in the Anglo-Saxon era before the Norman conquest of 1066. A consideration of the evidence from this earlier period assists in understanding the more popular Christianized beliefs in the werewolf in the later Middle Ages. Nicole Jacques-Lefèvre, for example, argues that 'belief [in werewolves] has most commonly and mistakenly been attributed to the Middle Ages and to peasants, but [. . .] the beliefs were in fact developed most thoroughly and explicitly during the Renaissance by intellectuals'.[4]

As early Christians encountered pagan werewolf beliefs, an answer had to be sought:

> In paganism, a man who could shift his shape was looked at with worship and thought to have divine nature [We can recall here the prehistoric shamans, druids or berserkers for instance]. However, Christian priests were suspicious of everything that belonged to pagan mythology and for this reason they condemned magic powers that were not acknowledged by the Church as devilry.[5]

The Bible is indeed full of examples of the evils committed by wolves, including Ezekiel 22:27: 'Her princes in the midst thereof *are* like wolves ravening the prey, to shed blood *and* to destroy souls, to get dishonest gain.'[6] In a twelfth-century compilation, *De Spiritu et Anima*, formerly attributed to St Augustine, it is recorded that 'it is very generally believed that by certain witches' spells and the power of the Devil men may be changed into wolves'.[7] In the fifth-century *The City of God*, Augustine himself tells how

> demons modify in appearance only those creatures of the true God so that they seem to be what they are not . . . I thus do not admit in any way that demons be capable, by their power or their tricks, to transform in reality not the soul, but simply the body of a man into parts and shapes of beasts.[8]

This argument mirrors the much later belief in the medieval werewolf tales that the soul of a Christian cannot become tainted by the devil, and that any transformation is merely a bodily imprisonment, a curse, placed on susceptible men through witchcraft and devilry.

Also from the fifth century are the writings of St Patrick, more famous for driving the snakes from Ireland than for his dealings with werewolves. The legend narrates how Ireland was suffering from a triple plague: 'a great abundance of venomous reptiles, with myriads

Statue of St Patrick with Croagh Patrick, the holy mountain,
in the background.

of demons visibly appearing, and a multitude of magicians'.[9] St
Patrick drove the snakes into the lake at the bottom of the mountain,
the Log na Deamhan (Demons' Hollow): 'laboured by prayer and
other exercises of devotion to deliver the island from the triple
pestilence [and] taking the Staff of Jesus into his hand, St Patrick
hurled the reptiles into Log na Deamhan'.[10] This episode most likely
represents the power of Christianity over the devil (embodied in the
serpent or dragon) that is regularly observed in early Christian sym-
bology. However, 'St Patrick and the Irish' from Giraud de Barri's
Topographia Hibernica relates how natives were displeased by the
saints' attempts to convert them:

> the Irish began to howl like wolves against St Patrick who
> was preaching to them about the Christian religion. (In
> punishment for their lack of faith) the saint obtained from
> God that certain among them would be transformed into
> wolves for seven years and they would live in the woods like
> the animals whose appearance they had taken on.[11]

Another story from Ireland from before the eighth century is mentioned in Algernon Herbert's letter to Lord Cawdor (dated 1831):

> among the Erse or Gael of Erin, the notion of lycanthropy
> was prevalent; we read of their voracious cannibalism on the
> ocular and undeniable testimony of St Jerome, and another
> author pretends that a certain Abbot in the district of Ossory
> had obtained from heaven a decree that two persons of that
> district should every seven years be compelled to leave the
> country in the shape of wolves.[12]

Dating this tale to some time in the eighth century is possible, for the district of 'Ossory' was an ancient kingdom of Ireland in the province of Munster until the ninth century. Crucially, though, the link is again drawn between those outside the Christian faith and the myth of the werewolf.

This link weakens through the Middle Ages to be replaced by a relationship between the devil and witches. Regino of Prüm, writing in 906, tells how

> certain wicked women, perverted and seduced by Satan's illu-
> sions and mirages, believe and say that they go out at night with
> the goddess Diana or Herodias ... (they allow themselves) to
> be taken over by this madness and wander off the straight and
> narrow path, and ruin themselves in pagan wrongdoing ...
> priests much preach to the men of their parishes that all this
> comes not from the spirit of God but from evil'.[13]

Burchard de Worms (*c.* 950/65–1025) recounts how these 'wicked' women or Fates can control susceptible men: 'at the birth of a man, they do with him as they please, so much so that this man can, at will, transform himself into a wolf – which common stupidity calls a werewolf'.[14]

Once this suggestion of seductive women under the influence of the devil became more widely accepted, it gave rise to the persecution of alleged witches. However, a less acknowledged result is the appearance of the early medieval werewolf tales that share the common theme of the 'dangerous liaison'. Generally, a man was said to become a werewolf through the influence and actions of a woman. But this woman is not the aged hag familiar in witchcraft tales, but rather a young, beautiful harlot. One of the earliest werewolf tales is the *Wulf and Eadwacer* written by a Christian monk and included in the tenth-century *Book of Exeter*. The poem is narrated by a woman who has been separated from her lover, Wulf (as we have seen, this is a common Anglo-Saxon or Viking name) and laments this parting. The poem's true meaning and its composition are, however, subject to debate. It could well have a much earlier oral origin that was adapted to conform to Christian doctrine:

> it stands to reason that the priest who wrote (it) vaguely remembered fragments of the 'Edda' and of 'Signy's Lament' and may have added Christian views to an originally Pagan story . . . (the combination of these) with the terms from ancient Norse and Anglo-Saxon legal texts make it very clear that the Kenning 'Wulf' stands for war, violence, treason, crime, cruelty, blood revenge, shape-shifting and bestial behaviour.[15]

In other words, it was a moral tale that took familiar folkloric pagan tales and wove them with Christian faith and ideology. In Christian times, crime, blood revenge and bestial behaviour were actively discouraged. The werewolf, widely popular amongst the pagan peoples, became a symbol of these taboo practices: to exercise 'evil' deeds was to become the beast. This is highlighted in contemporary penal codes, with a law drafted under the reign of Edward the Confessor in the eleventh century describing a man fleeing from justice (an 'outlaw') as a *wluesheved* (wolf's head).

During this period arose the allegation that Prince Vseslav of Polotsk (1039–1101), a city in Belarus, was a werewolf. He was also known as 'Vseslav the Sorcerer'. He became prince in 1060 after his father's death but as he was excluded from princely succession, he began pillaging the countryside and attempting to take the capital. In 1065 he tried to take Pskov in Russia but failed, and the

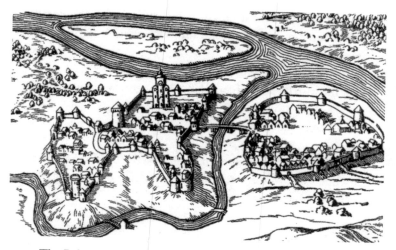

The Polotsk region, home to Prince Vseslav, *c.* 11th century.

year after, he pillaged and burned Novgorod, also in Russia. His opposition joined forces and defeated him at the Battle of Nemiga River in March 1067. Vseslav escaped but was later 'captured' rather unfairly during peace talks and imprisoned. In 1068 he was freed and declared Prince of Kiev during an uprising but subsequently lost the city to his enemies later that year. After a couple of years of fighting, he secured Polotsk in 1071, where he ruled for the next 30 years, dying in April 1101.

So why was Vseslav known as a werewolf? The *Russian Primary Chronicle* says that Prince Vseslav was conceived by sorcery and was born with the caul (the amniotic sac) on his head, hence his 'sorcerer' label. Throughout Eastern Europe, common folkloric belief held that a person born with a caul over their head was destined to become a vampire. As has been demonstrated, in this Early Medieval period there were no clear distinctions between vampires, werewolves and witches. In the twelfth-century document *The Tale of Igor's Campaign*, Prince Vseslav is mentioned and is labelled as a 'werewolf', perhaps precisely because of the caul.

Whilst there are numerous mentions of other people being linked with wolves, in these cases the wolf is used as a positive metaphor for some of the bearers' attributes. For example:

Prince Vseslav was a judge to his subjects, he appointed cities for the princes but he himself at night raced like a wolf from Kiev.[16]

For the wise Boyan ... [could] race like a grey wolf on earth.[17]

Gzak races like a grey wolf.[18]

Igor the Prince raced like an ermine to the brushwood, like a white duck to the water ... like a swift-footed wolf [and a] hawk in the mists.[19]

This last quotation shows that it is not just the wolf that humans are compared to, but hawks, ducks and ermines too. A contemporary account regarding the Scottish people, however, suggests that the idea of humans becoming werewolves was reasonably common. Bishop Patrick wrote that:

There are some men of the Scottish race,
Who have this wondrous nature from ancestry
    and birth,
Whensoever they will, they can speedily turn themselves,
Into the form of wolves and rend flesh with wicked teeth,
Often they are seen slaying sheep that moan in pain,
But when men raise the hue and cry,
Or scare them with swords and staves, they take flight
    like true wolves.
But whilst they act thus, they leave their true bodies,
And give orders to their women not to move them,
If this happens, they can no longer return to them.
If any man harm them or any wound pierce their flesh,
The wounds can be plainly seen in their own bodies,
Thus their companions can see the raw flesh in
    the jaws,
Of their true body: and we all wonder at the sight.[20]

Although this is an eleventh-century account, it seems that Bishop Patrick could have been drawing on earlier sources. In *The Wonders of Ireland* we learn that

> certain people in Ireland . . . who go in the shape of wolves when it pleases them, and they kill livestock in the manner of wolves. And they leave their own bodies . . . if they are wounded, those wounds will be in their bodies at home, and the raw meat which they devour will be in their teeth.[21]

These two examples demonstrate a continuation in the Christianized early medieval period of the Germanic practice of leaving one's body to become a werewolf (the 'double').

In *De Nugis Curialium*, a twelfth-century account, Walter Map advances the notion of the 'double' in Christianized society which lends weight to the later witchcraft 'fanaticism'. Map relates the successive deaths of a knight's children: each newborn child is found apparently strangled the day after birth. To defend the fourth child, a pilgrim keeps watch, when, during the night, an old woman approaches the cradle and tries to strangle the child. The pilgrim seizes the woman and burns her face with a poker. The local people identify her as the village matron. The watchful pilgrim sends them away to the matron's house to be sure of her identity and they return with the matron: they are one and the same, even down to the burn mark on the woman's face. The pilgrim, however, is still holding the culprit that he caught trying to kill the child. The pilgrim releases her and she escapes shrieking through the open window. He knew then that she was in fact the demon's messenger and had been created to *look* like the matron to ruin her reputation.[22] This story, and other collected evidence, show that by the end of the twelfth century, the werewolf seems to be succeeded by the witch. Yet it is in this period, as the witch craze begins to develop, that the classic medieval werewolf tales are composed.

There are four werewolf tales of note during this period that are known as the 'Breton Lais' (or 'Lays'): *Bisclavret* (Marie de France's 'The Werewolf', from the early– mid-twelfth century), *Mélion* (dated to *circa* 1190–1204), *Guillaume de Palerne* (1220) and *Bisclarel* (*circa* 1319–1342). It is generally believed that the tales emerged because of the increase in Christian scholars debating the nature of humanity by comparing man with beast. Their conclusion (which we have seen examples of earlier in the chapter) was that the change was impossible, or at least spiritually impossible. However, the peasants were not convinced. During the 11th and 12th centuries there was a growth in the number of folk tales with ecclesiastical imagery in the many bestiaries that were composed throughout Christian Europe. Kathryn L. Holten has argued that 'so much representation of the wolf within literature and legend is anthropomorphic that the rise of the werewolf myth [in the period] seems almost inevitable'.[23] However, the werewolf myth as it may be recognized today had already been established hundreds of years previously. What the four texts outlined above have in common is that they all share a similar theme: the wolf is the innocent, 'wronged' party and the woman is the cruel instigator of the male's downfall. Whilst this gendered thematic treatment may suggest a male author, at least one tale was penned by a woman – Marie de France, and *Bisclavret*. In *Mélion*, the main character of the same name is a knight in Arthur's court who vows never to love a woman who has loved another man. For this, he is ostracized by the court's women. Whilst hunting, he meets the daughter of the king of Ireland who says that she would never love another man but he, resulting in their swift marriage.

One day, again whilst out on a hunt, she says she will die unless she eats the meat of a stag, so Mélion turns into a wolf by using a ring with two magic stones to effect the mutation. The princess immediately runs away and travels back to Ireland with the ring, cursing Mélion to be trapped in wolf form. He follows her, all the while killing livestock, and all seems hopeless until Arthur learns of what has happened from her squire and demands the return of the ring, thus releasing Mélion.

The next tale in the four aforementioned tales is *Guillaume de Palerne* (or *William of Palerne*), a similar tale to the previous one, containing the passage that recounts

somme ther ben . . . that eten children and men, and eten no
other fleische from that tyme that thei ben acharmed with
mannes fleisch. For rather thei wolden be deed. And thai ben
cleped 'werewolves' for that men schulden be 'wer' of hem.[24]

In his 'Note on the word werewolf' appended to the translation of
the text, Sir Frederick Madden discusses the word's etymologies and
highlights the arguments of Algernon Herbert in 1831. Together, they
argue that the first part of the word (that is, *were* or *wer*) relates to
the Latin *bellum* from which the French word *guerre* and the Dutch
wer originated. *Bellum* is the Latin word for 'war', so the beast is
actually a 'war-wolf' and not a 'man-wolf', which is a perfect linguis-
tic and textual bridge between 'wolves' and 'warriors'. Madden further
points out that in the medieval period the term *waer-bod* meant a
herald, *were-man* a soldier and *were-wall* a defence in war. Indeed,
King Edward the First (1239–1307) had a war machine known as
a 'war-wolf'. This word *guerre* has some etymological links to a
description by the thirteenth-century chronicler Gervaise of Tilbury,
who mentions that 'we have frequently seen men in England transformed into wolves for the space of a lunar month, and such people
are called "Gerulphs" by the French and "werewolves" by the English'.[25]

Biclarel is a knight in the court of Arthur, and after he marries,
he turns into a wolf, although this time it seems his new wife does
not at first know about these transformations. Once Biclarel becomes
a wolf, his wife steals his clothes so that he cannot change back, and
then runs away to be with her lover. Arthur protects the wolf / knight
and discovers the truth from the wife, returns the clothes to Biclarel
and so he becomes a man again. These repeated themes enable modern readers to make clear links and hypotheses. Writing on medieval
courtesy, Rachel Kaufmann says that in the period being aware of what
was the 'right' thing to say, following the appropriate rules, and generally being a 'good' person were all types of expected comportment.
Kaufmann focuses on a set of instructions for table manners from the
Syon Monastery, for example, as well as a service book for inducting
a knight from *circa* 1000 that stressed the importance of bathing and
dressing properly and spending the night at Confession and Mass.

Beyond the 'assumption 'that Kings, monks, and knights were supposed to be exemplary human beings, these sets of instructions apply
not only [to them] but to all humans'.[26]

It follows that a mere mortal should be clean and clothed, have
good table manners, be spiritually minded, and exert self-control
over his inner urges. Yet the latter capacities are obviously not possessed by beasts: 'there is something inherently monstrous about a
werewolf, though Medieval writers seemed not to care most of the
time, treating the werewolf with interest rather than fear'.[27] Kaufman's
argument stresses that the pagan fascination with the werewolf was
difficult to destroy. In Kaufman's view, the medieval werewolf tales
were attempts to portray what would happen in society if rules were
broken, if people strayed from the straight and narrow path. They
depicted people, often 'good' people, who were cursed to live as a
beast, retaining their 'human understanding', as Gervaise of Tilbury
said, but condemned to remain in beast form, and as an outsider. This
reflection echoes the line of Christian scholars who said that the
form of a man could be changed but not his Christian spirit. Gervaise
of Tilbury also comments how a man

> became a wanderer . . . alone, like a wild animal . . . one night,
> perturbed by too much fear . . . he turned into a wolf, devoured
> infants (and) tore old people into wild beast's morsels'.[28]

By the thirteenth century, the Roman Inquisition in northern Europe
and southern France had begun to forcibly seek out such 'dangerous
folk' to end their apparently wicked, anti-Christian ways. In 1235
Étienne de Bourbon was charged with travelling around the area of
Valence in southern France and preaching to the heretics there. He
tells how a woman he met feared a *stryges* (a witch, or an ailed female
demon) was coming in the night to suck the blood of her child:

> the woman around the middle of the night saw a small, old
> neighbour woman riding a wolf and then saw her enter (the
> house) through the closed door.[29]

From this account

> there is a very archaic motif [that has been] found through-
> out Germanic tradition: that of the wolf as the witch's mount.
> Here this seems to be an accentuation of the evil nature of
> the old woman: she allies herself with wolves.[30]

Moreover, there are further links between witches and wolves in the
Germanic sagas. In Germany, for instance, a male witch (for not all
witches were women, contrary to popular belief) was someone who
could send out his double to attack other people, and who, in later
medieval times was referred to as a '*Trude*' or '*Drude*'. Indeed, the term
Drudenmensch is frequently used in contemporary sources. *Drudenmensch* is similar to the more widely known term 'Druid' that was
applied to early religious priests or shamans in pagan times, particularly in the Iron Age of Western Europe. The previous chapter examined the many links between the early pagan Germanic tribes, and it
seems logical for this term to be applied amongst the same Germanic
regions in later medieval times. Hence, those 'male witches' would
arguably be of a similar pagan ilk to their earlier Druidic counterparts.

The *Truden* apparently carried out their tasks as follows:

> after the Truden left at night to squeeze sleepers, they would
> lean their bodies against the wall or door of the sleeper's
> house. The soul would leave the body, go into the house,
> and press so violently on the sleeper's chest that he would
> almost suffocate.[31]

This would then explain how the woman in de Bourbon's account
gained entry to the house through the 'closed door'. In short, she
sent in her double, or soul (spirit) to do the work for her. As has
already been demonstrated, this action is repeatedly seen in the many
accounts from across Europe in the period and indeed beyond.[32]
Indeed, this practice is discussed at length in the fifteenth-century
Malleus Maleficarum: a key 'witch hunting' text, which will be discussed below.

There seem to have been specific methods employed in order for a witch to send out the soul / spirit / double: 'as a general rule, flight happens during a person's sleep exactly as in the Norse accounts [discussed in the previous chapter] of the alter ego (*hamför*). For Jean Vincent, the fifteenth-century Prior of Les Moustiers, a demonic sleep is what allows the women to imagine themselves being transported or metamorphosed into animals'.[33] (A French historian of Scandinavian culture, Regis Boyer, has argued that every man has, in fact, an 'animal double', something that [he] believe[s] later emerges within witchcraft trials as the witch's 'familiar'.) In the nineteenth century, Jacob Grimm declares that 'out of six girls born in a row to a couple, one is a werewolf'.[34] Textual sources provide many reasons for why a man or a woman, be they werewolf, witch or vampire, might send out their double, transform into a beast or generally have magical powers. Nevertheless, the most recurrent idea seems to be being born with a caul (as discussed in relation to Prince Vseslav earlier). This notion is prevalent in Eastern Europe, particularly in Romania, where people born with a caul are said to be potential-vampires. Furthermore, these people are said to be 'exactly like those born with a tooth, or a sixth finger on one hand . . . exactly like those designated to become shamans'.[35] Claude Lecouteux further adds that these people (those born with cauls or teeth) were the ones who had special powers and would later become magicians, sorcerers, seers or witches, and after death, their spirit would remain to haunt the living. As discussed in Chapter One, this would call for preventative methods to be exercised in burial to 'contain' the dangerous dead:

> 'In German-language countries, evil dead people called *Unhür* or 'ghost', and *Nohier* or 'he who draws the living into death', were born with a caul. To release them, it was said that the corpse was to be decapitated and the head put at the foot of it, or else they were to be buried facedown.[36]

Remaining with the Sagas for a moment, there is another specific area of society that would become the 'dangerous dead' after they had died: those who were traitors or outlaws. In the *Atlakviða* (*Lay of Atli*) there is a link between these traitors, or outlaws, and the wolf:

> what swayed our sister to send us a ring,
> all wound with wolf's hair? Some warning it meaneth:
> the heath-dweller's hair was hidden in the ring,
> wolfish would be our way to the Huns.[37]

Here, the two brothers in the poem, Gunnar and Hogni, are arguably, through the conduit of the ring wrapped in wolf's hair sent to them by their sister, being warned of betrayal.

With time, witchcraft becomes more of a widespread problem, and the 'folkloric' elements are replaced by more magical and sinister methods. Often, accounts focus on the witch's balm (discussed earlier). It is a particular feature of Christian treatises on witchcraft to cite this balm. Here, it should be recalled that by using Satan's 'balm', the witch is endowed with special powers. As previous chapters discussed, such powers include the use of trance-inducing states or catalepsy: 'I believe it served, above all, as a drug, a soporific, which allowed the witch to enter catalepsy that enabled part of her to escape her body'.[38] Arguably, that 'part' was her mind. Even as early as the fifteenth century, Alonso de Madrigal (or, Tostada of Ávila), who was Bishop of Ávila in 1449–55, argued that the so-called 'Witches' Sabbath' came about because of various drug experimentations using plants such as Atropa belladonna (deadly nightshade), henbane (stinking nightshade) and stramoine.[39]

The Sagas provide further rich examples of how these witches use their powers to become animals, and in particular, to become wolves. In *The Saga of Havard of the Ice Fjord*, Thorgrim, who is a sorcerer, is one of a group of people riding to kill Havard in Otradal. At one point, he goes into a sleep and thrashes continuously in a restless fashion. Upon waking, he says that during his 'sleep' he visited Havard's farm, which suggests he sent out his double. Meanwhile, Atli, one of Havard's men, also has a restless sleep and on waking, says, 'I saw some wolves coming from the south . . . eighteen in all, with a female fox running in front of them'. Thorgrim is the fox – or his double – and the wolves are his men, of which there are eighteen in the *Saga of Havard*. A similar tale in *Brennu-Njáls Saga* tells how Gunnar 'dreamed that [he] was riding [and saw] a great many wolves, and they attacked me'. Gunnar is subsequently ambushed and his brother killed, just as was foretold in his dream. Again, the wolves are the men's doubles. Finally, in the *Poetic Edda*, Odin says that 'if I see witches riding through the air, I do something to make them lose their way, and they never find their own skin again, and they never find their own spirit again'.[40]

Between the thirteenth and sixteenth centuries, evidence from witchcraft trials indicates that there were two types of people involved. On the one hand, these were the evil beings, the creators of dark storms, and on the other, the people who fought these, that is, the Livonian werewolves and the *Benandanti* ('those who journey to the Blessed Realm').The latter relate to an age-old battle between winter and spring. Throughout the sixteenth century in particular there are examples of the *Benandanti* (the 'Good Walkers') going out at night to combat witches.[41] In one trial in March 1575, Battista Moduco said he was a *Benandante* and went out to fight witches four times a year, at the start of each season. At the trial, Maria Gasparutto, the wife of one of the accused, told how her husband would not wake up one night even though she shook him and tried ten times to wake him. When he woke, he said that when a *Benandante*'s spirit came back to the body, it had still to be lying on its back because 'if the body were turned it would remain dead, for the spirit could not re-enter it'.[42]

This notion again echoes much earlier pagan traditions that relate to winter and spring and fertility, the harvest and the Earth Mother goddess. However, throughout this period, there are more remarkable enemies of the pagan witches and werewolves: members of the Church, or God's 'army'. The power of this army of priests, preachers, saints and bishops is poignantly highlighted in the four-teenth-century account of St Francis of Assisi and the wolf of Gubbio in Umbria in Italy. A fierce wolf apparently appeared in the country-side surrounding Gubbio and began attacking the livestock. Before long, it tired of eating sheep and turned its attention to humans as well. Finally, it ate nothing but human flesh. No weapon could harm the beast and anyone who tried to kill it was savagely devoured. St Francis duly travelled from Gubbio into the countryside to meet with the wolf:

> As he approached, the saint, making the sign of the cross, cried out: 'Come hither, brother wolf; I command thee, in the name of Christ, neither to harm me nor anybody else.' Marvellous to tell, no sooner had St Francis made the sign of the cross, than the terrible wolf, closing his jaws, stopped running, and coming up to St Francis, lay down at his feet as meekly as a lamb.
>
> 'Brother wolf, thou hast done much evil in this land, destroying and killing creatures of God without his permission

St Francis leads
the Wolf of
Gubbio towards
the town gates.

... for which things thou art worthy of being hanged like a robber and a murderer.'

St Francis requests that the wolf change his ways and live in peace, and in return the creature would be protected:

'As thou art willing to make this peace, I promise thee that thou shalt be fed every day by the inhabitants of this land so long as thou shalt live among them; thou shalt no longer suffer hunger, as it is hunger which has made thee do so much evil; but if I obtain all this for thee, thou must promise, on thy side, never again to attack any animal or any human being.'

The wolf knelt down, bowing his head, and, by the motions of his tail and of his ears, endeavoured to show that he was willing, so far as was in his power, to hold to the compact.

St Francis then returns to Gubbio with the wolf and preaches to the assembled townsfolk:

'How much we ought to dread the jaws of hell, if the jaws of so small an animal as a wolf can make a whole city tremble with fear.'

The town agrees to protect and feed the wolf, and the wolf fulfils his part in the pact, too:

The wolf lived two years at Gubbio; he went familiarly from door to door without harming anyone, and all the people received him courteously, feeding him with great pleasure, and no dog barked at him as he went about. At last, after two years, he died of old age, and the people of Gubbio mourned his loss greatly; for when they saw him going about so gently amongst them all, he reminded them of the virtue and sanctity of St Francis.[43]

This, the story seems to be saying, is the power of the Christians' God.

In *Of Wolves and Men* Lopez argues that

> beneath the popular, anecdotal appeal of the story is a common allegory: the bestial uncontrolled nature of the wolf is transformed by sanctity, and by extension those identified with the wolf – thieves, heretics and outlaws – are redeemed by St Francis' all-embracing compassion and courtesy.[44]

This is precisely the message from the medieval werewolf stories discussed above which depict the wolf as a symbol of the carnal, bestial wrongs of society, from which God alone can protect Man. Lopez continues that

> Medieval men believed that what they saw in wolves was a reflection of their own bestial nature; man's longing to make peace with the beast within himself is what makes this tale of the Wolf of Gubbio one of the more poignant stories of the Middle Ages. To have compassion for the wolf, whom man saw as enslaved by the same base drives as himself, was to yearn for self-forgiveness.

However, the problem was that the Church wanted to repress that ungodly nature in Man, and to do that, it had to repress the wolf, as well as the witch.

The fourteenth-century example of the wolf-child of Hesse, taken from *The Chronicle of Peter of Erfurt*, also stands out here. In 1344 a boy was rescued from a pack of wolves that had taken him three years previously and raised him as a cub:

> A certain boy in the region of Hesse was seized. This boy, as was known afterwards, and just as the boy told it himself, was taken by wolves for three years and raised up wonderously. For, whatever prey the wolves snatched for food, they would take the better part and give it to him to eat while

they lay around a tree. In the time of winter and cold, however, making a small pit, and picking up the leaves of trees and other plants, they placed them on the boy, and, putting themselves around him, they thus protected him from the cold; they also compelled him to creep on hands and feet and to run with them for a long time, from which practice he imitated their speed and was able to make the greatest leaps. When he was seized, he was bound with wood to compel him to go erect in the manner of a human. However, this boy often said that he much preferred to live among wolves than among men. This boy was conveyed to the court of Henry, Prince of Hesse, for a spectacle.[45]

An account of 1394, *Pierce the Plowman's Crede*, tells of the 'wilde wer-wolves that wiln the folk robben'.[46] Whether this represented *actual* werewolves or thieves and brigands who acted like wolves to rob people is not implicit, but another text penned in the fifteenth century was undoubtedly aimed at those who believed in such transformations. The *Malleus Maleficarum* (*Hammer of Witches*) of 1487 cites one authority who insisted that

whoever believes that it is possible for any creature to be changed for the better or for the worse, or to be transformed into any shape or likeness, except by the Creator Himself, who made all things, is without doubt an infidel, and worse than a pagan.[47]

St Antoninus also argued that the devil at times works to deceive a man's fancy, especially through an illusion of the senses, and he 'proves this by natural reasoning, by the authority of the Canon'.[48] The *Malleus Maleficarum*, which was in essence a manual for witch-hunters, was 'such an influential work that it was used by all, from clergy to judges, to hunt out, torture and condemn thousands of innocent 'witches' during the Middle Ages'.[49] The authors, two Dominican Inquisitors, Heinrich Kraemer and Johann Springer, argued how

The twelfth-century Doomstone carving from York Minster showing the cauldron depicted as the gateway to the underworld.

our bodies naturally are subject to and obey the angelic nature as regards local motion. But the bad angels, although they have lost grace, have not lost their natural power, as has often been said before and since the faculty of fancy or imagination is corporeal, that is, allied to a physical organ, it also is naturally subject to devils, so that they can transmute it causing various phantasies, by the flow of their thoughts and perceptions to the original image received by them . . . it is certain that devils can make some imperfect creatures . . . (but) when the body of a man is changed into the body of a beast, or a dead body is brought to life, such things only seem to happen, and are a glamour or illusion.

What is being argued here is that it is not *actual*, but *magical* actions that are at work. Curtailing the long-held belief in human-animal transformation must have been a difficult exercise, especially as accounts spoke so convincingly of such transformations. According to the Church, it was the devil, in all his so-called glory, and creating 'fog and filthy air' that masked reality, who seduced those that were susceptible. For example, *Macbeth*'s trio of witches who speak 'of the fog and filthy air' are themselves transformed into the messengers of the devil. Kraemer and Springer urged an understanding that

> this kind of witchcraft is more practised in Eastern countries than in the West, that is to say, in the East witches more often bewitch other people in this way, but it appears that the witches so transform themselves more frequently in our part of the world; namely, when they change themselves, in full sight, into the shapes of animals.[50]

Despite the teachings of the Church, society was in denial. For example, two years before the *Malleus* was published, Thomas Malory's *Morte d'Arthur* was published (1485), in which 'Sir Marrok the good knyghte, that was bitrayed with his wyf, for she made hym seuen yere a werwolf'.[51] Paracelsus, the Swiss physician, alchemist and astrologer, also advanced the idea that there are not one, but two spirits inside Man: an animal spirit and a human spirit. He believed Man's actions in life dictated which spirit flourished after his death. If he had lived a good, temperate life, his spirit resembled a man, but, had he indulged his carnal desires, the animal spirit would be released in the form of a wolf, cat or bear. In his *History of the Northern Peoples*, Olaus Magnus (1490–1557), Archbishop of Uppsala in Sweden, commented that:

> talking of wolves, I may do well to add that that species of them who are transformed from men, and which Pliny confidently says we should account false and fabulous, are to be found 'in great abundance' in the more northerly countries.

The Swiss physician, alchemist and astrologer Paracelsus (1493–1541).

In Prussia, Livonia and Lithuania, although the people yearly suffer a very great loss of cattle by the rapacity of the wolves, they think but little of that, in comparison with the damage done to them by men converted into wolves.[52]

It is then to be questioned how these men 'transform' themselves:

It immediately follows upon drinking a cup of beer, prepared by one who is skilled in such veneficious arts, and who at the same time uses certain words; provided always that he who drinks it is a party consenting. From that time forth, he has only to retire into some cellar or dark wood, whenever he is so disposed, and entirely transmute his human shape into the likeness of a wolf.[53]

A number of people were convicted of being a werewolf from this time onwards. The accusation of having anointed themselves with an ointment supplied by the devil were levelled at the defendants. The majority of those convicted were burned at the stake. As this was a male-biased exercise, it could be said to be the quasi-equivalent of the female witch trials, that took place across Europe and are much more widely known than the werewolf trials. Two Frenchmen, Pierre Burgot and Michel Verdun, were convicted for such 'crimes' in Besançon in 1521, as were Gilles Garnier in 1574 (the French believed the name Garnier to be synonymous with werewolves ('ce nom est comme fatal'), several people in Konstanz, Germany, under the reign of Sigismund, Holy Roman Emperor, and in France at Rennes in 1598 and Grenoble in 1603. In 1608 King Henry IV of France commissioned Pierre de Rosteguy de Lancre (1553-1631), a French judge, to wipe out witchcraft, 'werewolfery' and heresy. In just three years, he had nearly 600 people burned at the stake, and he wrote extensively on both witchcraft and lycanthropy. In *Tableau de l'inconstance des mauvais anges et démons* (1613), he documented how a young boy called Jean Grenier, who was just thirteen years old, had allegedly confessed to him in person about how he liked to eat young children, especially young girls. He claimed that a 'black man of gigantic stature', called 'Monsieur de la Forêt', gave him a magic ointment and a wolf skin, and that Forêt had visited him twice at the convent, where he was being detained. Another man, Gilles Garnier of Dole, also claimed Forêt was his master.[54]

The height of werewolf hysteria in Europe's Middle Ages occurred in the mid- to late sixteenth century, and in France alone, a high number of people were ready to confess to being a werewolf, including those in senior administrative positions of responsibility. Indeed,

> the judicial court, having its suspicions awakened, and, doubtless, fearful of sentencing so many important personages, acquitted the majority of the accused, announcing them to be the victims of delusion and hysteria.[55]

The French antiquary and Latin poet Jean-Jacques Boissard (1528–1602) told of how the Grand Duke of Muscovy had a man brought before him on charges of 'werewolfery'. He asked the man to demonstrate the stages of his metamorphosis and was escorted to a certain place by his prison guards, where he supposedly performed the rites taught him by the devil. Suddenly, he was transformed into a wolf with 'glaring eyes and horrid bristles'.[56] Incredible as this may seem, it is typical of the werewolf cases of the period and dozens of examples exist within the folkloric accounts of Europe, to which we shall now turn.

five
A Cruel and Savage Beast: The Werewolf in Folklore

Listen to the children of the night,
What sweet music they make.
Bram Stoker, *Dracula*

Whatever the cause of the werewolf phenomenon, the widespread accounts of the creatures reached all social strata between the sixteenth and nineteenth centuries. This was to the extent that it seemed that every village in Europe had its own tale to tell. How much this was a result of the witch 'craze' that occurred in the early part of this period is hard to gauge, but folkloric accounts of werewolves, witches, vampires and other fabulous creatures are unrivalled.

From the sixteenth century onwards a great deal of scholarly interest occurred in the werewolf myth. Demonologists such as Henri Boguet, Jean Bodin and Johannes Weyer all wrote treatises on the creature. These authors were not the first to tackle the werewolf myth: the *Malleus Maleficarum* had, for example, been published over a 100 years previously. Clearly, the werewolf question was a popular topic. From the Enlightenment scholarly interest also peaked. However, European peasants hailing from rural villages were no less avid 'consumers' of tales of vampires and it was precisely because of them that such tales reached the ears of scholars and academics, through the conduit of returning soldiers who had been stationed throughout Eastern Europe. How then did tales of this creature infiltrate the more learned circles of Europe? It seems, quite simply, that published stories were already on the shelves of libraries and personal collections across the lands.

In 1599 Beauvois de Chavincourt published his *Discours de la Lycanthropie* in which he told of the terrors afflicting the French countryside:

'the bloody incursion of wolves maddened with hunger'. He was not sure, however, if these were merely natural wolves, or rather

> men so denatured, that they have made bastards of their first origin, leaving this divine form, and transforming themselves into such an impure, cruel and savage beast.[1]

The preceding chapters have examined the debates of sixteenth- and seventeenth-century scholars on the existence of the werewolf. Whilst it is an accepted fact that Man cannot either be transformed or transform himself into werewolf form, this does not discount the existence of the werewolf. Arguably, a creature does exist, albeit not the shaggy-coated man-wolf that has mutated in the light of the full moon. Certainly, though, there remains some need in society to retain and fuel the werewolf myth. Whereas the vampire could be seen as a metaphor for society's fear of and fascination with death, the werewolf is the direct opposite: it is mankind's fear of and fascination with life. It may seem strange to suggest we fear life, but this precisely and plausibly stems from the notion that we do not yet understand life, that is, what creates life, what causes us to be alive, and whether death ends this life or merely opens up the next stage of life to us. These are all questions that mankind has been struggling with since our own species, Homo sapiens, emerged into Europe some 45,000 years ago.

Folklorist Harry Senn advanced the exact opposite explanation, when he said that 'nature was the ideal, and the wolf was a quasi-divine symbol of death and leader of souls to the other world'.[2] By considering all the evidence thus far, this too is a moot point. A point of convergence, however, is that the werewolf myth is more relevant to the villagers who believe in it than the towns and cities that study it:

> it is possible, that wolf warrior brotherhoods developed in agrarian communities that, having superceded hunting soci-eties, bestowed a magical-mystical status on hunting and warfare, gaining in religion what they had given up in their social and economic system.[3]

Most, if not all, religions are based on the worship of a deity or way of life that has passed. Worshippers also usually aspire to regain or at least protect the memory of the deity in question. (This idea will be comprehensively reviewed in the consideration of the Corsican dream-hunters.) In addition, 'wolf warrior brotherhoods' have been noted in the pagan societies of the Anglo-Saxons and Vikings, for example.

The nineteenth century was an interesting turning point in the werewolf myth as this was when the werewolf was suppressed into nothing more than a mythical and imaginary creature that 'haunts' literature and films rather than woods and graveyards. This was initiated in 1824 when Charles Robert Maturin published his tale *The Albigensis* about a knight who is locked in a cell with a werewolf. The knight relates how the man–beast pleaded with him to 'examine [him]; I tell thee I am a wolf. Trust not my human skin – the hairs grow inward, and I am a wolf within – a man outward only'.[4]

When Sabine Baring-Gould published his classic work, *The Book of Werewolves*, in 1865, werewolves were clearly still a popular subject, and more so than the vampire. However, by the time Bram Stoker published *Dracula* (1897), something had changed. Originally, *Dracula* contained a chapter that made clear references to werewolves. The publishers asked him, however, to omit the chapter. Whilst there are still references to wolves in the novel, they are not to werewolves, other than when the count assumes the form of a wolf. Here he is not a were-wolf, however, but merely a wolf, and no more emphasis is placed on this than when he transforms himself into a bat or into a veil of mist. Clearly, Stoker's point was that vampires can become other things. The chapter in question was later released as a standalone piece called *Walpurgis Night* (1914) and is now widely available under the title *Dracula's Guest*. In it is the famous line, 'a wolf – and yet not a wolf! ... no use trying for him without a sacred bullet'.

The original title of *Walpurgis Night* aligns it to the fact that 'Walpurgis Night' (or 'Walpurgis Nacht') is an ancient pagan festival, celebrated on 30 April, one that signifies the end of darkness (winter) and the return of light and the Sun (spring), and, traditionally, it is a time when bonfires are lit to keep away witches and evil spirits. The connotations of the festival can be noted in recent history, as Walpurgis

Night was the night in 1966 that the occultist Anton LaVey founded his Church of Satan and is also the night on which Hitler supposedly committed suicide. A debate amongst historians remains to the extent of the occult link surrounding Hitler's Nazis, with some claiming that Hitler's suicide was part of a bizarre occultist initiation that was tied to Walpurgis Night. In Hitler's private library it is also alleged that there was a book by Dr Ernst Schertel, a keen advocate of occultism, called *Magic: History, Theory and Practice* that was personally dedicated to Hitler. Passages in the book had been marked by Hitler including the phrase 'he who does not have the demonic seed within himself will never give birth to a magical world'. Hitler himself could be said to have some sort of 'link' with werewolves: for example, his secret 'werewolf bunker' was located in the Ukranian town of Vinnytsia.

By the end of the nineteenth century then, feelings towards the werewolf had changed dramatically. In fact, just ten years after Baring-Gould's book, the following passage in J. Greenwood's *Penny Packets of Poison* appears:

> there never lived an animal of prey of uglier type than this
> two-legged creature, who poisons the minds of little child-
> ren to make his bread. Never a more dangerous one, for his
> manginess is hidden under a sleek and glossy coat, and lips of
> seeming innocence conceal his cruel teeth.[5]

This description locates what is inside the werewolf, that is, his evil, and his ugliness as a creature. Clearly, it is a moralistic description, and is far removed from earlier medieval literature on the werewolf as a cursed and pitiful creature. How then did the werewolf come to be seen in this light? The folklore of Europe, from England and France in the west, Scandinavia in the north, and Romania and Greece in the east can provide an illuminating answer to this conundrum.

Evidence for this abounds in Romania, a country that is considered by the rest of Europe to be the 'homeland' of vampires and werewolves, and is, accordingly, steeped in superstition. During his folkloric studies of the region, Harry Senn described a number of festivals and parades that occur from Christmas to Epiphany in the many villages of Romania and beyond. Indeed, there are a great number of similar folkloric beliefs that occur in many of the villages of Eastern Europe that are linked by the Carpathian Mountains.[6]

One such parade sees young, unmarried men dress in animal masks, and in Romania folk dramas take place, where people wear animal costumes and masks which Senn believes have their origins in the age-old traditions of magic and human transformation. It is believed that these 'were-beings' appear at key festivals throughout the year such as Christmas, New Year's Day and Easter:

> according to legends, werewolves . . . emerge at a specific season of the year. Christmas and New Year appear to be the primary period, with Easter and the Pentecost as a secondary one'.[7]

Perhaps what we are seeing here is a specific 'season' that runs from Christmas to Easter and which is relevant or 'auspicious' to the propagation of the widespread werewolf legends. This is therefore a derivation from the age-old legend that reflects the final throes of winter before spring and rebirth arrives. The werewolf then 'represents' the death of winter, which allows the spring goddess (the Earth Mother) to come forth and revitalize the earth.

Senn further argues that there is a connection between the religious beliefs and festivals (such as the *Lupercalia*), the representative 'death' of winter and the physical death of the ancestors. This all, he believes, creates folkloric 'layers' surrounding the werewolf legend. One such Romanian folkloric tale tells of a man who:

> driving home from church on a Sunday with his wife, suddenly felt that the time for his transformation had come. He therefore gave over the reins to her and stepped aside into the bushes, where, murmuring the mystic formula, he turned three somersaults over a ditch. Soon after this the woman, waiting in vain for her husband, was attacked by a furious dog, which rushed, barking, out of the bushes and succeeded in biting her severely, as well as tearing her dress. When, an

hour later, this woman reached home alone she was met by her husband, who advanced smiling to meet her, but between his teeth she caught signs of the shreds of her dress which had been bitten out by the dog, and the horror of the discovery caused her to faint away.[8]

Were-Wolves is a story set in the Harz Mountains in northern Germany that recounts the magical transformation of the protagonist – the mountain-dweller Baron von Egenheim – into a wolf. After the carriage he was travelling in crashed in the snow and injured one of the horses, the baron and his band of men sought solace at a farm deep in the forest. As night approached, the baron went for a walk, when suddenly the farmer's brother was attacked and killed by a vicious wolf. One of the baron's men, Ludwig, had his suspicions and followed the baron the next night and witnessed the transformation – the baron was a werewolf:

> a man with the nature of a beast, who had the dreadful capacity to take the form as well as the nature of the wolf, and who in that form preyed on human flesh. These creatures changed their form generally at sunrise and sunset, and hardly any one had ever seen the actual moment of change...they sought blood always, warm blood of living people if they could get it. If not, they devoured corpses newly dead, and would tear open new graves in lonely churchyards'.[9]

When the werewolf returned to the farm that night, the farmer shot it dead, but as they looked on the dead beast, they did not see a wolf but the baron's lifeless body instead. They buried his body 'with many old ceremonies and prayers (and) drove a stake of holly through his heart (so that) his evil spirit was prevented from returning'.[10]

Although there is some uncertainty about the time of year that this event took place, the fact that the carriage crashed in the snow would logically indicate it to be winter. A Serbian werewolf legend speaks of the *vlkodlak* (werewolf), telling that they chiefly rage in the depths of winter: they hold their annual gatherings, and at them divest themselves of their wolf-skins, which they hang on the trees around them. If any one succeeds in obtaining the skin and burning it, the *vlkodlak* is thence forth disenchanted.[11]

Again, folklore 'aligns' the werewolf with winter. This particular description also recalls the imagery of the prehistoric Druid groves. For its part, the vivid imagery of Serbian folklore states that 'the power to become a were-wolf is obtained by drinking the water which settles in a foot-print left in the clay by a wolf'.[12]

Similarly, Polish werewolves were believed to haunt the land on two annual occasions: Christmas and midsummer. This both strengthens and weakens the link between the werewolf's presence in winter. Yet, this periodic 'haunting' is arguably firmly linked to the midwinter and midsummer solstices, which would again be due to religious beliefs and possibly fertility rites.

In Greece werewolf folklore is also linked to Christmas: a time when

participants dress up to resemble the monstrous *callicantzari* that emerge at the dark of the solstice to take control of the world. Modern-day Greek celebrants blacken their faces and cover themselves with feathers. The *callicantzari* are pictured as covered with shaggy hair, heads and sexual organs out of proportion to the rest of their bodies.[13]

This image of blackened faces echoes that of Monsieur de la Forêt, discussed earlier. It is also important to note that the *callicantzaros* are clearly linked to fertility, given the accentuated phallus and the links to the winter solstice that punctuate the 'death' of the natural world in winter and its rebirth in spring. The folklorist J. C. Lawson describes the *callicantzaros* as seized with a 'kind of bestial madness which often effects a beast-like alteration in their appearance . . . [with] all the savage and lustful passions of a wild animal'.[14] Another creature mentioned above is the Greek *vrykolakas* which, despite its being more akin to a vampire, was originally closer to a werewolf creature. The name

> *vrykolakas* has etymological links with the word *werewolf* (English and German), *warwulf* (Scottish) and *loup-garou* (French) ... some believe that the term *vrykolakas* was borrowed from Slavic, meaning 'wolf' or 'pelt', and was originally used in Greece to mean a werewolf.[15]

It may also have links with the 'wolf girdle' worn by potential werewolves to 'transform' into the beast.

The Greece-based research carried out by folklorist Demetracopoulou Lee involved interviews with a number of people in relation to the *vrykolakas*. He concluded that

> there is no agreement ... as to the form of the *vrykolakas*; apparently, though, he starts out as a dead human body, he can change his form, or even enter the body of an animal.[16]

He goes on to say that the Arcadians 'made no clear distinction between what we would call fact and fiction, or history and folklore'.[17] Demetracopoulou Lee documents several cases of folkloric beliefs in his work, for example:

> Antonious, 1934: 'the vrykolakas is the devil. The people hear about him in church and are afraid. (They) kill people ... look like a man, like a dog, like anything. He comes out at night'.

> Bill, 1934: 'in our village, on the outside of the church, they had drawn the outline of a wolf. And when anyone from another village became a vrykolakas, they would take earth from under the sketch of the wolf and would strew it all the way to the grave of the vrykolakas. And the wolf would go and eat the vrykolakas, and he would disappear'.

Superstitions such as these are feature in many of the rural, isolated villages across Europe. Yet archaeological evidence has recently enabled scholars to demonstrate how certain superstitions are more than just superstitions. The archaeologist Hector Williams has been excavating sites on the Greek island of Lesbos for the past 30 years. As well as finding artefacts from inside the area of the ancient city walls of Metholini relating to a Roman brothel and a Hellenistic 'industrial estate', excavations have also revealed over 50 burials from different periods. One corpse was found in the ancient wall itself: a section of the wall had been cut out and a crypt constructed, after which the coffin was inserted and heavy stones placed on top of it. The remains of a 40 to 50-year-old male were found inside. He had been nailed to the coffin with three long metal spikes: one through his throat, one through his pelvis and one in his ankle. Clearly, those who had buried him were concerned that he might otherwise return from the dead.

Furthermore, excavations in the late 1950s at the Roman villa site at Southwell, Nottinghamshire, unearthed several graves dating from the Anglo-Saxon period that had been inserted into the base of the villa, presumably as part of a church graveyard, though this has not yet been located. One of the corpses discovered bore large, metal nails driven through the heart, shoulders and ankles. The excavator at the time, Charles Daniels, jokingly wrote how the mouth was open wide as if the corpse were screaming. He also added that he had checked for eye teeth but they were normal. Presumably, his extra observations were prompted by the burial 'practices' surrounding the control of vampires, as the 'dangerous' body was ritually staked to the ground. Indeed, this was common practice in the Anglo-Saxon period when the 'dangerous dead' were feared, but the example from Greece demonstrates that the corresponding fear and practice were more widespread.

A second burial was discovered on the island of Lesbos at a church at Taxiarcis in 2000. The skeleton had deformities to the face, head, jaw and nose, which may suggest some form of disease, and again it was buried with metal spikes. This time, however, it was considered adequate simply to place the spikes alongside the corpse and not to

The Anglo-Saxon 'deviant' burial from Southwell,
Nottinghamshire, 1959.

drive them through the body. The reasons for this are unknown, but
they probably served as a means to prevent the dead person from
returning to haunt the living. In theory, the sharp, iron stakes could have
punctured the flesh if the body had begun to swell as a result of the
release of gases during decomposition. If the corpse was punctured,
the body would duly dry out and decay, and could not then 'return' after
death. In a slight but relevant aside, two examples from America
enable a better understanding of the Greek and English examples. In
1990 archaeologists working on a gravel pit in New England found
a necropolis that was over 300 years old. One of the burial plots,
intriguingly, bore the initials 'J. B'. The remains had been arranged
in the shape of a skull and crossbones. A study of the bones revealed
that the person had died from consumption (tuberculosis), which
would have given them pale skin, red, sore eyes and caused them to
cough up blood. These are also the 'symptoms' of a vampire or werewolf, according to folklore. Anastasia Tsaliki, who studied the bones,
believes they may have been re-arranged to prevent the person returning from the dead. Some 40 miles away, in a Rhode Island cemetery,
is a gravestone dating from 1841 with the inscription: 'Simon Whipple,

who died May 6th 1841, altho' consumption's vampire grasp has seized that mortal frame and mind'.[18]

In the 1860s Charles Newton wrote about Greece in his memoirs. He claimed that 'in Metilini the bones of those who will not lie in their graves are transported to a small adjacent island', presumably referring to the widespread European belief that the returning dead cannot cross water, or sometimes salt water. Furthermore, this reference may be where Stoker sourced the idea for *Dracula* from, since a circle of salt is drawn around his protagonist Mina Harker to protect her. The Greek island of Santorini has long been known as the 'Vampire Island': it is where dead vampires and other supernatural beings were 'transported' to protect the living. Hector Williams has long been searching for the island graves that Newton was referring to, and now believes he has located them on the small island of Pamphila. From the air, traces of several buildings can be seen that Williams believes are possibly mausoleums.

Whilst this evidence seems to relate more closely to the vampire, it should be recalled that it is only in western Europe that there are clear divisions between werewolves, vampires and witches: throughout much of Europe these divisions are not so clear-cut. The problem in locating the truth from all the 'hearsay' and folklore is original meanings of burial or other 'control' practices are now lost. In addition, they are placed in a modern context. Many beliefs have their roots in ancient times, and social 'development' has generally revised and discarded these old beliefs.

Corsica is, however, a unique phenomenon, in that certain 'ancient' beliefs are still known and even intact there. Dorothy Carrington's work *The Dream-Hunters of Corsica* is key here. The Corsican tradition of vendettas or death vengeance pacts are discussed, with the example of an elderly man chanting in a *voceru* (a song in honour of the deceased):

> may I see in a basket, the entrails of the priest, may I tear them with my teeth, and rub them in my hands, in the house of the priest, one hears the Devil, Infamous priest, excommunicated, Dog-eater of the sacraments.[19]

Carrington also deals with the *mazzeri* figures, the dream-hunters, who are 'mostly women, hunt in packs and tear their prey to death with their teeth, like hounds'.[20] However, this violence is based in and confined to a *mazzeru's* dreams only. For the *mazzeri* are seers, and their premonitions and dreamworld killings foretell the future: the animals they kill in their dreams are the representations of people from their village. Should a death occur in the *mazzeri's* dream, the corresponding actual death of that person quickly follows. Strangely, though, 'reliable witnesses have seen *mazzeri* walking abroad at night at an hour when they and their families swear they were sleeping in their beds'.[21] The Corsican folklorist Jean-Dominique Cesari explained this as a *'redoublement de la personnalité'*, or a 'doubling of the self'. The notion of the 'double' is, as has already been shown, widespread in Scandinavian belief.

Given the obvious pagan links of the *mazzeri*, it is curious that the predominant religion in Corsica is Catholicism. This religious 'adhesion' could, though, explain why islanders have not been persecuted for anti-religious beliefs and practices. In his *Histoire de l'Église Corse* (*History of the Corsican Church*) (1931), S. B. Casanova expressed a belief that the *mazzeri* were sorcerers and priests of the devil who anointed their bodies and could transport themselves to the ends of the earth, become animals and make themselves invisible. Casanova links the *mazzeri* to the Corsican *strege*: a witch / vampire creature.[22] Whilst the *mazzeri* might have the characteristics of witches, and Corsican folk belief holds that they can travel over greater distances than a non-*mazzeru*, they cannot fly, unlike witches in European sorcery traditions. Indeed, Corsican 'witches' are strictly speaking, and as stated above, *'streghe'* (the etymological roots to Romanian *strigoi* or the Classical *striges* are clear here) and are wholly distinct from the *mazzeri*. An elderly Corsican *mazzeru* who was shunned by villagers after she foretold the deaths of two local people, related how she was dunked in the local stream but broke free – an act that mirrors the 'swimming test' of the European witch hunts. The *mazzeru* explained that 'it still happens that I go out at night. I tear my flesh and my clothes. It is stronger than I (the need to hunt), the blood wills it so'.[23]

Carrington turns to 'Roccu Multedo and his work Le 'Mazzerisme' et le folklore magique de la Corse, which suggests that the mazzeri facilitate their access to this state (of Dream-Hunting) by dosing themselves with certain hallucinogenic plants that grow in Corsica, such as mandrake, datura and belladonna.' However, she 'ha[d] found no evidence of this'.[24] Nevertheless, in a Corsican trial of 1617, Catarina of Bastia was accused of visiting the dead by night and returning home 'blackened all over' by 'what they had given her'.[25] This is arguably the anointing of her body with a herbal salve. Jean Cesari also draws on a folk tale from 1933 of a woman who had a 'mad desire to kill' and 'went hunting at every full moon'. She was walking with her husband one night when she saw a large dog and felt the urge to kill it. Although her husband was not a mazzeru, he saw it too, perhaps, Carrington suggests, because he was touching her at the time. This sharing of the 'seer's' visions through touch is similarly detected and discussed by Sir John Rhys and J. G. Campbell[26] in relation to Welsh and Scottish accounts.

Is it possible for mazzeri to bring on these dreams themselves? Carrington's research suggests not: 'they were, to use the Corsican expression, "called" to hunt, "called" to kill; the order was absolute; they could not even choose their victims'.[27] The question is, who 'called' a mazzeru? A reflex answer here would be that it is the devil, especially as the mazzeri resided in Roman Catholic Corsica. The 'art' of the mazzeri is, however, extremely ancient: 'it indeed seems likely that mazzerisme derives from a period of Corsican culture considerably older than the Megalithic faith (that is, the Late Neolithic / Early Bronze Age); that of the hunting and food-gathering people, the first occupants of the island, as early as 7000 BC'.[28] For some villagers, the prospect of being a mazzeru, destined to kill (albeit in dreams) was a repulsive notion and one to ward against. Hence, the giving of amulets made from of the teeth of hedgehogs to children:

why it should be credited with magical powers seems now to be forgotten ... was it simply regarded as potent on account of its spikes, its wonderful natural protection? Teeth, more over, have been generally regarded in primitive societies as a symbol of strength.[29]

The wearing of amulets made from wolf and fox teeth was prevalent in early prehistory. As previously discussed, this practice suggested that, in some sort of religious rite, the wearer was trying to 'become' that creature. Perhaps, they were in fact attempting to ensure the protection of the wolf against the spiritual 'powers' that were being bestowed on them. It might then follow that those wearing wolf and fox teeth amulets were not shamans after all, but beneficiaries of the premonitory dreams and visions. Contemporary to the *mazzeri* are the Italian *benandanti*. Ethnologists Georges Ravis-Giordani and Carlo Ginsburg have similarly argued for the *mazzeri* of Corsica as comparable to the *benandanti*. Again, this may immediately appear to be the case, but Carrington has pointed out noticeable differences:

> the *benandanti*, by their own account, were predestined to their vocation by being born with a caul on their heads. According to an old belief of which I found no echo in Corsica [for the *mazzeri*], such people were endowed with exceptional powers: soldiers went through battle unscathed and lawyers always won their suits if they had been born with a caul. Witches and sorcerers were distinguished in the same way'.[30]

Both the *mazzeri* and the *benandanti* are, arguably, distinct from one another, as the shamans are too. The latter category wields greater power but suffers more for it. Initiation occurs, according to Corsican beliefs, through the shaman-to-be being taken by demons and rendered apart: his body is hacked to pieces and his organs ripped out. He is then subjected to a brilliant, bright light, that is the 'knowledge' he will then have as a shaman. Finally, he is recomposed, with new limbs, organs, bones and blood. Another folkloric tale from a woman shaman told how she was 'cut up' by a group of strange men and her body parts put into a cauldron and boiled. This is remarkably like the relationship between the cauldron of rebirth and the rites of

Nerthus. Incidentally, although the term 'cauldron' comes from the Latin '*caldarium*', meaning 'cooking pot' and 'hot', there are possible etymological links with the word 'caul'. Perhaps the term originally derives from the belief that the 'magical' cauldron is associated with rebirth, which would then link it to the caul, or amniotic sac, of childbirth.

The 'language' of the shaman originates 'in the beginning of time [and] was given by the lord of the universe so that men and animals might live together in harmony and exchange identities', according to Corsican folklore.[31] This could, perhaps, be said to be the case for the bear and the wolf, and possibly for other animals. It is a 'language' that is, of course, defunct. Montague Summers's book *The Werewolf* provides many examples of were-foxes, were-hyenas and were-leopards, and the Anatolian Çatalhöyük 'leopard men' enhance the dual creature 'catalogue'. In a shamanistic ceremony, the shaman uses their body to imitate the beast. This is his 'animal spirit'. Their voice imitates the animalistic sound:

> the shaman growls like a bear and steps with its heavy tread, whinnies and stamps his foot like a horse, and if his auxiliary spirit is a snake, as may happen, he twists and writhes on the ground.[32]

The engraved bone from the Pin Hole Cave at Creswell Crags and a 'masked ceremonial figure' might suggest a shaman whose animal spirit was a bear. A bear skull (currently on display in the museum at Creswell Crags) was also found in the cave during excavation. The animal mask that he is wearing could well be a bear mask? (it certainly looks bear-like). The Creswell bull roarer also was perhaps used to make trance-enducing sounds, much like the Corsican drums. There is another link between the shamans from Corsican folklore and the potential evidence of shamanism at Creswell Crags (and, one might assume, other early sites in Britain):

> only the shaman has access to the celestial world. There he purifies himself on the contamination of the nether regions

and intercedes with the gods on behalf of the tribe. To prepare for the ascent he erects a new yurt (his 'spiritual' house) and plants in it a birch tree, symbol of the Axis of the World. Nine notches are cut into its trunk representing the nine circles of heaven.[33]

The deer stag from the Church Hole Cave at Creswell is the main piece of engraved art found there. It has nine notches carved on the bottom that could relate to the Nine Circles that are so central to the shamans and shamanic. One problem is trying to comprehend beliefs that date back to 13,000 years without any modern practices to base opinion on or to compare with. Admittedly, shamanic practices still occur amongst indigenous tribes of South Africa, for example, but not in European cultures. However, Corsica and its beliefs and traditions are perhaps again the exception here and therefore unique in modern Europe.

After the notches are engraved in the bone, an animal is sacrificed and its flesh eaten by both the shaman and tribe members. This is because it is believed that the flesh contains the spirit. The shaman then does a ceremonial dance and sings to the rhythm of the drumbeat, which induces the trance state in him. Once the shaman reaches the trance state, 'ascends' the spiritual tree in ecstasy through each circle of heaven. When he reaches the ninth notch (the Ninth Circle), he falls to the ground, unconscious. His spiritual ceremony is complete.

The differing roles and practices of the the *mazzeri*, the *benandanti* and the shaman are clearly specific and differentiated. Shamans, for example, carry out acts and affect what happens; the *mazzeri*, on the other hand, merely convey messages or foretell death. This echoes Northern traditions. The *mazzeri* of Corsica bear similarities with figures from the Sagas who can send out their double: they both 'hunt' in dreams and have premonitions of death that become actual deaths in real life. Just as the shamans and the *mazzeri* cannot be 'grouped' together, folkloric figures who send forth their 'double' cannot be aligned in a comparable manner with the berserkers. The same could probably be said of members of early prehistoric cultures.

The question of who the 'werewolf' label should be applied to remains, however, uncertain. Prehistoric shamans tried to copy the wolf; berserkers dressed as wolves for battle and the *mazzeri*, whilst not adopting or becoming trapped in wolf form, certainly acted and hunted like wolves. Hence, the werewolf of tradition and folklore is an entirely different beast to that of the earlier 'spiritually-linked' werewolf. In Corsican folklore, the *mazzeri* are the night hunters, they 'become' the animal during the hunt; shamans seek out the spirit world above, and the *mazzeri* focus on the real world below. Folklore cannot present a werewolf that has one form, one role, or indeed, one name.

The wider and complex spiritual beliefs found until recently in Europe and perhaps even today link to those more ancient ones from many other regions. The Scandinavian region of Europe, as has already been discussed, has a rich history of beliefs and tales that surround and link to the werewolf. In Norwegian folklore, it is held that the power to become a werewolf was divulged not by the devil but by trolls:

> in a hamlet in the midst of a forest, there dwelt a cottager named Lasse and his wife. One day he went out in the forest to fell a tree, but had forgot to cross himself and say his pater-noster, so that some troll or wolf-witch (*varga mor*) obtained power over him and transformed him into a wolf.[34]

Several years later his wife managed to break the curse and change him back on Christmas Eve. This mirrors a 'pattern' of process seen in many other countries. Another tale from the region, from Sweden, tells how the queen had recently died, leaving the king and their daughter (the princess). A cunning handmaiden persuades the princess that she ought to become queen and so the princess confides in her father and monarch and maiden marry. An enemy then invades the kingdom and the king is forced to leave his new queen and the princess behind to go and fight. Once the king has gone, the new queen rapidly reveals her true personality and is hateful towards the princess. Meanwhile, the princess has been courted by a handsome young prince and the two have fallen in love. The queen, in her spite, wishes to break up this love and sets out on a destructive course of action. One morning, the prince departs for a day of hunting and

> while engaged in the chase he lost his way ... availing herself of the opportunity, the queen practised on him her wicked arts and transformed him into A WEREWOLF, so that for the remainder of his days he should be a prowler of the forest.[35]

The princess goes into the forest to search for him and meets an old woman who lives in a cottage. The old woman tells her that if she finds and picks a lily, all will be well. The princess eventually finds a prescribed lily but each time she tries to pick it, it moves further away into the forest. Eventually, she follows the flower to the top of a mountain from where she is finally able to pick it. The sun begins to set and she has no choice but to sleep on the mountain. Suddenly, a little old man appears and bids her to kindle a fire, fetch a pot of tar from further up the mountain, set it on the fire and place the lily into the boiling pot. On doing this, a terrifying howling is heard and a wolf emerges from the bushes. The old man then tells the princess to pour the boiling tar over the wolf, and

> scarcely has she done so when the wolf changed his covering, the great gray skin started off from him and, instead of a ravenous beast, there stood a comely youth with eyes directed towards the brow of the mountain.[36]

The princess realized that the 'wolf' was none other than her beloved who had turned into a werewolf.

The king then returned from battle where he found his queen apparently in mourning, but in fact pretending that the princess was dead. However, the king realised the trick when he ordered the coffin to be opened and found it empty. After this, the queen confessed everything and they went to search the forest for the missing princess. As the queen and her two daughters (who were complicit in the deceit) walked below the mountain, the old man told the princess to drop the wolfskin on them, and all three turned into werewolves and ran off into the forest. The prince and princess were then married and the entire kingdom feasted. The narrator explains how

> I, too, was at the feastings; and as I rode thru the forest I was met by a wolf with two young ones; they were ravenous and seemed to suffer much. I have since learned that they were no other than the wicked stepmother and her two daughters.[37]

This profoundly moral tale has clear similarities with the Breton Lays. As such, whilst there are (or were) beliefs and traditions that link to other esoteric traditions in places such as Corsica, the northern region also has moralistic and folkloric accounts that match those from France or Romania, for example. Britain, however, seems to be lacking in such folkloric accounts, perhaps because of the culling of wolves in the seventeenth century. Indeed, Algernon Herbert (quoted above) said 'no wolves, no werewolves', and Baring-Gould reiterated this point when he wrote that

> English folk-lore is singularly barren of were-wolf stories, the reason being that wolves had been extirpated from England under the Anglo-Saxon kings, and therefore ceased to be objects of dread to the people.[38]

Nevertheless, there are several folkloric accounts of big black dogs haunting various regions such as the Black Shuck in East Anglia (discussed above), or a similar beast that exists in legend at Whitby in North Yorkshire (in the UK), made famous by Bram Stoker in *Dracula*: when the count arrives at Whitby harbour, brought by the ship *Demeter*, he leaps from the deck. However, as he has become a large, black dog, he bounds up the steps leading to Whitby Abbey. Other folkloric tales of werewolves are often set in or occur in moorland – such as the so-called 'Beast of Bodmin' of modern times. Indeed, these earlier examples provided inspiration for Sir Arthur Conan Doyle's *The Hound of the Baskervilles* (1901–02). Doyle, it seems, took his inspiration from a local Devonshire legend that recounted how, in the seventeenth century, a man called Richard Cabell (who was by all accounts an evil man after reputedly selling his soul to the devil) died and was laid to rest in a sepulchre at the church. However, on the night he was buried a pack of phantom hounds was seen bounding across the moor and later heard howling and baying at his tomb. According to the legend, ever since that night Cabell's ghost can often be seen leading the hounds over the moors, or they can be heard howling from the graveyard.

These accounts demonstrate that it is large, fearsome dogs rather than wolves that are the 'stuff' of legend in UK-based folk tales. Baring-Gould also uses the story of two creatures appearing at a local village inn and drinking the cider, only for the landlord to shoot a silver button (not bullet) over their heads. No sooner had he done this, than the beasts turned into two 'ill-favoured' old ladies of his acquaintance.[39] Again, it does not seem that these creatures were werewolves – in fact, Baring-Gould simply refers to them as 'beasts' – but the parallels with wider European folklore involving werewolves is apparent.

There were, however, tales of cannibalism in both England and Scotland but, as Baring-Gould believes, owing to the disappearance of wolves and therefore the corresponding werewolf myth, people at the time did not connect this practice with werewolves. At the same time, it is not clear, despite Baring-Gould arguing to the contrary, why the two should have been connected. Nevertheless, Baring-Gould usefully argues that if the incidents had occurred in, say, France or Germany, , the culprits would almost certainly have been charged with lycanthropy, that is, sanctioned with being a werewolf and devouring their victim.[40]

France is a useful case in point, given that it is the 'breeding ground' for alleged 'werewolfism', and folkloric traditions from the country are especially significant in number. Montague Summers held that

in France the belief in werewolfism has certainly survived, and the tradition descends unbroken from the very dawn of history. Shape-shifting was part and parcel of the wizard lore of the Druids, of whose sacred shrines none was more secret and more evil than the little isle of Sain, off Finistère.[41]

It was on this Breton island, according to legend, that nine witches who often turned themselves into animal form lived and who worshipped He 'ro Dias, the mistress of witches. Furthermore, in the south of France certain humans were said to become wolves when there was a full moon and did so by

> leaving their beds, jumping out of a window and plunging into a fountain. After the bath, they come out covered with dense fur (and) walking on all fours, commerce a raid over the fields . . . biting all beasts and human beings that come in their way.[42]

According to French folklore, in specific parts of the country, a were-wolf would sometimes take the form of a big, white dog, and on other occasions, that of a wolf bound in chains.[43]

It was held that 'werewolfism was a very terrible and real thing, a sorcery which persisted through the ages'.[44] The Bretons believed that werewolves were in fact warlocks who dressed in wolf skins at night, or sometimes assumed the shape of wolves. To detect a were-wolf, the method was simple:

> a were-wolf may easily be detected, even when devoid of his skin; for his hands are broad, and his fingers short, and there are always some hairs in the hollow of his hand.[45]

In Normandy, to free a detected werewolf from the curse, it was said that three stabs in the forehead with a knife should be admitted, or in lesser cases, three drops of blood with a needle should be taken.

French werewolf tales are well represented throughout the ages. Indeed, the twelfth- and thirteenth-century Breton Lays are a useful example here. However, such tales go even further back with that of St Ronan, who was preaching Christianity in the early sixth century in the Lé region in Brittany. Certain witches who were practising in the region tricked King Grallon with their 'wicked lies' into believing the saint was a warlock who could transform himself into a ferocious wolf who had devoured a witch's chid. As St Ronan easily cleared his name and proved his innocence, and thus converted his enemies to the 'true' faith, the moral of the story is unambiguous.[46] On a similar moral note in which wolf form acts as a symbolic deterrent, in 1181 Hugues de Camp d'Avesnes, the comte de Saint-Pol, desolated the abbey at Saint-Riquier in northern France and burned it to the ground. His actions caused the deaths of more than 3,000 and razed the surrounding countryside. As a punishment for the massacre, he was cursed and haunted the region in the form of a large, black wolf loaded with chains and howling pitifully.[47]

It was, however, 'during the sixteenth century that in France especially the rank foul weeds of werewolfery flourished exceedingly'.[48] A 1558 account narrates the woes of a certain landed gentleman who was walking near his chateau in Apchon in Auvergne, south-western France, when he met a hunter he knew and asked him to bring some of his bounty back for him. Whilst hunting, the hunter was attacked by a large wolf. He wrestled with the creature and managed to take out his knife and cut off its paw, causing the beast to run yelping. The hunter put the paw in his bag and returned to the gentleman's chateau. On recounting his ordeal, he looked for the paw in the bag but instead found a woman's hand complete with a gold ring. Horrified, the gentleman recognized the ring as his wife's, and when he went into the house, he found her nursing a bandaged arm. He saw she had lost a hand and she confessed to attacking the hunter. The woman was burned at the stake for her crime at yRon. The account comes originally from Henry Boguet, who alleged that he was told the tale two weeks after the event. However, this time lapse fuels doubt to its accuracy.[49]

Jean Grenier, mentioned earlier, had been introduced to Monsieur de la Forêt by a youth called Pierre de la Tilhaire. Monsieur de la Forêt was described as a big, black man. Here Pierre de Rostegny de Lancre provides a useful embellishment He recounts how the lord is a 'tall, dark man, dressed all in black, riding a black charger', and offered the boys some wine and presented them with a wolf skin that when worn, turned them into wolves.[50] The lord accompanied them as they rampaged through the countryside, now mutated into leopards. In what has been shown as a frequent 'feature' of, or aide to, the man–beast mutation, de Rostegny adds that before wearing the skin, the boys had to smear themselves with an ointment. Grenier is depicted as a gaunt man, with small eyes that glared fiercely and long, sharp teeth. His hands appeared like claws with long, crooked nails, and he often went about on all fours, as he could move more easily in this posture than when he walked upright. He also, allegedly, preferred to eat raw offal. Rather than being a werewolf, Grenier is arguably more like one of the feral children discussed in Chapter Six. Of course, it is possible that he also had a form of autism, for example, making an absolute 'diagnosis' of his condition impossible.

In December 1764, the *London Magazine* ran a story about the so-called Wild Beast of Gévaudan (an area in the south of France) which was terrorizing the French countryside. The beast was variably described as a lion, a tiger or a large hyena, and it was said to have devoured over a 100 people in the Languedoc region including individuals and groups travelling in coaches. No-one was safe. According to eyewitnesses, the creature had large teeth and a powerful tail, could run at great speed and jump to an incredible height. Eventually,

An 18th-century illustration of the Beast of Gevaudan.

a Royal Proclamation was issued and a large reward offered.[51] Accounts of the tale are disparate in their descriptions and although some include anecdotes of several beasts, all creatures shared the common features described above. In addition, the beast was reported as having a reddish coat of fur and an offensive odour. Some reported seeing a smaller, female beast that appeared to be leading the pack but was never involved in any of the attacks on humans. King Louis xv took a personal interest in the matter and hired François Antoine to kill the wolf-beast. On 21 September 1765 he killed a large grey wolf weighing 60 kg, which was stuffed and sent to Versailles. Two months later, however, more people were attacked and the hunt for a second beast began.

This beast was eventually tracked down and killed by a local hunter called Jean Chastel. Human remains were allegedly found inside the animal's stomach. There is a strange addition to this killing that probably owes more to folklore than to actuality in that Chastel was supposedly reciting a prayer when the wolf appeared before him and stood staring at him. It would seem that the wolf kindly waited for Chastel to finish his prayers before allowing him to shoot him – hardly the actions of a ferocious, murderous beast. However, this is certainly a romanticized addition to the tale.[52] In his *La Bête du Gévandan*, Michel Louis suggests the beast may have been a cross between a wolf and a dog that had been purposefully bred by Chastel. This theory is supported by the fact that Chastel owned a large, red-coated mastiff, which would explain the reddish tint present in the beast's coat. Yet sceptics have suggested that this creature might have been a surviving species such as an Asian Hyena or Mesonychid (an early carnivorous mammal). The mystery remains.

Even a century after the case of the Beast of Gévaudan, people living in the French countryside still feared the threat of the werewolf. As the historian Douglas Starr recently wrote,

France (in the 1890s) was still largely a nation of peasants barely a generation away from medieval-era fears and superstitions. People lived in a world populated by wraiths and spirits, in which real and imaginary fears played a role in daily life.[53]

Locals were warned:

> do not believe in witches. Do not believe in ghosts, or spectres,
> in spirits, in phantoms ... do not imagine one can avoid harm
> or accidents with ... amulets, talismans, fetishes.[54]

The French, it seems, did not heed the advice, evidenced by a popular
folk song of the period:

> Return, my child, with eyes so soft, to your mother.
> Flee far from these woods; for in the bushes waits an
> assassin with black intentions.
> Fear this hyena.[55]

For an unknown number of years, the bestial assassin had lived in the
countryside, bringing fear to the French. Such wolf-induced fear had
also seized most of Europe.

six
Of Wolf and Man: Werewolf Cases from Europe

Even a man who is pure of heart
And says his prayers by night
May become a wolf when the wolfsbane blooms
And the autumn moon shines bright.
The Wolfman (1941)

The French fear of 'the assassin with black intentions', the hyena that waited in the bushes ready to pounce, might have seemed to the average Englishman no more than a peasant superstition, but to the Frenchman, it had more weight than that and the danger was very real. Whilst the vampire legend is awash with real-life monsters that have been 'immortalized' – Vlad Dracula (The Impaler)[1] is one such example, who tortured and murdered hundreds of people by impaling them alive in the 1400s – a less well-known werewolf myth is that of Gilles de Laval, the Maréchal de Retz. Henri Martin aptly encapsulated the full extent of the horrors committed by de Laval in saying that 'the most monstrously depraved imagination never could have conceived what the trial reveals'.[2]

In the trial referred to, a picture unfolded of the absolute terror that the *maréchal* inflicted on the French country people in the mid-fifteenth century. The trial came about because of the increasing belief that he was responsible for the disappearance of dozens of children. What was happening to those children could not have been imagined by anyone:

> During the year 1440, a terrible rumour spread through Brittany ... that one of the most famous and powerful noblemen in Brittany, Gilles de Laval, Maréchal de Retz, was guilty of crimes of the most diabolical nature.[3]

Gilles de Rais, 1835, by the French painter Éloi Firmin Féron.

It was precisely because he was 'one of the most famous and powerful noblemen' that his being brought to trial is so remarkable, yet alone his subsequent conviction. The *maréchal* is perhaps better known as 'Gilles de Rais', the Templar knight. Born in 1404, he inherited lands and wealth after the death of his father and spent the years 1426 to 1433 engaged in military action. He invested heavily in the cause of King Charles VII (who made him 'Maréchal of France' for his services in the Hundred Years War), had several celebrated victories including the re-capture of the fortress of Rennefort and the castles at Lude and Malicorne, and fought alongside Joan of Arc (he was by her side when she was wounded by an arrow in Paris). However, in 1433 he suddenly and unexpectedly quit the service of the king and retired to his estates. Within two years he had lost much of his fortune, ceding the majority to the Bishop of Nantes and to the chapter of the cathedral at Nantes.

Many people believed this was to prevent his excommunication for the atrocities he had committed, and whenever and wherever he travelled, people wept for missing children, babies snatched from their cradles and infants who had simply vanished. It was in the region surrounding the *maréchal's* Castle of Machecoul (also known as 'Bluebeard's Castle') that people suffered most as no-one had entered the sombre fortress and returned alive: 'tales of horror and devilry circulated in whispers'.[4] At night, a sole window remained alight, high up in the tower. Peasant stories attributed all kinds of terror:

> They spoke of a fierce red glare which irradiated the chamber at times, and of sharp cries ringing out of it, through the hushed woods, to be answered only by the howl of the wolf as it rose from its lair.[5]

Sometimes the castle gates would open and money and food would be given to those begging for alms outside. However, local gossip told how children would then be lured in with promises of food, never to be seen again. In 1440 the people rose up and charged the *maréchal* with child abduction and his offering them up to the devil. It got to the point where the Duke of Brittany had no choice but to order an investigation.

The person charged with this investigation was Jean Labbé, a *sergent d'armes,* and on his arrival at the castle in September 1440, the *maréchal* promptly surrendered. It is alleged that years earlier one of his astrologers had foretold how mankind would one day fall into the charge of an *abbé* (abbot), and he believed the prophecy had now come true, hence he surrendered. The people believed he would escape punishment, save for some forfeit of land, as surely the Duke would not find him guilty?. This would no doubt have been so if the Bishop of Nantes and the Grand Seneschal had not taken a personal interest in the case. Indeed, they ensured the Duke complied with their demand for a thorough investigation and a public trial.[6] Why then was the

Bishop of Nantes so intent on proving the *maréchal*'s guilt? Was it merely to bring justice for the people, or was there some other motive? Also, it was not clear what he stood to gain if the *maréchal* was found guilty. We have already seen the *maréchal* had ceded land to the bishop, and this provides some sort of explanation. Conspiracy theories abound as to the true nature of this case, and will be returned to shortly.

Witnesses gave evidence at the trial as to how certain children had been duped into going with the *maréchal*: the son of Perrine Loessard had been taken after expressing his wish to be a soldier; eight people testified that a young beggar named 'Jamet' had suddenly vanished at midsummer; the son of Jean Leflou had also gone to Machecoul and was never seen again, and Georges Lebarbier's son had disappeared whilst gathering plums. In total, some 38 children had fallen prey to the *maréchal*. The evidence appears damning, and might well have been sufficient to convict the *maréchal*, but more was to come. Whilst studying the evidence for the case, the duke received a letter from the *maréchal* claiming he was 'overwhelmed with incomparable repentance for [his] crimes which [he was] ready to acknowledge and to expiate as is suitable'.[7] This statement of guilt was, however, not necessarily given freely. It could have been obtained through torture, as was the standard practice of the period.

The evidence, it is alleged, caused the Duke to order a search of the castle at Machecoul. This resulted in the location of a great number of human remains. The verdict was out and the *maréchal* stood trial. The charge stated that he had

> seized several little children, not only ten or twenty, but thirty, forty, fifty, sixty, one hundred, two hundred and more, and has murdered and slain them inhumanly, and then burned their bodies to convert them to ashes.[8]

When his two personal servants were questioned, one of them, known as 'Henriet', broke down and said he must confess all, much to the disgust of the other servant who refused to speak up against his lord. Henriet claimed that when the *maréchal*'s castle at Chantonce was given over to his brother, he told him how he had discovered the bodies of children, some headless, others mutilated, in the tower. Henriet was charged, along with two helpers, to go and remove the bodies and transport them to Machecoul for disposal. He counted 36 heads and many more bodies forming a gruesome cargo. Yet is it feasible to believe that over 40 corpses were removed from the castle and transported to Machecoul, only to be burned like the others? It would surely have been simpler to have burned them on-site. As such, the 'evidence' is at best contestable.

Henriet explained how he was asked to go out and find new children to abduct and bring to the *maréchal*, and after doing this, he bore witness to their slaughter, watching their throats being slashed after which, the *maréchal* would bathe in their blood. Henriet claimed that he had seen over 40 children killed by the *maréchal* in this way:

> I used to read him the chronicles of Suetonius and Tacitus, in which [great] cruelties are recorded. He used to delight in hearing of them . . . it gave him great pleasure to hack off a child's head . . . sometimes he had all their limbs chopped off . . . I remember having brought three little girls . . . he bade me cut their throats whilst he looked on.[9]

On hearing the confessions of his accomplices, he had no choice but to confess:

> I have killed (these) children . . . either by cutting their throats with daggers, by chopping off their heads with cleavers, or else I have had their skulls broken with hammers or sticks; some-times I had their limbs hewn off, at other times I have ripped them open, that I might examine their entrails and hearts.[10]

On Wednesday, 26 October 1440, Gilles de Laval, Baron of Rais, Maréchal de Retz, was hanged and burned for his crimes. Was he a werewolf? No he was not. He was possibly a witch, in league with the devil and practised dark arts, as some have alleged. Was he guilty at all, or the victim of a campaign to ruin him and claim his lands and wealth? It is impossible to draw a conclusion. Nevertheless, his story was not made widely available until historian Jules Michelet attempted to pull together the remaining information (many of the documents relating to the case were destroyed in the French Revolution in 1789) and the French antiquarian Lacroix published a memoir of the *maréchal* based on an abridged version of the material collated prior to the Revolution. Whilst modern scholars dismiss Margaret Murray's *The Witch-Cult in Western Europe* (1921), she makes many speculations on Gilles de Rais. Murray classes Joan of Arc and Gilles de Rais as mutually necessary to each other's story, since scholars study them separately, and Joan of Arc is lent more consideration. It has to be said, however, that this was probably because of the destruction of documents relating to Gilles de Rais.

For Murray, there was a duality of religions occurring in fifteenth-century France and Joan of Arc might have had the backing of some 'unseen power':

> She first heard the 'Voices' at the age of thirteen, the usual time for the Devil and the witch to make 'paction'. One of her followers, Pierronne, was burnt as a witch, avowing to the last that she had spoken with God as friend with friend, and describing the costume of her Deity with a detail which shows the reality of the occurrence.[11]

Murray further argued that the rank-and-file soldiers, the men-at-arms, would have followed anyone believed to have been chosen by God and that Gilles de Rais himself attempted to belong to 'both religions'. Joan of Arc was eventually tried and convicted of being a witch and was burned. 'Like Joan of Arc, Gilles de Rais was tried and executed as a witch and in the same way, much that is mysterious in this trial can also be explained by the Dianic Cult', Murray claims.[12] The fact that Gilles de Rais did not attend Joan's execution, nor try to save her by offering ransom, is particularly curious, given how close they were and that she was under his protection. Indeed,

> it seems incredible that a soldier of Gilles's character and standing should have made no move to rescue Joan by ransom

or by force, when she was captured. She was not only a comrade, she was especially under his protection, and it is natural for us to think that his honour was involved. But if he regarded her as the destined victim, chosen and set apart for death, as required by the religion to which both he and she belonged, he could do nothing but remain inactive and let her fate be consummated.[13]

Moreover,

He could not decide to which religion he would belong, the old or the new, and his life was one long struggle. The old religion demanded human sacrifices and he gave them, the new religion regarded murder as mortal sin and he tried to offer expiation; openly he had Christian masses and prayers celebrated with the utmost pomp, secretly he followed the ancient cult.[14]

The reason for the extensive relinquishing of land to the Bishop of Nantes is now clear: he was indeed trying to expiate for the sins he committed as a Christian, and his practice of the 'old religion' is almost certainly the reason for the bishop's insistence on a thorough trial. The latter knew what would be found and he knew Gilles de Rais would burn for it. The moot point is that if a Maréchal of France was involved in a continuation of the 'old religion', how far did this go? The identity of others involved in it is to be questioned, as is the number of 'witches', 'werewolves' and 'devil-worshippers'. With this in mind, it is more understandable why there were so many French werewolf cases.

In 1521, nearly 100 years after the death of Gilles de Rais, two men, Pierre Burgot and Michel Verdun, were burned at Poligny for being werewolves. Burgot confessed that nineteen years previously, on the day of the Poligny fair, he was rounding up his sheep because of the heavy rain and thunder, when three horsemen appeared, all clothed in black and riding black steeds. One of the horsemen told Burgot that if he accepted him as his master, then not one of his sheep would be lost in the storm. In accepting, Burgot renounced God for which the horseman promised him money. As the years passed, he grew tired of this allegiance and attended a 'sabbat of warlocks' with Michel Verdun from nearby Plane. Verdun told him to strip and anoint his body with a special ointment. Once he had followed instruction, Burgot believed that he has undergone a transformation into a wolf: 'his limbs were hairy, his hands and feet the paws of a beast'.[15]

Verdun also turned into a wolf. The ointment was given to Burgot by his master (who he claimed was called 'Moyset') and Verdun, by his friend, Guillemin. Together, they attacked and killed a seven-year-old boy, a woman out collecting peas and a four-year-old girl, whom they ate except for one arm. Many more were killed by them, 'for they loved to lap up the warm flowing blood'.[16] They also claimed to have had sexual intercourse with a number of 'she-wolves'. Verdun was eventually caught, when in 'wolf form', attacking a traveller. The man wounded the wolf and tracked it to a hut, in which Verdun was discovered having his wound cleaned by his wife. A third man, Philibert Montot, was also charged for 'being' a werewolf and all three were executed for their crimes. During the trial, however, information was given that may support the argument that they were never in wolf form at all, but merely under the influence of the hallucinogenic cream (which, interestingly, they applied to revert to human form, or so they believed):

> one evening at dusk, Pierre leaped over a garden wall, and came upon a little maiden of nine years old, engaged upon the weeding of the garden beds. She fell on her knees and entreated Pierre to spare her; but he snapped her neck and left her a corpse, lying among her flowers. On this occasion he does not seem to have been in his wolf's shape.[17]

A case from 1572 is that of Gilles Garnier, the 'Hermit of Dole', who was finally executed on 18 January 1573. Garnier was described as being a sombre, ill-looking fellow, who walked with a stooping attitude, and whose pale face, livid complexion, and deep-set eyes under a pair of coarse and bushy brows, which met across the forehead, were sufficient to repel anyone from seeking his acquaintance.[18]

One evening, some peasants were returning from work when they heard the cries of a child and the howl of a wolf. They came upon a great beast who was attacking the child. The creature ran off, and as it was getting dark, they could not be sure if it had been a wolf or the hermit. Soon after, a young boy disappeared and the hermit was arrested.

Garnier confessed to all his crimes, but again whether this was freely or under duress we cannot be sure, although Summers wrote how he 'several times freely acknowledged and confessed' his crimes[19] – which included attacking a young girl whilst he was in the form of a wolf, stripping her naked and eating her flesh, before taking some home for his wife. On another occasion, he had killed a young girl and proceeded to eat her before being disturbed. This pattern was repeated on several other occasions. Whilst in prison, he was visited by Daniel d'Auge, who wrote of him being

> a solitary who took to himself a wife, and then unable to find food to support his family fell upon such evil and impious courses that whilst wandering about one evening through the woods he made a pact with a phantom or spectral man ... (who) taught him to become a wolf ... (and) received a salve wherewith he anointed himself when he went about to shift his shape.[20]

There is a marked difference in belief between the time of Gilles Garnier (and the other alleged werewolves of the period), and when Baring-Gould was writing on werewolves in mid-nineteenth-century France. Daniel d'Auge's acceptance of Garnier's transformation and Baring-Gould's comments on the case, relating that the 'the poor maniac fully believed that actual transformation into a wolf took place', highlight this contrast.[21]

A German print showing scenes from the case of Peter Stubbe.
Its date is unknown but is likely to be late 16th century.

In December 1573 the parliament of Franche-Comté issued a decree, because of the supposed problem of 'werewolfery' in France, that permitted

> those who are abiding or dwelling in the said places . . . to assemble with pikes, halberds, arquebuses, and sticks, to chase and to pursue the said were-wolf in every place where they may find or seize him; to tie and kill him.[22]

It took until the turn of the century for the condemnation and execution of alleged werewolves to decrease, but the preceding 25-year period featured many high-profile cases. The next case of note occurred in 1589 in Germany, when Peter Stübbe, or Peter Stump, was convicted of being a werewolf. According to a contemporary pamphlet, Stübbe was chosen by the devil as a 'fit instrument to perfourm mischeefe' and was provided with a girdle which, when worn, transformed him into a 'greedy devouring Wolfe'. For the next 25 years, Stübbe killed countless children, women and animals:

> Within the compass of fewe yeeres, he had murdered thirteene yong Children, and two goodly yong women bigge with Child, tearing the Children out of their wombs in most

bloody and savedge sorte, and after eate their hartes panting hotte and rawe.[23]

On one occasion, Stübbe came upon two men and a woman in the woods, and after killing the men (who were later discovered 'mangled in the wood'), he raped the woman, killed her and ate her. Eventually, Stübbe was captured after being chased in wolf form by men and dogs, and trying to escape by changing back into a man and pretending he was a traveller walking to the city. Some of the men had witnessed the transformation and he was arrested. When he was put on the rack, and fearing the torture to come, he quickly confessed to being in league with the devil, who had given him the wolf girdle, to killing and eating his victims and to being involved in black magic. He also confessed to having had sexual intercourse with a succubus which the devil had sent to him.

Stübbe was executed, rather fittingly, on 31 October 1589, by being put on the wheel (usually a large, wooden wagon wheel) and tortured with pincers heated in the fire that were used to tear flesh from several places, after which his arms and legs were broken with a blunt axe to prevent him returning after death. Finally, his head was cut off and his body burned on a pyre. Stübbe's head was displayed on top of a wooden post, with the wheel and an image of a wolf added, to warn potential 'werewolves' of their fate.

In 1598 Pernette Gandillon, a girl from the Jura, a region in the east of France, 'ran about the country on all fours in the belief that she was a wolf'.[24] Henri Boguet told how she had attacked two children and ripped out the throats of one of them. The community was shocked and 'tore her to pieces in rage and horror'.[25] Pernette's brother Pierre was subsequently charged with witchcraft and accused of becoming a werewolf. It is alleged he did this with the use of a salve from the devil. However, this salve was not just for turning into a wolf: on one occasion he reportedly took on the form of a hare.[26] During his trial, he admitted these actions, as did his son Georges, who told how he too had used the devil's salve to transform himself. He recounted how one night he had lain in his bed in a cataleptic state for three hours before recovering enough to get up. During this

Three 16th-century woodcuts portraying Peter Stubbe, the 'Werewolf of Bedburg', first on the loose, and his subsequent destruction by decapitation and burning along with his daughter and a female relative, with both of whom he had a sexual relationship.

time, he was a wolf and had attended a witches' Sabbat, or Sabbath. His sister, Antoinette, also claimed to have attended the Sabbat, and sold herself to the devil, who had appeared as a black goat. When imprisoned, Pierre and Georges 'behaved as maniacs and ran about on all fours howling dismally'.[27] All three were burned at the stake.

In the same year (1598), a man by the name of Jacques Roulet was also convicted of 'werewolfery', after the corpse of a boy who had been badly mutilated was discovered. Eyewitness accounts reported the sighting of two wolves running away from the scene. Having given chase, the men lost the wolves but came upon a half-naked man, who was crouching and shivering in the bushes. The man had 'long hair and beard, his hands dyed in blood, his nails were long as claws and were clotted with fresh gore, and shreds of human flesh'.[28] Roulet later admitted to having killed the boy and eating him. Yet *two* wolves were seen. At the trial, Roulet recounted how he used a salve that had been given to him by his parents. Local people recognized him as a beggar who was often accompanied by his brother John and cousin Julien. According to Roulet, they were the two wolves.

If two, and not three, wolves had been sighted, how could Roulet have been there? His parents were known to be respectable people and they testified that both John and Julien were working at the time of the crime. The judge asked Roulet whether he 'became' a wolf on applying the salve. 'No', he replied, 'but I still killed and ate the boy, so I am as a wolf'. Roulet claimed that his hands and feet became those of the wolf.

The trial was apparently abound in contradictions and the evidence was weak. Indeed, the only evidence to link Roulet with the murder was his own testimony, which is flawed and clearly issuing from someone who was confused, and probably mentally unwell too. He was, however, sentenced to death. An appeal then ruled that he be admitted to what would now be a psychiatric hospital for two years, as he was 'clearly more of an idiot than a malicious killer'.[29]

The 1603 case of Jean Grenier, the feral child discovered living wild in the woods, provides a further instance of wolf-like features 'embedded' in a human:

his hair was of a tawny red, thickly matted, falling over his shoulders and completely covering his narrow brow. His small, pale-grey eyes twinkled with an expression of horrible ferocity and cunning, from deep sunken hollows. The complexion was of a dark olive colour; the teeth were strong and white, and the canine teeth protruded over the lower lip when the mouth was closed. The boy's hands were large and powerful, the nails black and pointed like bird's talons.[30]

Grenier was discovered by three girls, whom he told he was the son of a priest. He said he was dirty and black because he sometimes wore a wolf-skin. The devil, incarnated in a man called Pierre Cabourant, apparently gave him the wolf cape, and 'wraps it round me every Monday, Friday and Sunday, and for about an hour at dusk every other day, I am a wolf, a were-wolf'.[31] Another girl, Marguerite Poirer, told her parents that when tending her flock, a boy called Jean Grenier would come and tell her horrific stories of how he would eat young girls. One day, a strange wolf-like creature had attacked her. It resembled a wolf but was smaller and stouter, had red hair, a stumpy tail and had a much smaller head than that of a wolf. Official investigation constructed a profile of Grenier: he had travelled around the countryside begging and carried out odd jobs, and had widely confessed that, when younger, he had been given, along with a friend, a salve and a wolf-skin by a black man called 'Monsieur de la Forêt'.

Grenier also admitted to having attacked and killed several girls and then eating them. However, of all the witnesses who gave evidence, only Marguerite Poirer said that a wolf had attacked her, and there was no proof that this was Grenier. The president of the Assize Court therefore dismissed

all questions of witchcraft and diabolical compact, and bestial transformation (and that) the age and imbecility of the child who was so dull and idiotic that children of seven or eight have usually a larger amount of reason than he ... Lycanthropy (is) mere hallucination, and the change of shape exists only in the disorganized brain of the insane.[32]

Grenier therefore escaped execution and was instead sentenced to imprisonment in a monastery, where he ran on all fours and ate a huge portion of raw offal in one 'sitting'. Seven years later, Pierre de Rosteguy de Lancre visited him and Grenier related how Monsieur de la Forêt had paid two visits since his imprisonment. Grenier died soon after de Lancre's visit, aged just twenty years old. From this time onwards, lycanthropy was understood in terms of a mental melancholy rather than a 'bestially-induced' transformation brought on by the devil. Moreover, it was treated as such, as the last two cases attest.

This shift is seen in *The Duchess of Malfi* (1614) by John Webster, which features a case of lycanthropy. However, whilst the illness is recognized as such by the play's modern audiences (that is, from today), the actual detailing of the source of the 'curse' responsible for Webster's werewolf has been much debated. Indeed, this is expressed as a case of either 'disease' or 'diabolism'. For Ellen Tullo, Webster

> makes frequent reference to contemporary Jacobean con-
> cerns about health and disease for dramatic effect. Most notably
> . . . lycanthropy, through the evolution of the condition of
> Duke Ferdinand.[33]

The source of the duke's curse is usefully described or deciphered by Tullo as an 'evolution'. This 'diagnoses' the deterioration he undergoes in the play – resulting in his eventually becoming 'mad'. The play's doctor describes Ferdinand's illness as 'lycanthropia', which, to quote Webster, 'in those that are possess'd with't there o'erflows, Such melan-choly humour, they imagine themselves to be transformed into wolves'.[34] Tullo argues that

> literature that involves the experience of health and disease
> in the form of a novel or play is . . . never entirely divorced from
> the lives of real doctors and patients and may draw directly
> from genuine experience.[35]

What then was Webster's source for lycanthropy, his 'genuine expe-rience'? The fact that there were no cases of lycanthropy in England during the period should not deter from the idea that his audience must have been aware of the disease and its 'supernatural origins' from the recent past. There were still reverberations of the 'Witch's Hammer' throughout Europe at this time. Webster's werewolf was, however, the only werewolf to appear on the Jacobean stage, suggesting it was still, on the whole, a rather taboo subject. Furthermore, Webster was arguably not entirely convinced that the devil was not absent: in Act One, scene Two, Bosola suggests that Ferdinand wishes to make her his 'familiar', which she describes as being a 'very quaint invisible devil in flesh: an intelligencer'.[36] As Tullo points out, the scene in which Ferdinand presents the duchess with a severed hand closely resembles a case discussed by Boguet in his *Discours exécrable des sorciers* that speaks of a witch who turned into a werewolf.

Brett D. Hirsch has argued that the last 'traditional' werewolf trial was that of Roulet and that subsequent cases

> affirmed the new approach by the courts, which tended to view the werewolf as no longer the product of a fleshy, demonic transformation, but of an unstable mind.[37]

Although Hirsch is referring to the case of Jean Grenier, Roulet too was deemed to be mentally unwell and referred to a residence for 'psychiatric' problems, in modern terms, even though he initially received a death sentence. Webster potentially had twenty years of 'werewolf' cases to draw on, albeit not English ones. Owing to the lack of 'homegrown' werewolves, it is not surprising that English treatises on witchcraft were even more sceptical in relation to the disease than those penned in areas where cases of lycanthropy occurred. Henry Holland, writing in 1593 argued, for example, that alleged transformations by man or woman into a wolf were brought about by delusional melancholy, as was the case in the Stübbe and Gandillon family cases.[38] So-called werewolves were not evil, they 'were victims, not considered blameworthy in the development of their disease'.[39] Is it from this point that the 'afflicted innocent' meant that the werewolf or its associated illnesses were no longer taboo? It could be argued that since werewolves did not exist, that is, not in the half-man, half-beast 'variety', they could be used as theatrical 'characters' for entertainment. The question of why the werewolf figure and its surrounding ambiguity were employed by Webster remains. For John Gunby,

> the form Ferdinand's madness takes is as appropriate as it is extraordinary, since to Webster's contemporaries lycanthropy not only betokened guilt and remorse, but was also associated with witchcraft and love melancholy.[40]

Hirsch has also commented that 'scholarship has established Simon Goulart's *Admirable and Memorable Histories* as the source for Webster's werewolf, in particular his report of a man in the "yeare 1541 who thought himselfe to bee a Wolfe"'.[41] This suggests the source, but does not explain why he chose it. Webster's audience would most likely have known about the more infamous werewolf cases, such as Peter Stübbe, if not the lesser cases, but

> motivation must surely have rested upon the consequences, dramatic and moral, of constructing a villain afflicted with lycanthropy. . . lycanthropy poses important questions of moral responsibility, but other mental affirmities would have had the same effect . . . Webster then must have chosen lycanthropy on other criteria . . . what is it about the werewolf that sets it apart from all other conditions? [42]

To answer the above 'dilemma', it is arguably what the *werewolf* represents and not what the *lycanthropist*, the 'madman', clinically is that supplies its uniqueness. For that to be the case, the audience need not know a great deal about werewolves, in fact, the less they knew the better, and the more Webster can employ dramatic imagining.

In Jacobean England what could the werewolf have represented? Unlike in Europe, there was an absence of 'werewolves', which meant the creature could represent almost anything, as long as it was immoral, heretical and a 'cruel and savage beast'. Some scholars therefore suggest it was a religious scapegoat:

For a Jacobean audience the werewolf and the Catholic were similar beasts; both were essentially 'wolves dressed as men', otherwise indistinguishable from the rest of society but still a threat to church and state and both as depraved, bloody, and ruthless as each other.[43]

Others have argued that it reflected national identity:

The figure of the wolf in early modern England is not only emblematic of Catholics, but often a topical allusion to the Irish as well . . . according to medieval authorities the Irish shared a special relationship to wolves.[44]

So perhaps Webster was using the werewolf as a metaphor for social 'deviants', the Catholics or the Irish, and also playing the role of 'prophet' in suggesting that the 'werewolf disease' would eventually drive you 'mad'. The cure to this 'disease' was of course the good old Church of England. After all, the reason there were no werewolves in England was obviously because of the Church of England, or so teachings said. A few years before Webster wrote *The Duchess of Malfi*, Shakespeare's *As You Like It* had given weight to the above theory with the line: 'Tis like the howling of Irish wolves against the moon.' And Edmund Spenser had described how the Irish were descended from the Scythians, who, as analysed in Chapter Two, have links with werewolves.[45] The Italians also took their share of the abuse from the play, given its Italian setting, and the fact that an Italian becomes a werewolf. For the moment, however, it is worth considering the Irish:

Up until the eighteenth century Ireland always had a problem with wolves . . . the country was largely covered by thick and almost impenetrable forest, which made it an ideal breeding ground and hunting place for the animals.[46]

The dog used to hunt wolves was even given the wolf's name to label it as such: the Irish Wolfhound. However 'the name . . . is probably something of a misnomer, because the dogs are not native to the island (and were) imported from England during Roman times'.[47] In addition, the Romans had acquired the breed from the indigenous Britons of the Iron Age tribes. These early wolfhounds are immortalized in a small bronze statuette from the Roman site of Lydney in Gloucestershire, dating from *circa* 365.

Of greater concern and interest is the question of how, in 1596, Lord William Russell was able to go 'wolf hunting'. Indeed, later records from 1650 show that a pack of hungry wolves attacked the town of Coleraine in County Derry in the north of Ireland. Whilst parts of Europe were concerned with wolf madness in the countryside, and England dealt with it on stage, Ireland was still 'plagued' by wolves. A travelogue entry from 1699 even described the country as 'Wolf Land'.[48] In 1652 Oliver Cromwell had to issue a prohibition which prevented the export of the breed from Ireland:

> Forasmuch as we are credibly informed that wolves doe much increase and destroy many cattle in several partes of this dominion, and that some of the enemie's party who have laid down arms, and have liberty to get beyond the sea, and others, do attempt to carry away several such great dogges, as are commonly called wolfe dogges, whereby the breed of them, which are useful for destroying of wolves would (if not prevented) speedily decay. These are therefore to prohibit all persons whatsoever from exporting any of the said dogges out of this dominion, and searchers and other officers of the customs, in the several partes and creekes of this dominion, are hereby strictly required to seize and make stopp of all such dogges, and deliver them either to the common huntsman appointed for the precinct where they are seized upon, or to the governor of the said precinct.[49]

Throughout the seventeenth century, the werewolf shifted in public consciousness from feared beast to pitiful creature, given that an increasing number of cases were recognized as mental illness. In addition, Europe ended its obsession with burning suspected werewolves at the stake, and documented werewolf cases all but disappeared. The use of the werewolf by Webster as a basis for entertainment set a precedent, and the Enlightenment replaced superstition with science. The werewolf of old was no more, or so it seemed. As the eighteenth century loomed, Charles Perrault continued what Webster had started with Perrault's publication of *Contes* ('Tales') in 1697. His Little Red Riding Hood character is the earliest literary version of the tale that is still familiar today. A form of the tale has probably existed, though, in oral tradition since medieval times. Perrault's version makes an obvious contrast between the safe confines of the village and the hidden dangers of the wood. The basic premise is that Little Red Riding Hood's grandmother is eaten by a wolf (although later versions tone this down by having her locked in the cupboard), after which it turns its attentions on her.

His tale opens with Little Red Riding Hood being instructed by her mother to take a cake and some butter to her grandmother's house. On the way, she meets a wolf in the woods. The wolf wants to eat her, but is afraid to do so because of nearby woodcutters. The wolf hurries to the grandmother's house and eats her before lying in wait for Little Red Riding Hood. When she arrives, the girl finds her 'grandmother' (the wolf in disguise) in bed:

> Little Red Riding Hood: 'What big teeth you have!'
> Grandmother / Wolf: 'All the better to eat you with!'

In Perrault's version the wolf does eat Little Red Riding Hood and moreover, he consumes her whole. The moral of the tale is that young children should not talk to strangers: if Little Red Riding Hood had not told the wolf where she was going, she and her grandmother would have been safe.

In 1812 the brothers Grimm wrote their version of the tale called 'Little Red Cap', which is virtually the same as Perrault's. However, after eating Little Red Cap, the wolf goes back to sleep in the grandmother's bed. A passing huntsman hears the wolf snoring and goes inside. He sees that the wolf has eaten the grandmother so he takes some scissors and cuts open its belly hoping to release her. But Little

Bronze statuette from a Romano-British temple at Lydney, Gloucestershire, depicting a dog very similar to an Irish wolfhound.

Red Cap jumps out as well, and they quickly fetch some stones and fill the wolf's belly with them. When the wolf wakes up, he tries to run away, but the stones are so heavy inside him that he drops down dead with the effort. Little Red Cap promises never to stray from the path into the wood again. Next time, according to the brothers Grimm, Little Red Cap goes to her grandmother's house and again meets a wolf, but rushes ahead to warn her grandmother. When the wolf arrives at the house, he cannot enter as the door is locked. Thus he climbs onto the roof. The grandmother tells Little Red Cap to fill the stone trough at the front of the house with water that she had used to cook sausages in. The greedy wolf, smelling the sausages, looks down from the roof, stretching down as far as he can over the edge. He slips, falls into the trough and drowns, and Little Red Cap returns home safely. A similar moral to that of Perrault's can be taken from this version, and this time, the proof is added to the end. This tale can easily be imagined as a 'device' to scare children into doing what they are told, and never to speak to strangers.

The century that divides these two versions of Little Red Riding Hood is somewhat 'quiet' in relation to the werewolf. This could again suggest, that once the so-called transformation into a werewolf was discovered to be a mental affliction rather than a physical one, the symbol of the creature departed society's psyche. The 'Beast of Gévaudan' of 1764, discussed in the previous chapter, was one (unsurprisingly French) instance when the beast 'returned'. Twelve years after the Grimm brothers' tale, however, was the case of Antoine Léger, dealt with by Dudley Wright in his *Book of Vampires* (1914). Léger was a veteran soldier who, in 1824, seized a girl in the forest, murdered her and drank her blood. He then proceeded to rape her, tore out her heart and mutilated her body before eating some of her flesh. At his trial, he showed remorse for his actions but was sentenced to death. Although documented in a book on vampires, Léger's case has arguably clearer affiliations with werewolves. Whilst he reportedly drank some of the girl's blood, there are numerous occasions where convicted werewolves have also done this, and the mutilation of the body and eating of the flesh are certainly not vampiric traits. Despite the passing of more than two centuries since the height of the werewolf trials, it can be assumed that these had not disappeared from public consciousness, especially in rural areas. Cases like that of Léger, and the 'Beast of Gévaudan', posed a threat to the modern moral stance on werewolves. Regardless of folk belief, Léger was still a murderer. The fact that he violated the girl and tore out her heart shaped the case as that of a sadistic killer rather than a person suffering from lycanthropy. Nevertheless, Étienne-Jean Georget argued in 1825 that Léger was

> not, as has generally been said, a great criminal, a monster, a cannibal, a man-eater, who wished to renew the feast of Atreus; this individual was, in my opinion, an unfortunate imbecile, a madman, who ought to have been confined as a lunatic.[50]

George W. M. Reynolds's *Wagner the Wehr-wolf* (1847), a magazine 'penny dreadful' story about Fernand Wagner who is penniless and starving in his hut in the forest, was a subsequent addition to the genre of werewolf 'literature'. Wagner is devastated by the disappearance of his granddaughter, Agnes, when Faust comes to him, sent by the devil, offering wealth, youth and intelligence. The requirement is that Wagner must accompany him for eighteen months and prey on

Illustration from *Wagner the Wehr-wolf* (1847).

the human race in the form of a *Wehr-wolf.* This is a tale written to entertain that also reflects the misery and belief of past times. Reynolds has adapted his subject-matter to make it relevant to his contemporary audience. Just like Webster, who rather than trying to force his audience into 'perceiving' a werewolf, chose to recreate the wider argument for the werewolf, Reynolds chose to present the traditional view of the man-beast that he knew would excite readers. It is unlikely that a story on a protagonist struggling with lycanthropy would have had the same effect. Readers of penny dreadfuls wanted savagery, bloodlust, danger and misery in their tales.

No novel created such hopelessness, such abject poignancy as Robert Louis Stevenson's *The Strange Case of Dr Jekyll and Mr Hyde* (1886), which was born out of marvellous madness. The story goes,

Illustration from
*The Strange Case of Dr Jekyll
and Mr Hyde* (1886).

whether it is true or not, that one night in September 1885, Stevenson
was woken from a dream by his wife:

> in the small hours of one morning, I was awakened by
> cries of horror from Louis. Thinking he had a nightmare,
> I woke him. He said angrily 'Why did you wake me? I was
> dreaming a fine bogey tale.' I had awakened him at the first
> transformation scene.[51]

This 'bogey tale' was the inspiration for the novel, and it is believed that
when Stevenson wrote the final draft, he was under the influence of
drugs. William Gray has argued that it was probably cocaine or, more
relevantly, ergot (though it is difficult to see why this would have been
the drug of choice, as opium or laudanum was usually preferred).[52]
Moreover, Stevenson himself explained how he had been dreaming
of a scene where Hyde took a powder and underwent a change.[53]

The novel is widely described as an investigation of good and evil, of the duality of nature, of man and beast:[54] 'If I do what I do not want to, it is not I who does it, but sin living in me that does.'[55] Louise Welsh described the novel as being

> intimately concerned with the failings of its own age. The antics of Jekyll and Hyde fitted the times so well that when Jack the Ripper started his bloody campaign a stage version of the book had to be closed in order to protect the actors.[56]

This mention of Jack the Ripper is useful, as the case of the Ripper perhaps best encapsulates the mood of the times: late nineteenth-century England was 'dark', horrifically violent and dea y. It follows that a great number of literary 'evils' were borne from then, of which Frankenstein and Dracula were the most well known. The werewolf had to almost be relegated, given all those other monstrous creations, yet it was never far away from consciousness, awaiting its 'release'. Whilst Stevenson's novel could not be argued to be a werewolf story, its topic is markedly similar: there is a beast in us all, fighting to be unleashed. Stevenson himself echoed those words when he wrote about the critics he deemed to be hypocrites:

> the hypocrite let out the beast in Hyde, who is no more sexual than another, but who is the essence of cruelty and malice, and selfishness and cowardice, and these are the diabolical in man.[57]

Stevenson goes on to explain how he had

> long been trying to write a story on this subject, to find a body, a vehicle for that strong sense of man's double being which must at times come in upon and overwhelm the mind of every thinking creature.[58]

Man's 'double' is thus perfectly described. It is as though a circuit of understanding that which is within us has been completed. In Stevenson's time, and indeed in our time, the werewolf was and is no longer the relevant 'vehicle'. In the present, we consider the werewolf as something totally separate from the question of Man's inner self, his spirit twin, his double. Today, the only werewolves that exist are those featured in films and novels. Belief in a 'double' has not vanished: it might not be understood, and it does not necessarily take the form of a wolf anymore. As Stevenson said, 'Man is not truly one, but truly two.'[59]

PART THREE

Darkness Visible

All good things were previously wicked things;
every original sin has become an original virtue
Friedrich Nietzsche, *On the Genealogy of Morals*

seven

Methods to the Madness: Medical Explanations of the Werewolf Myth

Spirits from the deep who never sleep, be kind to me,
Spirits from the grave without a soul to save, be kind to me,
Spirits of the cold and ice, patrons of crime and vice, be kind to me,
Wolves, vampires, satyrs and ghosts! Elect of all dark, wild hosts!
I pray you send hither, the great grey shape that makes men shiver!
Invocation from a Slavic werewolf ceremony

L ycanthropy, so-called wolf-madness, had been recognized from very early times. In his study of the werewolf creature, Montague Summers wrote that

> it should be remarked that in a secondary or derivative sense
> the word werewolf has been erroneously employed to denote
> a person suffering from lycanthropy, that mania or disease
> when the patient imagines himself to be a wolf, and under
> that savage delusion betrays all the bestial propensities of
> the wolf, howling in a horrid long-drawn note.[1]

There are various suggestions of the causes for this 'mania or disease', including medical conditions such as porphyria or rabies, ingesting food contaminated with ergot, pacts with the devil or the witch ointments he provides, inherited conditions and lunacy, or the 'melancholy' of the mind, as early writers termed it. All of these suggestions will be considered to understand the breadth of the werewolf myth.

Throughout history, religion, mythology and transformation into animal form have been inter-linked. Here, Sabine Baring-Gould comments:

the line of demarcation between this and the translation of a beast's soul into man, or a man's soul into a beast's [metempsychosis] is very narrow ... the belief in a soul-endowed animal world was present among the ancients, and the laws of intelligence and instinct were misconstrued. The human soul with its consciousness seemed to be something already perfected in a pre-existing state, and in the myth of metempsychosis, we trace the yearnings and gropings of the soul after the source whence its own consciousness was derived, counting its dreams and hallucinations as gleams of memory, recording acts which had taken place in a former state of existence.[2]

What could then cause these 'dreams or hallucinations', what, magic potions aside, might cause a person to believe they were actually a werewolf? Baring-Gould suggests that the evidence for this cause is all but lost, confined to the pagan realms, yet interpreted in the modern day:

it is only from Scandinavian descriptions of those afflicted with the wolf-madness, and from the trials of those charged with the crime of lycanthropy in the later Middle Ages, that we can arrive at the truth respecting that form of madness which was invested by the superstitious with so much mystery.[3]

Even the Christian Church could not give a definitive answer to the werewolf question:

church authorities reversed their attitude. In 1484, it was still officially a sin to believe in the pagan superstition of werewolves, but by the later sixteenth century it was disreputable not to believe in werewolves, by then considered in league with Satan.[4]

Writing in the seventh century, the Byzantine physician Paulus Aegineta (Paul of Aegina) described the physical condition of lycanthropes but not the manner in which they were inflicted:

On Lycaon, or Lycanthropia. Those labouring under lycanthropia go out during the night imitating wolves in all things
and lingering about sepulchres until morning. You may
recognise such persons by these marks: they are pale, their
vision feeble, their eyes dry, tongue very dry, and the flow of
their saliva stopped; but they are thirsty, and their legs have
incurable ulcerations from frequent falls. Such are the marks
of the disease.[5]

Earlier still, in the fifth century, the Byzantine physician and medical
writer Aëtius of Amida discussed lycanthropia, or 'wolves fury', in *On
Melancholy*, and told how sufferers would disturb graves, eat bones,
suffer a great thirst, howl and have a haggard, hollow appearance.[6]
Marcellus Sidetes (Marcellus of Side), in the poem *De Lycanthropia*,
explained how sufferers experienced their symptoms at night and in
cemeteries 'in a context removed both temporarily and spatially from
that of normal life'. Early knowledge of the disease was thus reasonably generalized but the causes could not be exactly pinpointed. By
the later Middle Ages, the disease was attributed to melancholy (as
were many other ailments), and in *The Anatomy of Melancholy* (1621)
Robert Burton dedicated his 'Subsect iv' to this and similar diseases.
He wrote that those suffering from lycanthropy, which he believed
was a form of melancholy, 'lie hid most part all day, and go abroad in
the night, barking, howling, at graves and deserts; they usually have
hollow eyes, scabbed legs and thighs, very dry and pale'.[7] This seems
almost to be an amalgamation of the descriptions given by Aëtius and
Aegineta, so whether Burton was merely repeating what he knew
from other works or whether, over 1,000 years later, the disease was
still occurring exactly as it had in earlier times, we cannot be sure.

In the *Letter to Lord Cawdor* (1831), the English antiquary Algernon
Herbert described how

atrabilious patients take a fancy that they are wolves, and go
about howling and biting, and in some instances committing
cruel acts of homicide. In all digests of medicine that malady
is regularly described, under the name of lycanthropia, and

remedies (in the nature of depletion and febrifuge) are prescribed for it.

These terms 'atrabilious' and 'febrifuge' again hint at melancholic suffering, or as it might be termed today, 'depression', or 'fever'. Both, however, suggest mental illness. Writing in 1557, Johannes Arculanus, a Veronese physician, believed that those suffering from melancholy 'seem in very truth to be men no longer but incarnate devils and ravening wolves'.[8] However, by the time the second half of the nineteenth century arrived, medical knowledge had duly advanced and new discoveries demonstrated that earlier theorists, such as Arculanus or Burton, were probably mistaken.

Sabine Baring-Gould argues that melancholy is not the main cause of lycanthropy, rather it is due to hallucinations that are brought on by fever ('disturbs the senses and causes visions'), possibly caused by typhus. As such, sufferers 'often believe their limbs have been severed due to a deranged nervous system'.[9] This reflects Herbert's thoughts , in regard to links with fever. Furthermore, as analysed by Baring-Gould, 'a disordered condition of mind or body may produce hallucination in a form depending on the character and instincts of the individual'.[10] An ambitious man, labouring under monomania, could, with this 'symptom tracker', imagine himself a king; a covetous man might be plunged into despair by believing himself to be penniless; or a naturally cruel man might suppose himself to be transformed into the most cruel and bloodthirsty animal with which he is acquainted.[11] The links between hallucinations and the werewolf myth have been exposed here at length, and although purposeful hallucinations were apparently brought on by mind-inducing substances, this 'newer' evidence suggests that sometimes it might not be self-imposed.

In *Études cliniques* (1852), Dr Bénédict Morel described the case of one of his patients, who seems to have been suffering from this hallucinatory mental illness:

See this mouth, it is the mouth of a wolf, these are the teeth of a wolf. I have cloven feet; see the long hairs which cover my body; let me run into the woods, and you shall shoot me.[12]

A 16th-century German werewolf illustration.

Morel believed that the individual was suffering from a disease he called '*lycorexia*' or '*lycorrhexis*', and mentions the man's constant craving for raw meat that he would greedily devour 'like a wolf'. This patient died in the Maréville asylum at Nancy. Summers stated, somewhat matter of factly, that 'there appears little doubt . . . that here we have a plain case of diabolical possession'.[13] In this statement Summers is clinging on to a medieval belief that the mental illness suffered by some lycanthropes was a satanic possession of the sufferer by the devil, a point that is considered below. Today, mental illness is recognized as such, and not as the control of the soul by the devil. Indeed, someone today claiming to be a werewolf would be diagnosed as suffering from a form of mental disease. Baring-Gould, however, argued for lycanthropy to be considered as a combination of blood-thirstiness, cannibalism and insanity.[14]

Many writers on the subject have shown that, should a person become a lycanthrope, all is not lost. The Italian physician Girolamo Mercuriale (1530–1606) claimed that this is a most terrible disease, and yet not necessarily fatal, not even if it lasts for months. Indeed, I have read that after several years it was completely cured. The treatment is the same as that when dealing with lunacy.[15]

Paulus Aegineta also gave a detailed method for treatment:

you must know that lycanthropia is a species of melancholy which you may cure at the time of the attack, by opening a vein and abstracting blood to fainting, and giving the patient a diet of wholesome food. Let him use baths of sweet water, and then milk-whey for three days, and purging with the hiera from colocynth twice or thrice. After the purgings use the theriac of vipers, and administer those things mentioned for the cure of melancholy.[16]

These ingredients would be dodder of thyme (*epithymus*), aloes, wormwood, acrid vinegar as a beverage, squills, poley, slender birth-wort, phlebotomy and cataplasms. Failing that, as Herbert writes, a blow from a pitchfork between the eyes works just as well.[17] In the period when witches were being persecuted for the use of such remedies, disease or infection seems to have affected both persecutor and persecuted:

among medical factors affecting witches, werewolves and / or their persecutors, syphilis was probably specific to witch-hunters. However, rabies (which was still being transmitted from wolf to man in Pasteur's day) may have been connected with the hydrophobia ascribed to witches and werewolves.[18]

Rabies proves an interesting case: amongst the many wolves roaming the countryside, any infected creatures would have proved a real threat to people. Indeed,

Rabid wolves become irritable, restless and nervous and show exaggerated responses to sudden stimuli of sight and sound.

These animals show no fear and charge relentlessly, often inflicting massive injuries and death.[19]

This sounds like a description of the Viking berserker warriors after they had consumed their intoxicating drink. Yet does rabies explain the medical cause behind the myth?

The horror of a crazed beast, frantically assailing people, is often amplified by the hair-raising sounds which rabid animals emit due to the paralysis of their laryngeal musculature. Could rabid wolves have contributed to the belief in diabolically possessed werewolves who fiendishly and relentlessly attacked, killed and sometimes devoured humans?[20]

If it is expressed in different terms, were the rabid wolves considered as more than just wolves by wider society? They certainly acted differently, were more fearsome and deadly, made strange sounds and foamed at the mouth. As such, were they wolves at all or servants of Satan; men turned mad by the devil's work, perhaps? It would have been enough for the mutilated corpses of a couple of travellers or local shepherds to be discovered for the already superstitious community, persuaded by religious ideologies on witches and werewolves, to think something monstrous was afoot. What if a person was merely bitten by a rabid wolf, and not devoured but left alive to tell the tale? They might then have started to suffer from the disease themselves and be suspected of being a werewolf once the signs of the disease began to manifest themselves: 'many human victims of rabies are reported to rage in delirium, howl like wolves in their agony, go into violent frenzies and attack and bite those around them'.[21] It is certainly possible that outbreaks of rabies could have fuelled the werewolf myth, but surely these outbreaks would not have been widespread nor so prevalent to have caused the myth itself? It is more likely that they added to the general belief and were part of a wider phenomenon than the root cause itself.

Elizabeth Page-Nelson argues that although some people who believe themselves to be vampires or werewolves do not necessarily believe they are suffering from any medical or psychiatric illness, certain doctors would diagnose a specific condition for self-identified vampires – 'clinical vampirism' (or Renfield's Syndrome) – and for self-identified werewolves – 'lycanthropy'. She further points out that both conditions can be clearly linked to the medical disorder called 'porphyria' and the psychiatric disorder of 'schizophrenia'.[22] The possibility of porphyria as one of the causes for the vampire myth in the Middle Ages was discussed briefly in my earlier book, *From Demons to Dracula*.[23] However, whilst some of the factors do indeed fit the vampire myth, they are more applicable to that of the werewolf. It is important to note that in many cultures (and indeed in many periods of history, particularly the Middle Ages) there is little difference between vampires, werewolves and witches. Western imagery pertaining to these creatures has arguably evolved from similar 'archaic' entities.

The suggestion that porphyria may be relevant to the werewolf myth was first popularized by Lee Illis in the 1960s, as he examined the symptoms of the sufferers and how these could relate to the werewolf. These symptoms include, but are not exclusive to, extreme sensitivity to light causing sufferers to go out at night, and skin damage. This is particularly in cartilage around the face (nose and ears) and in the hands and fingers, giving a 'paw-like' appearance. Illis argued that

> the so-called werewolves of the past may, at least in the majority of instances, have been suffering from congenital porphyria. The evidence for this lies in the remarkable relation between the symptoms of this rare disease and the many accounts of werewolves that come down to us.[24]

Another important factor for the porphyria / werewolf link is that some manifestations of the disease – notably, 'mixed porphyria' – show a marked sexual differentiation in favour of males.[25] Illis came to the conclusion that the following symptoms were relevant to the werewolf myth:

Severe photosensitivity in which a rash is produced by the action of light. This may be especially noticeable during the summer or in a mountainous regions.

The urine is often reddish-brown as a result of the presence of large quantities of porphyrins (such as heme, the pigment in red blood cells).

There is a tendency for the skin lesions to ulcerate, and these ulcers may attack cartilage and bone. Over a period of years structures such as nose, ears, eyelids, and fingers, undergo progressive mutilation.

On the photosensitive areas extreme hair growth and pigmentation may develop.

The teeth may be red or reddish-brown due to the deposition of porphyrins.

The bone marrow is hyperplastic, which can cause enlargement.

Illis's research positions the sufferer in relation to the werewolf:

such a person, because of photosensitivity and the resultant disfigurement, may choose only to wander about at night ... the unhappy person may be mentally disturbed, and show some type or degree of abnormal behaviour. In ancient times this would be accentuated by the physical and social treatment he received from the other villagers, whose instincts would be to explain the apparition in terms of witchcraft or Satanic possession. The red teeth, the passage of red urine, the nocturnal wanderings, the mutilation of face and hands, the deranged behaviour: what could these suggest to a primitive, fear-ridden, and relatively isolated community?[26]

Twenty years later, David Dolphin suggested that sufferers of porphyria might have been the reason for the early vampire myth.[27] From both Dolphin's and Illis's research, sufferers, whilst admittedly having an aversion to sunlight (photosensitivity) and very pale skin (both hugely important traits to the modern vampire myth), can also suffer from skin discolouration, a growth or thickening of body and facial hair, and sores on the body. All these factors are remarkably similar to the accounts discussed earlier issuing from contemporary writers who attempted to document lycanthropy. If the disease progresses, as well as the cartilage becoming affected which leads to facial disfigurement, sufferers could also have experienced mild hysteria or delirium brought on by mental disturbances in the brain. Again, the disease could explain the potential for the 'launch' of the myth, but again, another factor in the myth itself is arguably responsible. This is largely owing to Illis's description of porphyria as a 'rare disease', unlike the 'many accounts' of werewolves. There simply cannot have been enough cases of porphyria to have caused the werewolf phenomenon alone.

Another factor that may also have contributed to the werewolf myth from a medical perspective is the outbreak of ergotism, which coincided in a widespread manner with the werewolf accounts in the medieval period. Ergot outbreaks were quite common throughout medieval Europe, and occurred because of the ergot bacteria contaminating rye and wheat, which was then used to make bread. The hallucinants contained in the ergot could have persuaded those who had eaten the contaminated substances that they were a werewolf, or produced visions of man-beasts, amongst other side effects. It has been suggested that there are two types of ergotism that may relate to the werewolf myth.[28] The first is convulsive ergotism, with symptoms such as trembling, twitching and shaking, and the second, gangrenous ergotism, which creates a burning sensation and gangrene. Ergot poisoning has occurred as recently as the 1950s in Pont-St-Esprit in southern France, where 135 people were hospitalized and six died. All had eaten bread contaminated by ergot. Reports recounted how victims had experienced horrible visions of tigers and snakes and some believed they were actually turning into beasts. One victim even asked bystanders to cut open his skin, presumably to allow the beast to escape, or perhaps it was to release the fire inside him, if he had been suffering the horrible burning sensation.[29] Interestingly, the demand to have the skin cut open also occurs in *The Duchess of Malfi*, and is expressed by Duke Ferdinand. As was the case above, too few incidents of ergotism are documented to support its being the cause of the myth.

Autism is a medical explanation that has been cited as a possible cause. Bruno Bettelheim, formerly of the Sonia Shankman Orthogenic School at the University of Chicago, argued that autism might have been mistaken for 'werewolfism' in the Middle Ages, particularly in the sixteenth and seventeenth centuries. According to Bettelheim, severe cases of autism in children makes them shy and reclusive in the day, but at night they often prowl around like animals. His research showed how such children crawl on all fours, refuse to wear clothing, urinate as they run, and snarl, bite and howl when angered. In extreme cases, they can attack with their hands and fingers in a clawing motion.[30] Bettelheim also proved that it is possible to link autism with so-called wild or feral children, and that some like to lick salt from their hands for hours on end (as a form of personal grooming), whilst others build dens in dark corners. One attacked a staff member over a dozen times in one year, biting her in the process. Sidky compared this behaviour to the famous werewolf case of Jean Grenier, the child believed to be a werewolf and sentenced to life imprisonment in the early 1600s.[31]

In 2007 the UK *Daily Mail* newspaper ran a story titled 'werewolf boy', which documented a young boy who had been reportedly rescued after living with wolves in a remote forest in Central Russia. He was described as having 'wolf-like traits and behaviour, toenails like claws and very strong and sharp teeth'. Doctors said that the boy looked about ten years old but that medical tests suggested he was in fact much older, although this was not confirmed. They also said he appeared intelligent but did not seem to understand Russian or any other language. A police spokesman commented that

it was simply unbelievable. He doesn't react when we call him, medics gave him clothes (but) he sprang down the corridor, bursting into his room . . . (he) devoured his food like an animal'.

After 24 hours, he managed to escape from the clinic, with a doctor commenting that 'its quite possible he is dangerous with psychological problems but also a source of viruses and infections'.[32] Was the boy a 'werewolf', was he suffering from severe autism, based on Bettelheim's theories, and how would he perhaps have been perceived by society a few hundred years ago?

The most obvious of all the medical explanations, though, is 'werewolf syndrome', or Congenital Generalized Hypertrichosis Terminalis (CGHT). The disease is also sometimes known as 'Ambras syndrome', for reasons that will become clear shortly. The main feature of the disease is extreme hair growth, which usually covers the entire body, including the face and hands. Those suffering from it will generally have excessive dark hair on their bodies and faces and some have large ears, mouths and thick lips, giving them a wolf-like appearance. The first documented case comes from the sevententh century, when four generations of the Gonzales family suffered from it, starting with Petrus Gonzales and documented by Altrovandus in 1648.[33] Altrovandus nicknamed them the 'Ambras Family', after discovering their portraits at Castle Ambras, in the Tyrol region, in western Austria. Curiously, in the very same castle is a fifteeenth-century portrait of Vlad Dracula, the Impaler, the (wrongly) suggested originator of the vampire myth.[34] Two other famous cases are those of Fedor Jeftichew, the 'dog-faced boy' in P. T. Barnum's travelling circus, and Julia Pastrana, 'the bearded lady', both from the nineteenth century. In 1857 the medical journal *The Lancet* described Pastrana as a 'peculiarity', but it is now understood that she and many other 'freaks' were suffering from werewolf syndrome.

Recent research in China has shown that werewolf syndrome is an extremely rare but highly heritable disease (as evidenced by the Gonzales family) but the research team have nevertheless discovered 30 cases so far.[35] Geneticist Xue Zhang found three families who have the disorder and compared DNA from both affected and unaffected family members. Those with werewolf syndrome had gene mutations in Chromosome 17, where copy number variations reflected 'missing' DNA. Zhang suggested that missing genes may affect 'neighbouring' genes, and one of these, sox9, is linked to hair growth. If this gene is missing, it can cause hair loss, or alopecia.[36]

Furthermore, research at Dalhousie University in Canada has shown very similar results. Brian K. Hall tested nineteen patients at the university and found a mutant gene in all cases. This sometimes occurred over several generations.[37]

Several medical explanations for the werewolf myth are available, and yet they are too inconclusive to explain the werewolf phenomenon. However much searching for the possible causes is undertaken from a modern medical perspective, a huge number of the werewolf accounts already explain the 'bringing on' of the beast: the 'witch ointments'. *A Restitution of Decayed Intelligence* (1605) recounts that

> the *were-wolves* are certaine sorcerers, who having annoynted
> their bodyes with an ointment which they make by the instinct
> of the devil; and putting on a certaine inchanted girdle, do
> not only unto the view of others seeme as wolves.[38]

Reginald Scott, in *A Discoverie of Witchcraft* (1584), says that 'here have I place and opportunitie to discover the whole art of witchcraft; even all their charmes, periapts, characters, amulets, etc', and then, quoting Virgil:

> These herbs did Meris give to me,
> And poisons pluckt at Pontus,
> For there they growe and multiplie,
> And doo not so amongst us.
> With these she made hir selfe become,
> A wolfe, and hid hir in the wood,
> She fetcht up soules out of their toome,
> Remooving corne from where it stood.[39]

Many witches were imprisoned, tortured or put to death for their practices, and yet there were defenders who continually argued that

Johann Weyer (1515–1588).

the witches were innocent. The most famous of these is Johann Weyer, a Dutch physician, occultist and demonologist, who was the first to publish *against* the persecution of witches – something that was as controversial in the period as witchcraft. Weyer even provides evidence of what was causing the hysteria of the period:

> About forty people at Casale in Western Lombardy smeared the bolts of the town gates with an ointment to spread the plague. Those who touched the gates were infected and many died. The heirs of the dead and diseased had actually paid people at Casale to smear the gates in order to obtain their inheritance more quickly.[40]

No doubt the witches were blamed for this before the truth came out. These three writers, discussed above, retrospectively offered their opinions on the 'witches ointment'. Indeed,

In 1545, the Pope's physicians first tested the idea (that it caused hallucinations) and modern findings confirm the hallucinogenic sensations of flying like witches or being furry like werewolves.[41]

What exactly was in these ointments? In a paper for the *National Library of Medicine*, Jaroslav Nemec wrote that

> There are records of the examination . . . of the so-called witches' ointments. They contained many extracts from hallucinogenic and poisonous herbs and plants, like aconite, belladonna, poison hemlock, henbane, wormwood and mandrake root. Most of them were well-known to physicians, but their effects were either unknown or not well understood.[42]

Jean de Nynauld also lists the ingredients for the ointment that aids 'transformation' into a werewolf:

> belladonna root, nightshade, the blood of bats and hoopoes, aconite, celery, soporific nightshade, soot, cinquefoil, calamus, parsley, poplar leaves, opium, henbane, hemlock, varieties of poppy and the crustaceans.[43]

For his part, Baring-Gould gave the composition of the ointments as:

> narcotics, to wit, *Solanum somniferum,* aconite, hyoscyamus, belladonna, opium, *acorus vulgaris, sium.* These were boiled down with oil, or the fat of little children who were murdered for the purpose. The blood of a bat was added, but its effects could have been *nil.* To these may have been added other foreign narcotics, the names of which have not transpired.[44]

If the witches' ointment was the primary factor for human transformation 'into' werewolves, albeit metaphorically, then the social ramifications of the act must also be considered. In pagan times, the transformation, or rather the potion, were welcomed and revered.

By the medieval period, however, hundreds of witches died for their 'sins'. The most common explanation for the whole act of witchery, as has been shown, was the devil, and those who doubted the charge of witchcraft accepted that the devil played some part. Amongst all the magic and mischief came the consequences of cavorting with the devil, the madness of the mind:

> Say, can you laugh indignant at the schemes,
> Of magic terrors, visionary dreams,
> Portentous wonders, witching imps of hell,
> The nightly goblin, and enchanting spell?[45]

Speaking of witches in the seventeenth century, Robert Burton said that 'to my purpose, they can, last of all, cure and cause most diseases to such as they love or hate, and this of melancholy amongst the rest'.[46] Weyer, as supportive as ever, argued against this general belief and publicly attacked the witch hunters and, in particular, the *Malleus Maleficarum*. His belief was that the witches were mentally ill and (as Burton believed) suffering from melancholy, rather than afflicted by a 'blanket' disease. Weyer argued that the supposed examples of magic and the notion of *physical* witchcraft were literally impossible, so those accused, or admitting to the charge, were in fact suffering from some form of mental disorder.[47] The physicians' response to this is valuable. Many of the witchcraft examinations (where 'seekers' would look for tell-tale witch 'marks' or teats used to suckle their 'familiars') had a physician present and often found the accused to be ill, in which case the charges were usually dropped.[48] Physicians of the time often recorded their beliefs on the subject. From such accounts, two types of lycanthropy generally emerge: one relating to possession by the devil and the other to a more natural occurrence.[49] In fact, Sennert discusses at length the question of whether 'diseases can be brought upon a man by means of spells and black magic, so that one will wither, consume and decay',[50] or perhaps be cursed into 'madness'.

What is strange, with regard to Weyer's beliefs, is that although he believed witches were mentally ill and not messengers of Satan as was held by others, he did accept that magicians (perhaps implying men) could in fact create illusions, and that they were heretics who used the devil's power to effect these. Sennert argued that such people were 'controlled by demons' (that is, possessed) and needed to be exorcized. As Nemec points out,

> belief in possession has been fairly common throughout the history of religion. Tales abound of people into whose body, it was believed, another being or creature had entered, causing hysteria, convulsions, and aberrant behaviour.[51]

Only a small leap of imagination is arguably, therefore, needed to imagine a person being transformed into a werewolf. Concerns with and interest in the 'beast within' are long-standing, and the most famous literary depiction of this is *The Strange Case of Dr Jekyll and Mr Hyde* (1886). This 'beast within' could be termed our 'personal Satan'. In the sixteenth century, when

> all the forces of organized religion had been deployed for centuries in formulating the notion of a personal Satan, he had a reality and immediacy which could not fail to grip the strongest mind.[52]

The Reformation almost certainly strengthened this view. The notion of a 'personal Satan' is gripping. Indeed, Hamlet himself warned that he had 'that within which passeth show'. As Keith Thomas has argued, 'the belief in the reality of Satan not only stimulated allegations about diabolical compacts; it also made possible the idea of demoniacal possession'.[53]

The 'treatment' for a patient diagnosed is valuable and curious in its simplicity and 'trickery':

> the doctor called in a priest and a surgeon, meanwhile equipping himself with a bag containing a live bat. The patient was told that it would take a small operation to cure him. The priest offered up prayer, and the surgeon made a slight incision in the

A 17th-century woodcut showing Father Urbain Grandier being burned alive. Note the demons circling in the smoke – this may reflect possession by spirits.

man's side. Just as the cut was given, the doctor let the bat fly into the room, crying 'Behold, there the devil is gone!' The man believed it and was cured.[54]

The series of exorcisms performed by John Darrell in Nottinghamshire and Derbyshire in the UK in the late sixteenth century provided a useful adjunct here. Darrell was born in Mansfield in Nottinghamshire in 1562 and was educated at the University of Cambridge, although he returned home before he finished his studies, to farm land he had been given. When he returned he claimed to be a Puritan minister, and soon had a reputation for being an exorcist, one 'able to drive out evil spirits that witches had cast upon people'.[55] His first exorcism in the area was on Catherine Wright, who claimed that Margaret Roper had sent a 'legion of fiends' into her. Roper was arrested and brought to trial but the magistrate declared her innocent and Darrell was threatened with prison. Darrell then moved to Burton-upon-Trent in Staffordshire, where he attempted to exorcize Thomas Darling, the 'Boy of Burton'. In February 1596 the boy fell ill and suffered a series of fits and visions of green cats and angels, a man emerging from his chamber pot and the flames of hell. The local doctor was sent for but could only diagnose a case of the worms. For the next three months he continued to suffer these fits.

Finally, he told how he had met a witch named Alice Gooderidge, and on bringing the woman to the household, young Thomas immediately attacked her and scratched her face – known as 'scoring over breath', this was an act repeated in many witchcraft cases.[56] It was believed that by wounding a witch in this way the demon inside would have to emerge to suck clean the injury. On examination, several 'witch marks' were found on her body and she was imprisoned in Derby Gaol. Whilst imprisoned, Gooderidge confessed to putting a spell on Darling and to having a series of 'familiars'. However, her confession may have been forced as she was placed near a hot fire, until 'being thoroughly heated desired a release, and she would disclose all'.[57]

Sir Edward Anderson, Chief Justice of the Common Pleas, was the judge at her trial and commented that 'their malice is great, their practices devilish, and if we shall not convict them . . . they will in a short time overrun the whole land'.[58] Gooderidge was thus found guilty and was to be sent to the gallows, but died in prison before her hanging could take place.

The most infamous case in which Darrell was involved was that of William Sommers. Sommers was allegedly possessed, and Darrell was asked to perform an exorcism on him. However, Sommers was found to be faking his convulsions after being brought before a magistrates' panel. Darrell was referred by Chief Justice Anderson (who had presided on the Burton case) to Archbishop Whitgift and was degraded from the clergy and imprisoned in 1599. Darrell argued that if neither possession, nor witchcraft, contrary to that hath been so long generally and confidently affirmed, why should we think that there are devils? If no Devils, no God.[59]

This was, it can be said, a valid point. The Church had backed itself into a corner here, and whilst it could be that it agreed with Darrell's stance, he was undoubtedly becoming too much of an inconvenience and drawing unwanted attention to the Church. In 1603 Samuel Harsnett published *A Declaration of Certain Egregious Popish Impostures*, in which he attacked figures like Darrell and branded their work 'devil theatre'. In response, Darrell released his own pamphlets that argued against the Anglican Church. Copies of these works were presented to James I on his accession to the throne later that year. Over the next decade, the Church regulated exorcisms and Parliament attempted to bring in new taxes (in 1616) but failed, so King James instead sought to raise revenues by granting new monopolies. Ben Johnson produced his 1616 play *The Devil is an Ass* in response to this, with many historians remarking how he cleverly linked 'spiritual' possessions with an insane desire for monetary possessions.

One of the more positive elements to issue from the witch craze was that it aided medical knowledge, particularly in regard to psychopathology or mental disorders. Whilst Johann Weyer was the most well-known advocate of this area of medicine, Girolamo Visconti, a Dominican monk and Professor of Logic at the University of Milan, wrote in 1490 that 'many men of learning and authority think that these (witches') illusions arise from a melancholic humor, depriving women of reason and freewill'.[60] Robert Burton also gives the example of someone, identified only as 'F.H.D.', who wrote how, when consulted by a man suffering from melancholy, he assessed the disease as 'partly magical, partly natural', as the patient vomited pieces of iron and lead and spoke in languages he did not know.[61]

As has been demonstrated, in the modern period 'melancholy' is no longer a single diagnosis or ailment. Today, it is a series of disorders including schizophrenia and other psychological problems. Katharine Ramsland has noted how 'lycanthropy has long been considered a form of lunacy that compels people to eat raw meat, attack others, grow their hair, and run on all fours'. This would arguably relate more to patterns of autistic behaviour described by Bettelheim, if his theory is to be believed. Ramsland asserts that 'popular stories play up the idea that the transformation (of man into wolf) is affected by the cycles of the moon, with the night of the full moon having the power to physically turn a person into a marauding wolf'.[62] A more popularized view of such symptoms is provided by Bram Stoker's *Dracula*:

> a dog began to howl somewhere in a farmhouse far down the road – a long, agonising wailing, as if from fear. The sound was taken up by another dog, and then another and another, till borne on the wind which now sighed softly through the pass, a wild howling began . . . from the mountains on each side of us began a louder and a sharper howling – that of wolves . . . just then the moon (appeared) . . . I saw around us a ring of wolves, with white teeth and lolling red tongues, with long, sinewy limbs and shaggy hair. They were a hundred times more terrible in the grim silence which held them than even when they howled . . . it is only when a man feels himself face to face with such horrors that he can understand their true import. All at once the wolves began to howl as though the moonlight had some peculiar effect on them.[63]

Montague Summers wrote that during his travels in Greece, he noted how there are generally known two types of the *vrykolakas* creature that variously represent a vampire, or a werewolf:

> one sort being men already dead (vampires) the other living men who were subject to a weird somnambulism which sent them forth ravening, and this particularly on moonlight nights.[64]

For Summers, those affected by the 'moon madness' or lunacy are the cursed servants of the devil, whom he has betrayed:

> often it is that Satan has betrayed his servant the sorcerer, the werewolf, has plagued him and driven him mad to make

him more miserable in life and to involve him even more irretrievably in perdition, for the sorcerer is one who has made a pact with the Devil.[65]

The devil can itself inflict this madness or disease on man, if the writings of King James I in his *Dæmonologie* (1597) are to be believed. The work reminds the reader of the example in the Scriptures that says if the devil

> layed sicknesse upon JOB, why may he not farre easilier lay it upon any other. For as an old practisian, he knows well inough what humor domines most in anie of us, and as a sprite he can subtillie weaken up the same.[66]

'Lycanthropy or wolf-madness (is) a variety of Isania Zoanthropica',[67] it has been argued by clinical psychologist Richard Noll, whereas Daniel Hach Tuke believed it to be 'endemic insanity'.[68] In terms of society dealing with sufferers in different ages, Illis indicates that:

> it is of interest that in pre-Christian days the insane were kept in beautiful gardens and tranquillised with music. With Christianity and the dreadful doctrines of heresy, the insane were thought to be possessed by evil spirits and were treated with appropriate inhumanity.[69]

Moreover, Illis demonstrates that the etymological roots of the term 'epilepsy' come from the Greek 'to seize or attack', and 'upon' and 'take hold' of by a spirit. In this manner, Montague Summers's comment that 'it is now quite generally recognised that insanity is very frequently nothing else than diabolical possession'[70] is particularly illuminating. In *Vampires, Werewolves and Demons*, Richard Noll highlights the eighteen documented cases of lycanthropy between 1975 and 1992, for which the most common diagnosis was bipolar disorder, with some cases relating to delusional depression and schizophrenia (and not to 'diabolical possession' as Summers would have us believe). Noll advances the theory that lycanthropy is closer to and resembles 'zoanthropy' (in line with Parker above), which is 'the delusion that one has been transformed into an animal'.[71]

A 1988 study in *Psychological Medicine* records twelve people being diagnosed with lycanthropy out of a survey of 5,000 patients at McClean Hospital in Belmont, Massachusetts. Whilst most were diagnosed as having 'delusional depression' or 'schizophrenia', this was not the case for all. As such, lycanthropy was said not to be exclusive to any particular disorder:

> like other curious and memorable syndromes . . . lycanthropy persists as an occasional but colourful feature of severe and occasionally factitious psychosis. However, it appears that the delusion of being transformed into an animal may bode no more ill than any other delusion.[72]

Three modern cases discussed by Katherine Ramsland all display different results: Mr H. had been using drugs; Mr W. was deemed mentally unwell; and Ms B. was diagnosed as being deluded – notably during full-moon phases. Such symptom and behavioural diversity make for an interesting study, given the pre-existing knowledge of werewolves. Before the relevance of the cycles of the moon is considered in more detail, it is worth considering two particular cases. The first involves 'Il Mostro', the Monster of Florence, who killed at least sixteen people between 1968 and 1985. Most of the victims were killed on nights of a full moon. Many of the victims were mutilated or torn apart, and some of the female victims had had their breasts cut or their genitals removed.[73]

The second case is that of Bill Ramsey from London, who claimed that when he was nine years old, he experienced a 'strange sensation and an accompanying foul odour', and began to think he was a wolf. He suffered seizures that made him snap and bite like a wolf, and in 1983, while being treated in hospital, he suddenly bit the nurse who was treating him, ran into a corner, crouched on all fours and started growling at people. He was sedated and admitted to a psychiatric institute, where demonologists Ed and Lorraine Warren visited him and strongly believed that Ramsey was 'possessed by a demon'. Bishop Robert McKenna was brought to perform an exorcism and recognized that a demon spirit was indeed inside Ramsey. During the exorcism, Ramsey claimed he felt 'a force leaving his body'. Afterwards, Ramsey said he felt at peace.[74] One commentator suggests that the ceremony may have had a powerful psychological effect on Ramsey, which led him to believe he was in fact cured. A final case of note, albeit a fictitious one, is that of the patient Renfield in Bram Stoker's *Dracula*, as exposed in the diary entry from Dr Seward's diary on 25 April:

> he is so unlike the normal lunatic . . . Renfield, aetat. 59 – sanguine temperament; great physical strength; morbidly exciteable; periods of gloom ending in some fixed idea which I cannot make out. I presume that the sanguine temperament itself and the disturbing influence end in a mentally-accomplished finish; a possibly dangerous man, probably dangerous if unselfish.

The 19 July entry records that:

> when I came in he ran to me and said he wanted to ask me a great favour – a very, very great favour; and as he spoke he fawned on me like a dog.

In this two-part account, Renfield appears to display the symptoms of what would today be diagnosed as bipolar disorder, which also aligns with modern studies on lycanthropy. As his behaviour is 'like a dog', the animalistic quality is in no doubt. Indeed, as will be discussed, he becomes more like the wolf. The exact reason for the inclusion of the Renfield character is unclear. Nevertheless, the persona is given much emphasis through his slow transformation. It is entirely possible that during the research stage of the novel, Stoker came across evidence of lycanthropy, especially as the links to wolves and werewolves are prominent. The wolves in Transylvania in the novel have already been discussed, for example, whilst Count Dracula himself turns into a wolf. Dr Seward's diary entry from 19 August states that:

when we closed in on him he fought like a tiger. He is immensely strong, and he was more like a wild beast than a man. I never saw a lunatic in such a paroxysm of rage before; and I hope I shall not again.

In this extract Renfield has become the beast. The following day's entry describes that

he has now so far quieted that there are spells of cessation from his passion. For the first week after his attack he was perpetually violent. Then, one night, just as the moon rose, he grew quiet, and kept murmuring to himself . . . after a while I left him. The attendant tells me that he was quiet until just before dawn, and then he began to get uneasy, and at length violent . . . three nights has the same thing happened – violent all day, then quiet from moonrise to sunrise.

The impression is that Stoker is trying to suggest something specific in terms of Renfield's diagnosis, but at this point the reader cannot be sure what it is. It seems that the author is insinuating that Renfield may be a lycanthrope, but gives evidence to the contrary: Renfield becomes aggressive, agitated, transformed into a quasi-beast when the moon *sets* and the sun rises and acts in an animalistic fashion throughout the day, before becoming calm again once the moon rises. This is contradictory to what we know of werewolves. Yet, there are more obvious discrepancies in Stoker's narrative that should alarm the reader. Renfield's attack occurs on 19 August, and yet on 20 August Stoker claims a week has passed between the attack and the diary entry. Also, in the 20 August entry, he claims that Renfield has acted in this strange manner for 'three nights', yet how can this be so if only one day has passed (19–20 August)? It is therefore possible that Stoker wanted to make the point more than be precise with material facts. Strangely, Stoker attempts to account for this discrepancy later in the 4 September entry:

I wish I could get some glimpse of his mind or of the cause of this sudden passion. Stop; there may be a clue after all, if we can find why to-day his paroxysms came on at high noon and at sunset. Can it be that there is malign influence of the sun at periods which affects certain natures as at times the moon does others?

This is surely the crux of the matter: Stoker was clearly aware of the theory that some mental disorders are affected by the moon, but he made this more complex by altering it to represent the pattern of the sun. Either Stoker was trying to demonstrate his intelligence or there was a particular significance for the modification. A clear conclusion is, in any case, difficult to reach.

Research in 2009 has assisted the understanding of behaviour and mental disturbances in relation to cycles of the moon. On 14 December 2009 *The Daily Telegraph* ran a story entitled 'Full moon brings out inner werewolf' in which it claimed that 'some people are more violent and exhibit tendencies comparable to werewolves during a full moon'. It referred to research carried out at Calvary Mater Newcastle Hospital in Australia which documented how 'some of the patients attacked staff like animals, biting, spitting and scratching . . . one might compare them with the werewolves of the past'.[75] In the *Medical Journal of Australia*, Leonie A. Claver, researcher and clinical nurse in toxicology, explained the findings:

the favoured belief that phases of the moon ('Luna') and extreme human behaviour are closely linked is alive and well within the health care system. This folklore, which links behavioural disturbance with the full moon is not easily explained by modern science but is regularly observed . . . those most enthusiastic about the link between disturbed behaviour and the full moon are mental health care workers (and) nurses in dementia units.[76]

Moreover,

although defining degrees of behavioural disturbance may be somewhat subjective, this is a particularly important factor in analyses involving human behaviour . . . we therefore postulated that the phase of the moon may be associated with only extreme violence . . . to investigate the possible association between lunar phases and extreme aggression and agitation, we studied a group of patients with violent and acute behavioural disturbance . . . and compared these patients to a group with less severe behaviour.

The study's sample was based on two groups of patients observed between August 2008 and July 2009. The first group was composed of a selection of patients who had presented at the emergency department and had required sedation and physical restraints, while the second group comprised patients from disparate hospital departments whose behaviour was less violent, but for whom hospital security calls had been made. The team determined the lunar phases. Four days from each month were chosen for study, based on the fact that there are eight phases of the moon with a periodicity of 3.69 days (rounded up to four days for simplicity). Some 91 patients fitted into the 'severe' category and 23 per cent of these occurred during a full moon (incredibly, double the number for other phases). It was also noted that 36 per cent of these patients had alcohol or drugs in their system. Five of the 91 had physically attacked staff, in a breakdown of biting (2), spitting (1), scratching (1), kicking (1).

In the 'less severe' category, 512 patients were observed. Perhaps surprisingly, a reasonably even distribution is discernible throughout the lunar phases, with no statistically significant increase during the full moon. The study suggested that 'violent and acute behaviour disturbance manifested more commonly during the full moon and most patients (in this category) had indulged in alcohol, recreational drugs or both'.[77] There are various theories on why this might have occurred including the notion that full-moon nights are twelve times brighter than other nights, leading people to stay up longer. However, this is not a particularly tenable argument. (The fact is that the body is made up of 70 per cent water and may be influenced by the moon's gravitational pull – as with marine tidal movements.) Calver and her coauthor-researchers point out that Thomas Aquinas argued this point in the thirteenth century, believing the brain was the 'most moist part' of the body.[78] Whilst this is accurate, Aquinas was actually quoting Aristotle here: 'the brain is the most moist of all the parts of the body.'[79]

In *Summa Theologia* (1274) Aquinas pondered 'whether heavenly bodies can act on demons' themselves. He believed that

it would seem that heavenly bodies can act on the demons. For the demons, according to certain phases of the moon, can harass men, who on that account are called lunatics.[80]

Here he could have been reflecting on Scripture. For example, Matthew 4:24 says: 'And his fame went through all Syria. Those possessed with devils, those which were lunatick, and those that had the palsy. And he healed them'. Similarly, in Matthew 17:15: 'Lord, have mercy on my son: for he is a lunatick, and sore vexed: for oftimes he falleth into the fire, and oft into the water.'[81] In Aquinas' time it was believed that the disease of the mind, lunacy, was affected by the increase in or decrease of the moon. Today, opinion is divided, although the term 'lunatic' is still used, albeit not as a technical term. The term is used on just two occasions in Matthew (4:24 and 17:15 above), but certain biblical translations use 'epilepsy' instead, and thus the two possibly refer to the same disease. Aquinas explained that the devil brings forth the disease for two reasons. The first is to 'defame God's creature' (the moon) and the second is because demons can only affect things through natural forces. As such, the demons gather in the brain: 'wherefore the demons, according to certain phases of the moon, disturb man's imagination, when they observe that the brain is thereto disposed'.[82]

Returning to Calver and her colleagues' research, their findings that the use of stimulants has an effect on behavioural disturbance, could be said to mirror the act of 'bringing on' the werewolf 'transformation' with a substance such as an ointment. However, stimulants alone cannot, arguably, be responsible for this. Indeed, there is evidence for a dramatic rise in 'werewolf-like' incidents during a full moon. Furthermore, the use of substances and stimulants probably occurs on nights other than when there is a fall moon. Perhaps people prone to mental disturbance that leads them to commit violent acts are the ones who are more susceptible. In the past, people in such a category were considered to be werewolves because of their behaviour. It is possible that they believed they were wolves because of the side effects of the stimulants consumed. The consumption of substances still results in the release of the 'beast within'. However, there is no longer a wolf population. How and why are werewolves still 'relevant'?

eight
Evolution Creates Dissolution: The End of the Myth?

And out come the wolves . . .
Junkie Man, *Rancid*

This final chapter considers the multiple images of the werewolf today and its representation as a creature, as a monster, and in myth. It is presently debated whether the werewolf myth has any relevancy to modern society, largely because it is a myth from medieval times that 'haunted' the minds of a peasantry throughout Europe. Today, the werewolf is confined to the book and the screen in imaginings that recycle the tale of an age-old monster. Many scholars and folklorists alike argue that science finally eradicated the beast, and that Charles Darwin's theory of evolution was the silver bullet that destroyed the myth forever, and replaced it with a new monster in the form of the cryptid Bigfoot or Sasquatch, and the Yeti. Even the names for these strange ape-like beasts – cryptids – are terrifying. Yet the werewolf is still, arguably, very present, as this chapter will show.

Historian of science Brian Regal suggests that

> for most of recorded history, the half-man, half-wolf lycanthrope reigned supreme as the creature travellers most feared encountering in the woods and along dark roads at night . . . but while the werewolf still holds a place in fiction and films, few people actually fear meeting one in reality. Many individuals and groups actively search for cryptids, but there are no werewolf-hunting organisations'.[1]

Regal further argues that from the nineteenth century onwards belief in creatures such as Bigfoot and the Yeti replaced that of the were-wolf, and cites Darwinism as the cause. To counter this hypothesis, the background to *The Origin of Species* (1859), Darwin's 'guide' to evolution, is crucial. Although the work assisted with the addition of the cryptid into the 'catalogue' of so-called monsters, it did not in fact destroy those that already existed. The point that Regal and others use to formulate their argument relates to Darwin's belief that it is scientifically impossible for one 'creature' to metamorphose *directly* into another. That is not to say human *evolution* into a wolf is not technically impossible, but it would need to occur over many evolution-ary 'stages': 'one cannot have a simple species intermediate between two great families', Darwin argued in 1843.[2] When the theory of evolution took hold (that is, an evolution from ape into man), claims of monstrous ape-men began to appear, most notably from the mid twentieth century onwards. Regardless of whether these beasts actu-ally did exist, what science had done was to prove that they *could* exist. However, never in these claims did the ape-men transform from man into ape or vice versa; they were rather continually in 'monster' form as a half-man, half-ape hybrid. As long as they had evolved into this form gradually, theoretically speaking, there is no reason why they could not exist. There is, however, no *physical* proof that they do exist. Has evolution therefore banished the werewolf myth to fantasy – to the realm of film and fiction?

The acceptance of evolution and the discovery of our early ances-tors coincided with serial killings such as those committed by Jack the Ripper in England and Joseph Vâcher in France. The archaeol-ogy behind the evolution must however be examined first. Prior to the release of Darwin's work, many believed that the world was just under 6,000 years old (created in 4004 BC). Although this theory was widely accepted, the archaeological record appeared contradic-tory. Darwin himself had been convinced of the theory of evolution long before he published his work in 1859, but was concerned that society was not ready to accept it. Rumours that other scientists were writing on the same theory and were ready to publish led him to hurriedly release his own work. It was by no means widely accepted and Creationists argued against it. For them, the animal remains that were being uncovered in caves, for example, were evidence of the Great Flood and related to the story of Noah in the Bible. This debate had been raging in Britain and in France long before Darwin's work was published. In the 1830s the French archaeologist Boucher de Crèvecœur de Perthes had been excavating the river gravels on the Somme and had uncovered evidence that linked flint tools with the bones of extinct animals. In the same decade, Sir Charles Lyell had advanced his 'doctrine of uniformity' in which he argued that geology and its processes were similar in the period to those in the distant past. According to Lyell, a few million years ago rivers wore away at their banks, glaciers carved out valleys and volcanoes erupted, just as they did in the present. His theory meant that a 'great flood' could not possibly have covered the highest mountains – an argument that contradicted that of religious belief.

In 1854, five years before the publication of *The Origin of Species*, quarrying in the Neander Valley near Düsseldorf in Germany revealed some strange 'human' remains in a small cave. The report of the discovery described the remains as those of a barbarous and savage race and was met with much scepticism. Professor Mayer of Bonn said they were probably the remains of a Mongolian Cossack suffering from rickets who had crept into the cave and died in 1814 during the Napoleonic War. He explained that the bowed leg bone proved that the man was a horseman, and that the large brow ridges reflected the dying man 'frowning in pain'. This example helps a modern audience to understand why Darwin feared the public were not ready for his theories. In 1863 the Irish anatomist William King suggested that the skull from the Neander Valley was distinct enough to indicate a separate species of human and proposed '*Homo Neanderthalensis*' (Neanderthals). Neanderthal remains were subsequently discovered across Europe, in Britain, France, Belgium and Croatia – precisely the countries or areas that revered the wolf and the bear, as discussed in Chapter One.

The extent of evolution began to be grasped, when, in 1907, a thick-set jawbone was discovered at a quarry at Mauer near Heidelberg in Germany. The teeth were intact but the jaw had no chin,

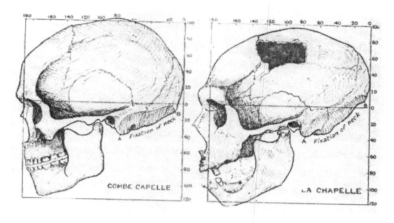

Skull comparison of a Neanderthal (La Chapelle) and Homo
sapiens (Combe Capelle).

and reflected a much earlier ancestor than the Neanderthals: *Homo
heidelbergensis*. Britain did not feel that it was a part of the evolution-
ary story until 1910, when Charles Dawson, a solicitor and amateur
fossil hunter, claimed he had been given a thick, darkly stained piece
of human skull. By 1912 he had obtained several more pieces of skull,
all reputedly 'sourced' from a quarry at Piltdown in Essex. Excavation
of the site led Dawson to discover additional fragments of skull,
along with fossilized animal bones, stone tools and the fragment of
a lower jaw. The skull fragments were reconstructed into a quite
modern-looking skull, apart from the fact that it had an ape-like jaw.
Was this then the missing link? Dawson believed it was, and claimed
that it was one million years old. In 1913–14 further discoveries were
made, including a canine tooth that appeared in size to be between
that of a human tooth and that of an ape, and a carved artefact made
from elephant bone. The following year another tooth and more
skull fragments were unearthed. These finds were, in many ways,
revelational. Although African and Asian finds from the 1920s and
1930s were exciting in their content, nothing arguably matched the
value of the 'Piltdown Man' from England. In 1949 new chemical test-
ing techniques were applied to the remains. This enabled scientists
to see that whilst the animal bones were quite old, the skull and jaw

were more modern. In 1953 even more stringent tests were carried out that proved the jaw to be a forgery. Moreover, further tests showed that all the bones had been stained to appear ancient. Although the skull was human, the jaw was that of an orang-utan with filed-down teeth. Ironically, in 1935–6 genuine early human remains *were* discovered in southeast England, at Swanscombe in Kent.

During the Piltdown fiasco, the Australian anthropologist Raymond Dart wrote about early mankind and suggested that early man was more beast than human. He discussed early man's bestial practices and the evidence of cannibalism, and in this saw parallels with modern man, claiming how 'we are Cain's children, all of us'. The archaeologists Mark Roberts and Mike Pitts suggested that the

> creatures that Raymond Dart described as 'human . . . in their love of flesh, in hunting wild game . . . slaking their ravenous thirst with the hot blood of victims and greedily devouring livid writhing flesh'; such chimeras, it seems, are dead.[3]

This was an erroneous judgment, as will be shown. Raymond Dart's suppositions that humans have 'a love of flesh' and 'slaking hot blood' are not to be discounted, however. Indeed, such a statement could have value and accuracy if applied to any of the werewolf stories of the past thousand years that have been discussed thus far. Yet stories that have resonance with this statement are to be found much closer to Dart's time. In fact, Dart was born in the aftermath of two of the most horrific killing sprees of the period. In 1893, when Dart was born, Britain was still reeling from the Ripper, and France was about to experience Vâcher, the 'Killer of Little Shepherds'. While the Ripper murders are well known, this is not the case with British audiences and the Vâcher case that occurred in the French countryside in the late nineteenth century.

Joseph Vâcher, the son of a farmer, was born in 1869 in Beaufort, in the Rhône-Alpes in France. He was sent to a strict Catholic school which had a profound impression on him. Later, whilst serving in the army, he fell in love with a young woman named Louise whom he wrote to constantly. When he left the army, Vâcher proposed to her but she turned him down. For this, he shot her four times before shooting himself in the face. However, both Vâcher and Louise survived the shooting. Vâcher was left with facial disfigurement and was plagued by an infected ear for the rest of his life. After the incident, Vâcher took to wandering the French countryside, looking for work and playing his accordion. In 1894 a 21-year-old woman went missing from her job at a silk mill on the outskirts of Beaurepaire, in the same region. She was found later that afternoon, lying in a hedge looking as if she 'had been attacked by a wild beast'.4 Eugénie Delhomme, the factory worker, was Vâcher's first victim. Over the next three years he would kill a further ten times.

In 1897 Vâcher was trying to find a twelfth victim. Whilst in the nearby Ardèche in the Rhône-Alpes region, he came across a woman in a field and attacked her. Her cries alerted her husband and her son and they went to her aid, overpowered Vâcher and took him to the police. Despite the police not having any substantial evidence to link Vâcher directly to the murders, he confessed everything and was sent to trial. The full ferocity of his murders transpired in court as

Contemporary drawings of Joseph Vâcher killing his victims in the French countryside.

judges heard how he had slit some of his victims' throats, mutilated their bodies and raped some of them after their deaths. Other victims had been sodomized, but their number could not be verified as this act was not always checked for during postmortem examinations. Hence the full extent of Vâcher's sexual violations remains unknown. The public were deeply shocked by Vâcher's killings and a popular verse from 1898 reflects this: 'The werewolf of legends, Has now been surpassed.'[5]

While there are neither any claims from Vâcher that he assumed 'form' of a werewolf as he killed, nor from any other parties that he was one, there are numerous instances where the evidence could have convicted him for being a werwolf, had he lived just 300 years earlier. Firstly, Vâcher's appearance at the trial led a reporter for *La dépêche de Toulouse* to describe him as a 'wild animal with a human face ... a monster, yes; the most odious and dreadful of monsters'.[6] And 'his raggedy beard, which came to a point under his chin, made him appear slightly Satanic ... with his clawlike fingernails and hyperactive limbs, he seemed less a martyred saint than a barely controlled animal'.[7] Secondly, Vâcher's own comments during his interrogation would have convicted him for being a werewolf, particularly as he claimed that he killed because of a rage – a possession – that came over him: 'I feel as though I am possessed by something evil. I'm afraid if I met someone I might do them harm.'[8] Vâcher further alleged that this 'possession' came upon him after he was licked by a 'suspected' rabid dog. He told the court that his mother quickly sent for a folk remedy which he drank and that his character changed after this incident. Clear parallels with traditional werewolf accounts relating to the salve are in evidence here, and although Vâcher did not claim he became a werewolf, he did allude to and even describe the metaphorical transformation he underwent.

However, during his trial, Vâcher altered his story slightly, claiming he was bitten by the dog, and not licked by it: 'I was bitten by a rabid dog ... I remember taking a remedy ... I always believed ... that it was the medicine that corrupted my blood.'[9] In one outburst during the proceedings Vâcher also linked his behaviour to the 'dog' incident: 'Do I know what got hold of me? I was like a beast!'

'A ferocious beast', added Judge Adhémar de Coston. 'Yes, because I was bitten by a ferocious beast', replied Vâcher.[10] Asked to elaborate on his temperament during the killings, Vâcher replied that

> at certain times, and especially when I'm exposed to the sun
> ... I would feel this rage and an immediate violent insanity
> ... the sickness would take me ... (and) terrible battles raged
> within me.[11]

In this last admission Vâcher's condition can be aligned with that of Renfield in Bram Stoker's *Dracula* (see Chapter Five), which had been published the previous year (1897). Stoker could not have been aware of Vâcher's alleged 'condition', and it is extremely unlikely that Vâcher would have been familiar with the novel. Yet the similarities between Vâcher and the fictional Renfield are striking. As has been demonstrated, it is the moon, if anything, that produces werewolf 'symptoms' in susceptible humans. However, this remains somewhat imprecise in definition. During the trial, it emerged that Vâcher had once attacked a fellow soldier, and had roared like a beast: 'it was a terrible cry, the likes of which I have never heard and which I will never forget.'[12]

After Vâcher's conviction and his execution on 31 December 1898, Alexandre Bérard, a public official, wrote how the scene on that day was like 'a monstrous Saturnalia ... an orgy (of) the most horrible and base instincts of the raging beast'.[13] Modern readers can only ponder how this 'Saturnalian orgy' and others took place across the centuries at the hundreds of werewolf trials throughout Europe. Indeed, the extent to which beliefs in werewolves and related superstitions affected the French people during the period of Vâcher's killings and trial has to be imagined. The criminal's confessions and their echoes in public opinion, along with wider discussion of werewolf beliefs in the press, provide some idea of the impact. For example, one newspaper in Lyons in 1895, alluding to earlier beliefs surrounding the devil, commented 'What demon pushed this monstrous murderer to tear his victims to shreds?' This remark conjures up images of Monsieur de la Forêt visiting Vâcher. It is curious to note that during the scientific

Laccassagne's autopsy of Gouffe.

advancements of the period, the British surgeon George Gulliver discovered that in the animal world, humans have the largest red blood cells at 1/3200, closely followed by dogs (and wolves) at 1/3395. The effect of such figures on an already superstitious public can again only be imagined.

Opinions on the Vâcher case were divided, and although he was found guilty of murder and subsequently executed, some people argued that he should have been classed as insane and treated thus. As Douglas Starr points out, 'this was the era of Darwin and Pasteur, and the conceptual mixing of evolution and contagion gave rise to harsh judgements about those whose existence would harm the greater good'.[14] Indeed, the physician Gustave Le Bron commented that

> if I am bitten by a viper or a rabid dog, I do not care to know whether the animal is responsible for its misdeed or not. I try to protect myself by preventing it from doing any further harm or harming others.[15]

In the same line of thinking, Maurice de Fleury asked whether

> it [is] really human to allow these monsters, these creatures of darkness, these nightmarish larvae to breathe? Do you not think, to the contrary, that it would be more pious to kill them, to do away with that ugliness and unconsciousness that cannot be made noble, even by suffering?[16]

The press response was 'It doesn't matter if he is a degenerate or not. It is necessary to rid society of whatever threatens it'.[17]

Another French killer of the time, Charles Double, who had killed his own mother over an argument about money, described himself (he was homosexual) as

> a kind of monstrosity, a castoff, something out of step with the rest of the world, a subject of study and wonderment for science. Society does not admit these beings. It rejects and condemns them ... (I am) stuck between the angel and the demon (and) crawl in the fetid ruts of shameful and criminal joys ... such is the destiny of poor, sick creatures like myself.[18]

Clearly the empathy surrounding lycanthropy, from which Double suffered, as a mental illness, was beginning to recede. As Starr summarized:

> the deepest and most troubling questions about human nature stubbornly remain rooted in the spiritual and moral worlds. Perhaps it is part of the human condition that we cannot analyse or explain that which most frightens us. We will never understand why (some) people arise to bring chaos and violence into a world that we strruggle to keep orderly and safe. We cannot account for the source of that impulse.[19]

Perhaps, from the werewolf's point of view, we tried to be empathetic, but cases like that of Vâcher made us question why we bothered.

Front cover of *Le Petit Parisien* (31 October 1897) documenting Joseph Vâcher's killing spree.

In 1898, the year Vâcher was executed, Henry Beaugrand published his short story *The Werwolves*. This little-known tale was subsequently adapted for the cinema in 1913 by Henry MacRae for the Bison Film Company and released by Universal Studios as *The Werewolf*. All copies of the eighteen-minute film were probably destroyed in a fire in 1924. The film related the story of a Navajo woman endowed with the power to turn into a werewolf and who duly seeks revenge on the invading white man. She teaches the skill to her daughter in order for her to carry on the tradition. The film bears little relation to the original book, which was set around Fort Richelieu in the American West and is supposedly attacked by werewolves that are in fact cunning Indian warriors who can transform into beasts. The importance of *The Werewolf*, whatever the plot, was its status as the first-ever 'werewolf film'.

In 1918, the debate surrounding the idea of lycanthropy as a 'mental illness surfaced again when Sigmund Freud published 'From the History of an Infantile Neurosis' concerning a patient he called the 'Wolf-Man'. The case concerned a Russian patient by the name of Sergei Pankejeff. Pankejeff had already received some initial treatment before he was referred to Freud, who saw him twice: between February 1910 and July 1914 and then again in 1919. Pankejeff was then referred to psychiatrist Ruth Mack Brunswick (1926–38) and was later analysed by Kurt Eissler and Wilhelm Solms, the latter the president of the Vienna Psychoanalytic Society. Freud's analysis of Pankejeff remains, however, the bestknown. Freud believed that his patient had suffered a severe neurotic disturbance in his early life which began just before his fourth birthday as an animal phobia. In later years, he developed a 'manic-depressive insanity'. Initially, Freud argued, his illness started as a sexual problem after his sister, two years his elder, tried to seduce him. It is not necessary to go into detail regarding Freud's opinions on the case, especially to the sexual element, for it bears no relevance to the 'Wolf Man' tag. However, at around the same time, Pankejeff's beloved nanny was replaced by a harsher English governess. On one occasion the governess gave the children chopped-up sugar sticks, telling them they were chopped up snakes. This may have been an innocent act, but young Pankejeff recalled a story told to him by his father about when he had once beaten a snake to pieces with a stick. Also, he was familiar with the popular children's tale *Reynard the Fox*, in which a wolf tried to go fishing in winter, used his tail as bait and subsequently lost it. Whilst Freud used this information to suggest castration anxiety on the part of Pankejeff, of more interest to this study is the presence of the wolf at such an early age in the patient's life.

Indeed, Pankejeff was also familiar with the story of *Little Red Riding Hood* (it seems more likely that he would have been familiar with the tale *Little Red Cap* by the Grimms) and also *The Wolf and the Seven Little Goats*, both of which featured children coming out of the wolf's belly. This confused him as he thought only women could have children inside them. Otherwise, did it perhaps mean that men could too?[20] Just before his fourth birthday, Pankejeff had had a dream that he recounted to Freud:

> I dreamt that it was night and that I was lying in bed. (My bed stood with its foot towards the window; in front of the window there was a row of old walnut trees. I know it was winter when I had the dream, and night-time). Suddenly the window opened of its own accord, and I was terrified to see that some white wolves were sitting on the big walnut tree in front of the window. There were six or seven of them. The wolves were quite white, and looked more like foxes or sheep-dogs, for they had big tails like foxes and they had their ears pricked like dogs when they pay attention to something. In great terror, evidently of being eaten by the wolves, I screamed and woke up.[21]

Until his eleventh or twelfth year, Pankejeff added, he was always afraid of something terrible in his dreams. During this time, he had a fear of wolves, and particularly an image of one in a book of fairy tales that his sister took great delight in showing him. In the picture, the wolf was standing up on two legs and was striding out with one leg. It had its ears pricked and its claws stretched out in front.[22] This posture is more akin to a werewolf than to a normal wolf, and a similar picture appears in *The Wolf and the Seven Little Goats*, which was also a Grimm tale. Hence, a clear foundation for his dream comes from his early experience with wolves in the stories that his father told and those that he read in his books. Freud, however, devoted the rest of the paper arguing for a sexual motive to the dream. Two questions relating to the dream arise. First: why were the wolves white? Pankejeff recalled that shortly before his dream, an epidemic had broken amongst flocks of local sheep and many of them died. Perhaps this was in Pankejeff's subconscious and the wolves represented or partly represented the sheep. Second: why were they in the tree? Again, Pankejeff recollected a story that his grandfather had told him about a tailor who was in his shop when a wolf burst through the window. The tailor hit the wolf and grabbed the tail, pulled it off and the wolf ran away. One day, as the tailor was walking through the woods, a pack of wolves came towards him, one of which one had no tail. He escaped by climbing a tree.[23]

Here then is one reason not only for the wolves being in the tree, but also for the window opening. Instead of the wolves coming in through the window, they sat in the tree instead. Finally, why were there six or seven wolves? This may simply relate to the pack of wolves from his grandfather's story. Freud initially suggested that it could have related to *Little Red Riding Hood*, but as there is only one wolf in that story it probably cannot be the case. Of more likelihood (and given the fact that the image from his childhood can be considered to be from this tale too) is the story of *The Wolf and the Seven Little Goats*. In this tale there are indeed seven goats, as well as seven wolves in the tree. The tale also includes the incident where the wolf's paw is turned white by the baker's flour. Is this then why the wolves are white in the dream? Ample evidence exists to explain Pankejeff's dream through the werewolves tales that his family recounted and that he read in his books. A further link between Pankejeff's memoirs and the dream is made as he explains that

> my sister and I both liked to draw. At first we used to draw trees, and I found Anna's (his sister) way of drawing the little round leaves particularly attractive and interesting.

The Wolf-Man's drawing of his wolf dream.

But not wanting to imitate her, I soon gave up tree-drawing. I began trying to draw horses true to nature, but unfortunately every horse I drew looked more like a dog or a wolf than a real horse'.[24]

The point that it was Freud who labelled the animals sitting in the tree as 'wolves' has been raised, since Pankejeff was unsure of this. It was suggested that they 'were not wolves at all but white Spitz dogs with pointed ears and bushy tails'.[25] Although this could be possible, owing to the sheepdogs that Pankejeff saw locally, the sheer volume of wolf tales to which he had been exposed before and around the time of the dream suggests, rather, that they were indeed wolves. According to Freud's analysis, Pankejeff's wolf-phobia disappeared by the age of four and a half, only to be replaced by a 'religious obsessional neurosis'. In this, he would say endless prayers, attend confession to expiate his sinful thoughts, and conduct a bizarre ritual each night where he went round the room kissing holy pictures. This ended around the age of ten years old, but not before he had had another curious dream. In it, he saw the devil, dressed all in black and in the same upright stance as the wolf from his sister's storybook. He recognised the devil as the demon from Lermontov's poem *The Demon*, in which Princess Tamara neither recognizes angel nor demon in him, but a tortured soul. Perhaps this was how Pankejeff saw himself. Towards the end of his religious neurosis, his mind was full of such blasphemes as 'God-shit' and 'God-swine', and how if he saw three piles of horse dung in the street, he would think of the Holy Trinity.[26] Eventually, his religious neurosis gave way to a military one.

Sufficient evidence could support the theory of the dream as related to Pankejeff's fear of wolves. Yet Freud sought to justify a sexual reason for the dream. Stephen Greenblatt has argued that Freud was creating an element of 'improvisation' here, that is, 'the ability to capitalise on the unforeseen and to transform given materials into one's own scenario'.[27] This 'improvisation' is explained in Freud's theory of *Nachträglichkeit* – the 'deferred effect'. In brief,

it is thought that when we make sense of something here and now, and when we say it's important to us here and now, we're actually channelling some past material, and reconfiguring it into terms of our current experience.[28]

Freud used this theory to argue that it related to a 'primal history' for Pankejeff, or the 'primal scene' of seeing his parents having sexual intercourse when he was eighteen months old. There has been much debate on the Wolf Man, and claims that both Freud and Pankejeff created false fronts and used the information to their own ends. Johnson similarly expresses this point and quotes Nicholas Rand who said that 'the Wolf Man is himself only when he creates himself as an enigma'.[29] However, Carlo Ginzburg's point is valuable as a final comment here. Ginzburg pointed out that Pankejeff's nanny, Nanya, was herself East European, and she would have been the first to comfort him after his dream / nightmare.[30] As he no doubt would have recounted the dream to her, she would have drawn her own conclusions that would also have differed greatly from those of Freud and others. Indeed, her belief in and observance of specific customs and traditions probably had an influence on the young Pankejeff. Moreover, he supposedly had a somewhat 'special' status as he was born on Christmas Day. According to Eastern European cultures, babies born on this day are destined to become werewolves, as are those born with a caul, which Pankejeff also was. Imagine the double-prophecy of his being born with a caul on Christmas Day, and then having a vivid dream just before his birthday (so very close if not on Christmas Eve) and seeing wolves outside his window. For Nanya, Pankejeff would have been looked upon as a werewolf, and those waiting in his 'spirit world' or dream were his pack, and had come to claim him as one of their own. What is perhaps more telling is that Freud makes no mention of this in his analysis.

In 1935, when the remains of our 'ape-like' ancestors were being excavated at Swanscombe, the werewolf was featured in celluloid form in *The Werewolf of London*, a Universal Pictures production that followed the 1931 success of *Frankenstein*. In the film, Dr Glendon (played by Henry Hull) is bitten by a werewolf whilst travelling in Tibet. When he returns to London with a sample of a rare flower that only blooms in moonlight, the villain of the film, Doctor Yogami, tells him that only the plant can stop him from transforming into a wolf. This echoes earlier folk belief that links transformation into a werewolf with the consumption of certain plants. (The original intention had been to use special 'wolf make-up' designed by Jack Pierce, but Hull refused it, saying that it took too long to put on. It was eventually used on Lon Chaney Jr. in *The Wolfman* of 1941.)

The discoveries of ancient human remains and the debate on Man's origins were clearly having as much an effect on film produc-ers as they were on those interested in the subject of the werewolf. A series of 'ape-monster' films were released. *Son of Ingagi* (1939) featured an 'ape-man' kept in a cage (played by Zack Williams) who eventually escapes and kidnaps a young woman, but ends up killing himself by drinking poison, whilst *The Ape Man* (1943) features a Dr James Brewster who invented a potion that could turn him into an ape-man. Despite such releases, the werewolf retained its 'hold' on the cinema, as 1941's *The Wolfman* proved. Released by Universal Pictures and pairing Lon Chaney Jr and Bela Lugosi (who starred as

Poster for *The Werewolf of London*, 1935.

Dr Brewster in *The Ape Man*), the film centres on Lawrence Stewart Talbot (Chaney), who returns to his ancestral home in Wales and is bitten by a werewolf whilst trying to rescue a young girl. He soon learns that he has been cursed and will turn into a werewolf. Only silver or objects made from it can destroy him.

Although it might seem that the werewolf was being banished further into the realms of filmic fantasy, and that it no longer had a 'place' in wider society, this is far from being the case. Documents released by the National Archives in Britain in 2011 show that during World War Two, 'a Nazi organisation called "Werewolf" apparently planned to spread death and fear in the closing stages of the Second World War through mass poisoning'.[31] 'Operation Werewolf' has long been known about, but its purpose and impact are usually downplayed. The declassified papers reveal that the list of items that would be used to poison British and American forces include chocolate, powdered coffee, poisoned aspirin and even a 'deadly cigarette lighter'. The Nazis also apparently planned to place 'sleeper agents' around the world to 'make the Allies' post-war task as hard as possible so that the Nazi party could, in time, reappear in a suitable disguise and build up a Fourth Reich'.[32] The operation was named after the novel *Der Werwolf* by Hermann Löns (1910), in which the main character, 'Harm Wulf', creates a militia known as the '*Wehrwölfe*' after his family was killed by marauding soldiers. Strangely, Adolf is an etymological variant of '*adal*' ('noble') and 'wolf'. Just as Hitler named his Ukrainian field headquarters 'Werwolf', his Eastern Front headquarters was the 'Wolfsschanze' ('Wolf's Lair').

Back in England, an alleged (and rare in any case) werewolf 'sighting' occurred in England in the 1940s, as the Shirley family was picnicking in an area of woodland on the East coast. They saw a huge animal, with 'flaming red hair all over it' and large, powerful jaws. The beast disappeared into the woods and nothing more of it was seen.[33] Just a couple of years later, in 1951, the ergot outbreak occurred in Pont-St-Esprit, in France (discussed in Chapter Three), where victims had hallucinogenic visions of werewolves. This phenomenon was soon followed by another alleged werewolf sighting in Scotland in the mid-1950s. An eyewitness reported seeing a 'hairy man with a wolf's head' near Loch Morar, that 'walked on two feet but ran on all-fours'.[34]

In 1960, cinema audiences could see werewolves for themselves in close-up, when Hammer Studios released *The Curse of the Wolfman*. The plot involves a servant girl in eighteenth-century Spain who is raped by a beggar, becomes pregnant and gives birth to 'Leon' (played by Oliver Reed). The boy becomes a werewolf, and is eventually killed by a silver bullet. (The werewolf make-up was created by Roy Ashton, but this is only seen in close-up in the final stages of the film.) This controversial film was banned in Spain until 1976, and cuts were made before it was released in Britain and America. The interlinking of fact and fiction again came to the fore when, in 1967, after the film's release, there was another alleged werewolf sighting in Scotland. This occurred in Oban, on the west coast, in the early hours of the morning, as a postman on his way to work saw 'a tall, man-like figure with wolf-like features' running in the opposite direction at an incredible speed.[35]

A further English werewolf sighting allegedly happened in 1970:

I encountered a werewolf ... in England in 1970. I was 20 years old when I was stationed at RAF Alconbury. I was in a secure weapons storage area when I encountered it. It seemed shocked and surprised to have been caught off guard and I froze in total fright. I was armed with a .38 and never once considered using it. There was no aggression on its part. I could not comprehend what I was seeing. It was not human. It had a flat snout and large eyes. Its height was approximately five feet tall and weighed approximately 200 lbs. It was very muscular and thin. It wore no clothing and was only moderately hairy. It ran away on its hind legs and scurried over a chain link fence and ran deep into the dense wooded area adjacent to the base. I was extremely frightened but the fear developed into a total commitment of trying to contact it again. I was obsessed with it. I was able to see it again a few weeks later at a distance in the wooded area. I watched it for about 30 seconds slowly moving through the woods and I will never forget my good fortune to encounter it.[36]

These alleged sightings could be categorized as either false or examples of urban myths. However, a study by Surawicz and Banta published in the mid-1970s could upset this facile categorization. The study showed that the mental illness of lycanthropy was still prevalent and occurring on a regular basis.[37] However, the developing fields of psychoanalysis and psychotherapy and tendency to apply analytical readings from these areas to lycanthropy cases meant that

> nineteenth and twentieth century case reports are exceedingly rare. Attention was turned instead to an examination by psychotherapists of the relevance of dreams and suspicions of werewolves.[38]

Robert Eisler, author of *Man into Wolf,* had argued that lycanthropy was a representation of the 'emergence of an archetypal carnivorous beast which is also expressed in sadistic behaviour'.[39] Earlier still, Carl Jung had suggested that it was rather a 'delusion' that allowed the sufferer to express a 'primitive identity' from which he 'struggles to free himself'.[40] In addition, it seems clear that Freud's 'Wolf Man' paper had influenced their beliefs. Moreover, the paper is arguably and ultimately flawed in terms of the werewolf connotations proposed earlier in this chapter.

For their part, Surawicz and Banta identified four modern cases of lycanthropy. Two of these cases were in young males, both of whom had suspected forms of schizophrenia: one male had a brain syndrome, the other abused hallucinogenic drugs.

The presence of 'wolves' in modern cases of mental illness re-affirms the wolf's 'relevance' to society. In another reasonably recent case, from 1978, a 56-year-old woman behaved like a wild dog and later developed Capgras syndrome (a delusion that makes the sufferer believe that a close friend or family member has been replaced by an identical 'impostor').[41] A second woman, from 1977, was recorded as having dreamed of wolves and suffered delusional thoughts of turning into a wolf.[42] A 1988 study documented a further twelve cases of lycanthropy:

> to gain an understanding of certain bizarre psychiatric symp-toms it may be helpful to consider the effects of religion and culture. At the time of the Inquisition . . . the incidence of lycanthropy peaked. These beliefs may be revived in those suffering from severe depressive illness (in the present) where they are incorporated into delusions of guilt and sinfulness.[43]

Scientific researchers have indeed recognized and confirmed that

> despite the passage of time, the werewolf remains a power-ful and evocative image. The influence of myth and legend has been filtered and obscured with the passage of time but it is likely that the symptom of lycanthropy will continue to be seen as long as tales of the wolf-man can frighten us.[44]

The twentieth-century role and presence of the werewolf in society was bolstered and maintained by 'werewolf' films, and the occasional sighting that refreshed society's curiosity in the creature. In fact, the late 1970s and early 1980s were 'boom years' for the beast. Further-more, in the 1970s a number of 'wolf children' were reported, as well as a 'real-life' Little Red Riding Hood. In 1970, in Azerbaijan, a six-year-old girl, Elmira Godayatiova, tried to follow her mother who was crossing through a wood that was en route to the house of the little girl's grandmother in the next village. On seeing the child, her mother sent her home. However, Elmira never reached home. She was discovered 23 days later, when a forest ranger found her sitting under a tree. The girl said she had 'eaten berries and grass, drank from the stream and played with the doggies and puppies'. She had in fact spent the period living with wolves. Wolves, moreover, 'are known never to attack near their home'.[45] In 1978, again in Azerbaijan, Mekhriban Ibragimov, aged three years, got lost in the snow. She was found sixteen hours later in a cave with a wolf and its three cubs. She told how the wolf had 'licked her face'.[46] As has been shown in the two cases above, wolves do not tend to attack children; indeed, they are not known to attack humans at all. This is despite the accounts claiming the contrary that have fuelled the werewolf myth over the centuries.

By far the most bizarre English case of a werewolf is arguably that of a sighting in Hexham, Northumberland, in 1976. In that year, BBC *Nationwide* (a magazine-style programme that followed the early evening news) ran a story about a werewolf that had supposedly been terrorizing a local family, the Robsons, after their children had unearthed two small, mysterious stone heads from the garden. Soon after the discovery, Mrs Robson said she was woken in the night by loud crashes apparently coming from her neighbour's house. The next morning, her neighbour, to whom Mrs Robson had shown the heads, claimed she had been in her daughter's room, when a strange creature 'like a werewolf' walked past the door. She screamed and her husband rushed to her just in time to hear something padding down the stairs. The crashes heard by Mrs Robson were never explained. The property in Hexham was not far from Hadrian's Wall. It was believed that the heads found by the children dated from Celtic or Roman times. Anne Ross, a specialist in Celtic mythology at the University of Southampton, examined the heads. A discrepancy in the date of this incident is apparent, for Ross wrote a description of the heads in 1972, which was included in *The Reader's Digest Compendium of Folklore, Myths and Legends of Britain* of 1973. According to Ross, carved stone heads are well known from many Celtic sites throughout Europe and are easily recognised through their distinctive features. Generally they date from the Iron Age or Romano-British period

Here, Ross is suggesting a period from *circa* 700 BC– AD 410. On an emotional note that has nevertheless links to the 'magic' of 'werewolfery', and which can even have an effect on scientists, Ross related that

> although there was nothing unpleasant about the appearance of the heads, I took an immediate instinctive dislike to them. I planned to have them geologically analysed, and then return them as soon as possible to the north [of the country].[47]

However, while the heads were still in Ross's possession, there was a strange occurrence. The researcher woke about 2 am one morning and felt 'chilled and extremely frightened'. She then saw a strange apparition in her room:

> I looked towards the door and in the corridor light glimpsed a tall figure slipping out of the room. It was about six feet high, stooping and black against the white door. My impression was that the figure was dark, like a shadow, and that it was part animal and part man; the upper part, I would have said, was a wolf and the lower part human. I would have said it was covered in very dark fur. Although I was panic stricken, I felt compelled, as if by some irresistible force, to follow it. I heard it, whatever it was, going downstairs, and then I saw it again, moving along the corridor that leads to the kitchen; but I was too terrified to go on. I went back upstairs to the bedroom and woke Dick, my husband. He searched the house, but found nothing. We thought I'd had a nightmare'.[48]

Several days later Ross and her husband returned home one evening to find their daughter distressed and upset. After calming her down, she eventually told her parents what had happened:

When she had come in from school, the first thing she had seen was something huge, dark and inhuman on the stairs. It had rushed down towards her, vaulted over the banisters and landed in the corridor with a soft thud as though its feet were padded like those of an animal. It disappeared into the music room, and she had felt that she had to follow it. At the door, it had vanished. Suddenly she realised she was terrified, and this was the state in which we found her. Feeling puzzled and disturbed, we searched the house. Again, there was no sign of any intruder. More than once since then I have heard the same soft thud of an animal's pads near the staircase. Several times my study door has burst open for no obvious reason. And on one other occasion, when Bernice and I were coming down stairs together, we both thought we saw a dark figure ahead of us – and we heard it land in the corridor after vaulting over the banisters'[49]

At this point Ross was unaware of the similar experience that the Robson family had undergone. When she contacted them in relation to the heads, they related the strange incident. Ross finally made the link between the heads and the strange wolf-creature, and finished her investigation of the heads. Examination proved that they had been carved from local Northumbrian stone around 1800 years ago (which would date them to *circa* 170–200). Moreover,

they had possibly come from a military shrine or temple of the Celtic legionaries who made up a large part of the garrison on Hadrian's Wall. Celts were head hunters who believed that severed heads could convey fertility and ward off evil spirits. Similar powers were vested in the stone heads. Once, those sent to Dr. Ross may have guarded over a god who has long disappeared.[50]

However, this scientific explanation does not end the mystery of the Hexham Heads. Their current whereabouts are unknown, and only Don Robins's description provides an idea of their appearance: they were about the size of a tangerine ... dense and heavy, but each had a very distinct appearance. The first head had a vaguely skull-like appearance with the carved lines of features only faint and vestigial. Nevertheless, its features were vaguely masculine, if gaunt and bony, and were crowned by a typically Celtic hairstyle with faint stripes running from front to back on the crown. The carved stone itself was greenish grey and glistened with quartz crystals ... the second [head] was more rounded and infinitely more expressive. The features were those of a formidable old wall-eyed woman with a strong beaked nose with hair combed severely backwards off the forehead into a bun. Unlike the skull-head the old woman, or hag, showed traces of red or yellow pigment on the hair.[51]

Controversy also surrounds this description as well as the dating evidence given. A recent BBC news article from the institution's website claims that the previous owner of the Hexham house where the Robsons lived, Desmond Craigie, had made the heads himself. Craigie claimed that he had carved the heads for his daughter in 1956. However, when Ross heard these claims, she apparently asked Craigie to reproduce them. Yet the results were poor and bore little resemblance to the originals.[52] The article further claims that Bill Dearman from Newcastle University sectioned the heads and found they were artificially moulded and not made from stone. After examining the heads, Ross gave them to the British Museum, where they were put on display, although they have since disappeared.

The werewolf link to the Robson and Ross case can be made through an incident related in the local *Hexham Courant* newspaper on 10 December 1904, under the headline: 'Wolf at large in Allendale'. It was necessary to shelter sheep in a barn at night after a shepherd had found two of his sheep dead, with their entrails hanging out and organs missing. Many other animals had been bitten around the legs and neck. Although the 'Hexham Wolf Committee' was set up to hunt down the beast using specialist hunting dogs, the wolf could not be found. An article of 1931 describes the community's difficulty:

We have impressions of the capacity of a large and hungry dog, but, upon reading these accounts, one has to think that they were exaggerations, or that the killer must have been more than a wolf. But, according to developments, I'd not say that there was much exaggeration. The killings were so serious that the farmers organised into the Hexham Wolf Committee, offering a reward, and hunting systematically. Every hunt was fruitless, except as material for the special correspondents, who told of continuing depredations, and revelled in special announcements. It was especially announced that, upon December 15th, the Haydon foxhounds, one of the most especial packs in England, would be sent out. These English dogs, of degree so high as to be incredible in all other parts of the world, went forth. It is better for something of high degree not to go forth. Mostly in times of peace arise great military reputations. So long as something is not tested it may be of high renown. But the Haydon foxhounds went forth. They returned with their renown damaged.[53]

A trained tracker was subsequently brought in, but to no avail. It was as if the wolf was but a ghost. Over the Christmas period, more livestock were attacked, and then finally, on 29 December, the wolf was allegedly spotted. Soon after, the body of a wolf was found on a railway line at Cumminton, Cumbria (about 30 miles west of Hexham), but the *Hexham Courant* reported on 7 January that this was a different wolf. Sure enough, more livestock were found dead and the footprints of a wolf were observed. Some people believed that there must have been several wolves, whilst others were convinced that it was the work of a werewolf. In theory, neither should have been possible, for wolves had long been extinct in Britain. Suddenly, the sheep killings ceased, and there were no more reports of the wolf (or werewolf). Not, that is, until the early 1970s. When the Robson children found the ancient heads, they were just ten minutes' walk from where the 'Wolf of Allendale' had stalked its prey.

The werewolf in the 'public eye' continued in the 1980s, albeit on film, with the release of three of the most successful films ever in the werewolf genre: *An American Werewolf in London* (1981), *The Howling* (1981) and *The Company of Wolves* (1984). The first of these films, directed by John Landis, featured two male American backpackers travelling through the Yorkshire Moors. Hungry, they find a small public house, 'The Slaughtered Lamb'. The pub's locals are anything but friendly, and the two soon notice the pentagram (a five-pointed star, of which the points are constructed from a continuous line) is painted on the wall. They start asking about it and are told to leave. As they make their way over the moor, they are attacked by a werewolf. One of the men, Jack, is killed but David survives, although he is badly wounded by the beast. When David awakes, he finds himself in a London hospital. The rest of the film focuses on David's mental deterioration. He finally becomes a werewolf himself. The film portrays the disease as a mental affliction, as well as a physical one. This approach is interesting and noteworthy, especially given the renewed interest in lycanthropy as a medical illness in the late 1970s. The way David's mental state deteriorates is reminiscent of that of the Duke in *The Duchess of Malfi*. Landis's take on the 'werewolf syndrome' depicts David as unable to control his bestial urges (a point that has been much contested about lycanthropes throughout the ages) and leaves him with no recollection of what he has done whilst in wolf form. The film almost blends the werewolf with a *Jekyll and Hyde* twist.

Despite the film being habitually labelled as a 'horror comedy', there is little to laugh at. Even if the presence of a decomposing 'undead' that Jack provides has some comedy value, he is essentially a metaphor for the devil, seated on David's shoulder, as he struggles to maintain his grip on reality. It is almost as if the devil is toying with him, and slowly claiming him as his own, leaving him cursed and as desperate as a wolfish beast. This is practically a historical 'rendition' of the treatment and suffering of 'werewolves', who were left burning at the stake. A further dimension is added as a group of Nazi 'beasts' feature in one of David's nightmare scenes, no doubt to comment on Hitler's links with the werewolf. In an interview with Landis,[54] the source for the film is recognized as a group of gypsies in Yugoslavia, whom he saw performing burial rites over a grave to prevent the dead person returning to haunt the living. Although this appears more vampiric than werewolf-related, it is sufficient to consider the numerous accounts of the 'dangerous dead' to grasp such a concept. The film remains an intelligent, 'accurate' and relevant commentary on the werewolf, especially as it foregoes a needless 'gore' element that is so often resorted to in the genre. *The Howling*, directed by Joe Dante and loosely inspired by the novel of the same name by Gary Brandner (1977), stars Dee Wallace as 'Karen White', the victim of a serial-murdering stalker. Karen agrees to work with the police in order to capture the killer. When he is eventually shot by the police, Karen is sent to a secluded resort known as 'The Colony' to recover from the ordeal. Her husband Bill (played by Christopher Stone) accompanies her. After he is bitten by a werewolf, he, too, is transformed into the beast.

It transpires that there are many werewolves at The Colony. Karen's friends Teri and Chris come to her aid, but Teri is then killed. Eventually, however, Karen and Chris succeed in burning The Colony to the ground. Karen's anguish does not end, though, as she too becomes a werewolf. Her bestial transformation is captured by television cameras filming her and broadcasting live. Her tragic fate is curtailed as Chris shoots and kills her with a silver bullet. As with Landis's *An American Werewolf in London*, *The Howling* played its part in shaping the cinematic werewolf.

The Company of Wolves, the final in this werewolf 'trilogy', directed by Neil Jordan and starring Angela Lansbury and Sarah Patterson, is a complex multi-layered and historically angled 'werewolf film'. Jordan blends werewolf folklore, modern horror and age-old fairy stories to create an intricate web of Gothic eeriness. The film itself is based on Angela Carter's short story of the same name, and from her book *The Bloody Chamber*. Carter's narrator warns that wolves are worse than ghosts, hobgoblins, ogres and witches, as these are at least part-human whereas wolves are not, and therefore, cannot listen to reason. The film shows the dreams of a young girl. Through these dreams, the audience follows the story of Rosaleen, who listens to the many werewolf tales that are told to her by her grandmother. *Little Red Riding Hood* is omnipresent and each of the stories that the grandmother tells serves as a warning, with its own moral.

In one of these stories, a young woman marries, only for her husband to soon disappear. Believing him gone, she remarries and bears children. One night, her husband returns. When he sees that she has forgotten him, he becomes a werewolf. Before he can attack her, the woman's new husband comes home and cuts off the werewolf's head. The woman is filled with pity and sadness, though. She is not horrified by the werewolf curse on her first husband. In another of the grandmother's stories, a young man is travelling through the forest when he meets the devil, who is not dressed in black and riding a black steed, as folkloric accounts would have it, but driving a shiny white car. Deception and symbolic colour reversal are the key here: black does not equate to evil but white does. Although he is not pure, he is evil, and the illusion has worked. The devil gives the boy an ointment, which he applies and duly becomes a werewolf. A third story features a she-wolf crawling up a well from the underworld who is soon sent back to the bowels of hell. Women too, this story is saying, can be werewolves.

Deception is at the core of the whole film: the husband was not the person his wife thought him to be; the devil in disguise; and the female werewolf. Indeed, the grandmother tells Rosaleen that wolves are not as dangerous as might be thought, for they are hairy on the outside and easy to see. It is those wolves that are hairy on the inside that pose the greatest threat, as the danger they pose is not known until it is too late. In short, the film's moral is: beware the beast within, not without. The grandmother also says that for a man to become a werewolf, or the beast within, he must strip naked in preparation for the transformation, and on turning back he will remain naked. Hence, were one to see a naked man in the woods, run away, 'as if the Devil himself were after you'. To prevent even a sighting of such a creature, one should 'never stray from the path'. On the surface, this is a warning against the werewolf, but it is also a warning to young women that men are dangerous, they are but wild beasts, the devil in disguise, and so you must never stray from the path (of righteousness). Clearly, this is a warning against sexual deviancy, further evident when analysing consider the character of Rosaleen. In Carter's novel, the child (Rosaleen in the film) has cheeks that are 'emblematic scarlet' and her periods

Poster for *An American Werewolf in London*, 1981.

have just begun. On screen, this is metaphorically 'translated' as the bright red lipstick that Rosaleen applies. Also, her grandmother makes her a bright red cloak that has 'the look of blood on snow'. The film, in this sense, is a modern take on the *Little Red Riding Hood* tale but with the innocence of the children's fairy story removed.

The Company of Wolves' final moral relates to the pity shown at various stages throughout the film. This pity is not shown by all characters, however – rather it is reserved exclusively for certain people to create the desired effect. The first to show pity is the wife who sees her werewolf husband killed. Next is Rosaleen herself, when in one of the dream stories, she meets a huntsman in the woods who turns out to be a werewolf. This huntsman tricks her into giving him a kiss (again, an instance of the man-wolf) before Rosaleen submits to his sexual demands, she shoots him with his own gun. Instead of being killed, however, he becomes a werewolf. Rosaleen, though, is neither horrified nor disgusted: she feels pity for him and becomes a wolf herself in order to be with him. Behold the cunning of men is nevertheless the segment's renewed caution. The final act of pity is that of the vicar who sees the she-wolf after she emerges from the well. The local people are chasing her and wound her, but the vicar protects her and helps her return from whence she came.

Save for the vicar, only women show pity towards the werewolf, and this is part of his deceit. You must be strong, and not succumb to his powers or the beast shall devour you. The overarching moral here is that all the stories end in pain, death and sadness, except those where there is an expression of pity and empathy. Further still, only God has the power to understand and forgive and, most importantly, protect if the path to God is accepted.

Despite the strength and extent of moral Christian teaching, and the power of God, the devil, supposedly, would not give up. The Hexham heads case and a similarly strange incident from 1985 in Glossop, Derbyshire, draw this theory together. Glossop is in an area known as 'Mouselow'. Today, there is a large mound where an early medieval castle once stood. Occupation of the site goes even further back to the Iron Age and the site is linked to the nearby Roman fort of Melandra. Curious carved stones, recalling the Hexham heads,

Poster for *The Howling*, 1981.

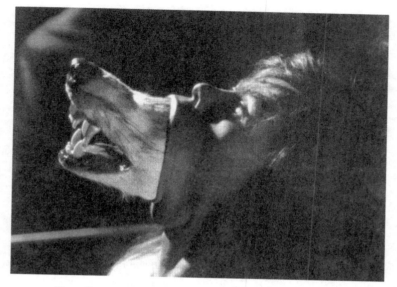

Transformation scene from *The Company of Wolves*, 1984.

have been discovered here that seem also to have mysterious links. Today, the stones are on view as they are built into the wall above an arched doorway at Buxton Museum in Derbyshire. According to museum staff,

> their precise origins are unknown but the consensus of opinion is that they are of Celtic (Iron Age) origin, and may have belonged to larger groups of carvings of cult significance.[55]

The stones were first discovered in 1840 by the Revd George Marsden, who described them 'curiously marked stones'. He removed them from the site and had them set into the wall of his house in nearby Hadfield. They returned to Glossop when the Glossop Antiquarian Society took charge of them, before they were eventually passed on to Buxton Museum.

Academic David Clarke believes that in the early nineteenth century they might have been linked to witchcraft.[56] One of the stones bears a carving of a man's face with horns and is similar to other carvings from Roman times. Although modern readers may attach this description to the devil, the figure is more probably the Iron Age god Cernunnos.

When the stones were brought back to Glossop in 1985, archaeologist Glynis Reeve had just begun excavations at the site where they were found. Soon after commencing their dig, Reeve and her volunteers received phone calls asking why they were digging there and issuing threats relating to 'horned figures' and 'the Old Ways'.

Reeve arranged for the stones to be displayed on site in a special exhibition. One visitor, after spending some time quietly staring at the stones, said to her that she had not yet 'found the entrance to hell'.[57] Reeve postponed the dig until the following year because of the hostile attitude towards her and the excavation. When the dig was relaunched the following year, all those who worked on the site suffered an accident. Reeve called an expert to examine the stones. The expert was Anne Ross, who had worked on the Hexham heads. Ross confirmed that they were Celtic *in style* but not necessarily in date, and that they would not be out of place in a pagan Celtic shrine. Reeve decided to try and appease the 'Old Gods' and on the eve of Beltane (1 May), she went to the site with a colleague and pronounced 'you have nothing to fear'.[58] They returned to their car, where another team member awaited them. He informed them that he had seen a number of torch lights moving on the hillside close to where they had been, and after that night, all was calm: there were no more hostilities and no more telephone calls.

One of the Mouselow stones has a Roman-style phallic symbol carved on it, while others bear Celtic 'roses' and another the letter 'A'. Interestingly, a Celtic goddess known as 'Arnemetia' was known to have been worshipped at nearby Buxton, so the stone perhaps relates to her. When viewed upright and cross-lit, one stone's patterning reveals a female figure wearing a tartan-style garment. Her hair is done up in a bun – just as the Hexham figure's hair is styled, if Robins's description is accurate. Archaeologists have also compared the image to similar examples from Denmark dating from the Bronze Age.[59]

In 1905 a local historian expressed his belief that the stones were not Celtic but Anglo-Saxon and that some of the symbols could be recognized as representing the river of life, the wind blowing from the four quarters of the earth, Thoth, one of their Gods, and other objects which they worshipped.[60]

As David Clarke quite rightly points out, Thoth is in fact an Egyptian god, not an Anglo-Saxon one, and as such he dismissed this information. In 1962 quarrymen working at Mouselow uncovered several large stones that surrounded a larger central slab (five feet by four feet) that seemed to be an altar. Under this 'altar' stone they found a small bronze and gold disc. The disc itself is copper, but the decorations are in gold and show a boat underneath the sun. They would appear to be Egyptian in design and examples of a classic Egyptian image known as the 'solar barge'. However, this is arguably the moon and not the sun. Looking carefully at the disc, the central circle reflects the full moon, and the crescent moon to the side of this. The arcs along the side may mark the solstices (initially, there was also probably a second arc along the opposite edge), and the small, circular dots form the shape of the constellation known as Orion's Belt. To see the striking parallels between this and other discs and to draw the above conclusions, it is worth considering a very similar disc known as the 'Nebra Sky Disc' from the Saxony-Anhalt region in Germany. The Nebra disc was found by (illegal) metal detecting in 1999 at a known prehistoric settlement on top of a hill. It is believed that the site was deliberately aligned to maximize the fall of the solstice rays, because on each solstice the sun sets behind the 'Brocken', the largest peak in the Harz Mountains. Associated artefacts were dated from between 1600 and 1560 BC, and the disc, dating from the Bronze Age not the Iron Age, as was initially suspected for the Mouselow disc.

The Mouselow disc was tested by Cookson PLC in Birmingham. The company found that the copper was from Egypt but the provenance of the gold was North Africa, and Carthage (near Tunis, Tunisia) the place where the disc itself was most likely made. Incidentally, the Nebra disc was European, as the copper was sourced in Austria and the gold was from Cornwall in England.[61] Certain researchers argue that the Mouselow disc is in fact Roman because it was found near the Roman fort Melandra. Melandra was a subdivision of the

Manchester Roman fort, and the legion at Manchester had arrived there from Carthage via Portugal. The legion in question was the 3rd Cohort of Bracara Augustani, composed of Iberian Celts, and known to have assisted with the construction of Melandra. This would make the Roman origin of the Mouselow disc a possibility. Although the exact legion that was stationed in Melandra is not known, it seems likely that this would have been Bracara Augustani, as its soldiers were used to hilly terrain, which is what they would have found in and around Glossop.

The Mouselow disc could have been a Roman division symbol, but this is extremely unlikely, given that it almost exactly matches that from Nebra. This makes dating the Mouselow disc all the more

The Glossop Stones.

important. Moreover, given the rarity of such discs, it seems incredible that one could have been made in North Africa and one in Northern Europe. With this geographical separation, perhaps the materials were sourced from diverse locations but the items themselves were made in the same region, and even by the same craftsman. Yet that would not explain why the metals were sourced from locations that were so distant from one another. Clearly, the Mouselow disc is much older than Roman. The fact that it may 'relate' to the Mouselow stones and a pagan religion seems a likely supposition.

As was the case with Hexham, perhaps this is why this area of Derbyshire has its share of werewolf legends. A creature known as the 'Speed Wolf' has often been spotted around the A6 road, just north of Buxton, and is supposedly a wolf-like creature that moves at incredible speed. Coincidentally, perhaps, the nearby village of Wormhill claims to be the very place where the English last wolf was killed. Another legend, supporting this theory, is that of the 'Edale Werewolf'. This was reputedly a large black creature that had killed dozens of sheep in the 1920s. Locals claimed the beast 'howled like a fog horn'.[62]

Germany also had its fair share of 'werewolfery'. In 1988, at the Morbach munitions base near Wittlich in western Germany, an alleged werewolf sighting took place. Wittlich is reportedly the place where the last 'werewolf' was executed in Germany, as Wormhill in Derbyshire was in England. Owing to this 'status', a small shrine was erected in the town, which contains a candle that is never extinguished. Local legend holds that if the candle goes out, the werewolf will return. In 1988 some policemen were making their way to the munitions base when they noticed that the candle had blown out. The group joked that the werewolf would come and get them. Later that night, the base's alarms sounded and when the guards checked the perimeter fence, they saw a huge, dog-like creature that leaped over the fence:

> I was stationed at Hahn Air Base in Germany from May 1986 to August 1989 as a security policeman, and it was my group that witnessed the Morbach Werewolf . . . the

creature that we saw was definitely an animal and definitely dog or wolf-like. It was about seven to eight feet tall, and it jumped a twelve-foot security fence after taking three long steps.[63]

After the sighting, a guard dog was brought to the fence but it went crazy and refused to track the creature. Three years later, in 1991, alarm bells sounded again, but this time at Broadmoor Prison in England. James Saunders, the 'Wolfman', a convicted sex offender, had escaped and was on the run. A local resident at nearby Bagshot village recounts the escape:

the siren went off at about three or four am. I was up at the time feeding my twin newborn daughters and I rapidly shut any open windows and double checked the doors were locked. 'Wolfman' was caught a couple of days after his escape after the entire area was covered by roadblocks and police searching vans.[64]

The following year, in 1992, another werewolf sighting was reported in Wales. This werewolf, it seems, had been plaguing the region of North Wales since the eighteenth century:

Records of an enormous wolf-like animal in North Wales date back to 1790, when a stagecoach travelling between Denbigh and Wrexham was attacked and overturned by an enormous black beast almost as long as the coach horses.[65]

The beast then killed one of the horses. Apparently, the attack took place just after dusk on the night of a full moon. The following year, in 1791, a farmer at Gresford, in Wrexham, North Wales, found the footprints of a large wolf-like creature in the snow in one of his fields. He followed the tracks for two miles and came upon a mutilated body (though it is not defined as man or beast). Another farmer's field was strewn with the corpses of sheep and cattle, and when the farmer was later found in his home, he was extremely distressed and

The Mouselow disc depicting Egyptian imagery.

The Nebra Sky Disc from Germany, dated to the Bronze Age.

claimed he had seen an enormous black animal that looked like a wolf. Seven years later (in 1798), two men walking over the Bickerton Hills in Cheshire saw a creature running towards them. They ran to the nearest inn and the next day a search party found the bodies of two vagrants dead in the woods. The attacks then stopped, until 1992, when newspapers claimed a large bear-like creature had been sighted. One farmer claimed he had seen it on the night of a full moon and that it had killed two of his sheep. In 2001, the *Evening Leader*, the local newspaper, carried several stories about large, cat-like animals that had been sighted near Wrexham and Mold.

Discussion of these latest sightings prompted 'Paul' from Barnsley to write to the *Evening Leader* with the following story:

> Whilst serving in the Royal Marines an incident occurred when I was on an exercise on Dartmoor. I was due to relieve a Forward Observation Post at 00:30am and made my way across the moor (which took about ten minutes in daylight). Obviously at night this took about fifteen to twenty minutes. After walking for about eight minutes I heard what can only be described as a low guttural noise, this made me stop instantly and lower myself on one knee, weapon ready (it was loaded with blanks but it still made me feel a bit secure). I heard the noise again on several occasions, I was in this spot

for about two minutes, but each time it came from a different position, as though I was being weighed up. If I was weak, if I would run, I think whatever it was wanted me to run. Once the guttural sound seemed to come from only a few yards away ... I honestly believe that something that wasn't fully human was with me, circling me, wanting me to run, make a move.[66]

A different kind of werewolf 'came to light' in 2000 in the film *Ginger Snaps*, directed by John Fawcett and starring Katharine Isabelle and Emily Perkins. The film used lycanthropy as a metaphor for puberty. In *Ginger Snaps*, the Beast of Bailey Downs initially preys on local dogs until it attacks Ginger (Isabelle) who then becomes a werewolf. The modern nuance of the 'silver bullet' werewolf fable is when Ginger hears that silver will cure her. She duly gets her navel pierced. This act arguably drags the werewolf myth into the twenty-first century. However, the piercing has no effect. Ginger then 'infects' Jason by having unprotected sex with him, after which she turns her attention to Sam, her sister Brigitte's friend (played by Perkins). Meanwhile, Sam has helped Brigitte make a cure for Ginger by using the plant moonbeam. Sam rejects Ginger's advances, causing her to become deeply angry and a fully fledged werewolf. She also breaks Sam's arm in the process. At the end of the film, Ginger kills Sam in front of Brigitte before attempting to kill her too. Brigitte has the life-saving serum in one hand and a knife in the other, and in the ensuing struggle she accidentally stabs Ginger. The closing scene shows Brigitte sobbing with her head resting on Ginger-wolf as she slowly passes away. There is no happy ending to this film, which is a true-to-life reflection of the perils of modern puberty (at least in a metaphorical sense).

Dog Soldiers (2002) is a gritty, 'no-holds-barred' werewolf shoot-out film by Neil Marshall. Set in the Scottish Highlands (although filmed in Luxembourg), the film features a group of six British Army soldiers who are sent on a training mission, where they are attacked by a pack of werewolves. They soon discover the remains of a Special Forces squad who have all been killed except for Captain Ryan, who is wounded. Ryan later becomes a werewolf. A long battle ensues until the werewolves are destroyed. The only surviving soldier is Private Cooper (played by Kevin McKidd), along with the army dog, Sam. At the end of the film, a newspaper article focuses on the headline 'England 5 Germany 1'. Aalthough this is a reference to the recent football result, it may be a brazen reference to the large number of werewolves reportedly found in Germany, in contrast to those in England. It may then be a means of saying that when werewolves do attack in Britain, the British are robust enough to see them off.

A smaller feature in the newspaper carries the headline: 'Werewolves ate my platoon', and this sums up the partly comic dimension of *Dog Soldiers*. Indeed, the film has the perfect balance of humour and action so that it remains mostly lighthearted. Despite the narrative, there is the possible influence of the many accounts of alleged werewolves and encounters with the military, of which a few have been discussed here. Additionally, the term 'Dog Soldiers' may be a reference to the Native American warriors of the same name who were renowned as being fierce in battle and who would 'pin' themselves to the ground during conflict using a 'sacred arrow' fixed through their long clothing.

On the morning of Wednesday 28 June 2006, the UK Highways Agency was inundated with calls from motorists reporting that a large 'wolf-like' creature was running between lanes on the M6 motorway near Junction 10A. It was described as being around 'three-feet long and greyish-black'. The Highways Agency and the police later claimed that it was 'probably a husky dog'.[67] Nick Redfern, a renowned paranormal investigator, commented that

> many big cats . . . were kept as pets until a couple of decades ago. The Dangerous Animals Act of 1976 put an end to that . . . many were released into the wild.[68]

This explanation did not, however, explain or rationalize the sightings of a similar creature, the so-called 'Beast of Cannock Chase', which date from the seventeenth and eighteenth centuries. This was not the end of the alleged 'husky dog' incident, as fresh reports of the beast occurred in 2007. On 26 April 2007, the *Stafford Post* featured an article that documented how

> a rash of sightings of a 'werewolf'-type creature prowling around the outskirts of Stafford have prompted a respected Midlands paranormal group to investigate. West Midlands Ghost Club says they have been contacted by a number of shocked residents who saw what they claimed to be a 'hairy wolf-type creature' walking on its hind legs around the German War Cemetery, just off Camp Road, in between Stafford and Cannock. Several of them claim the creature sprang up on its hind legs and ran into the nearby bushes when it was spotted.[69]

The werewolf-like creature was seen walking across woodland by a Scout Association leader and then inside the war cemetery by a postman. Both witnesses said the creature was initially on all fours but stood up and ran off when it saw them. The Scout Association leader claimed it was about seven feet tall. It did not end there, as the *Birmingham Post* ran a story on 28 September 2008 relating to a national paranormal report that was released that same day.[70] The *Fringe Weird Report* was a 25-year study of reported paranormal activity in Britain. It documented 21 separate werewolf sightings over the 25-year period. Of the 21 sightings, twenty of them were in the area of Cannock Chase (in the Midlands), and the other was in Southend, in Essex. Nevertheless, this does not account for the many other supposed sightings that have occurred since the seventeenth century.

In 2009 the third instalment of the *Underworld* series was released, called *Underworld: Rise of the Lycans*. Directed by Patrick Tatopoulos, and starring Michael Sheen, Bill Nighy and Rona Mitra, the film sets Lucian (Sheen) as the first werewolf, and who was also raised by Viktor (Nighy), the vampire elder. In the story, werewolves are depicted as slaves governed by vampires. This is until Lucian falls in love with Sonja (Mitra) and she helps him escape along with the other Lycans. The Lycans attack the vampires but Sonja and Lucian are captured, and Sonja is executed for her betrayal. Lucian takes revenge by killing Viktor, but at the end of the film, Viktor is seen alive and being put in a hibernation chamber on a boat and escaping. The third instalment was less successfully received than the two previous films. Whilst vampires are still a popular subject-matter in film and other entertainment formats, werewolves are becoming less so, although the *Twilight* saga is 'helping' to keep them in the public consciousness.

Indeed, the werewolf's public presence has not wholly been vanquished by the vampire. However, its favour with the public may be on the wane. For example, *The Wolfman* was remade in 2010, and despite starring Anthony Hopkins and Benicio Del Toro, and the latter half of the film being modified and extended for a modern audience, it was still a box-office failure. In addition, *Red Riding Hood*, a (loosely) updated, modified version of the classic tale was released in 2011. This was also a disappointing release, with *usa Today* claiming that it was a 'foolish story, marred by a strange blend of overacting and bland, offhand performances'.[71]

In a sense, the werewolf is, in the early decades of the twenty-first century, in limbo, and requiring its re-introduction into society. The werewolf does, nonetheless, still exist in public consciousness, despite the best efforts of Darwin and his evolutionary theory that tried to prove the creature could not possibly have existed in the first place. Exterminating 30,000 years of history with just one single silver bullet would be a difficult task.

REFERENCES

Introduction

1 Chantel Borgault du Coudray, *The Curse of the Werewolf* (London, 2006), p. 1.
2 Charlotte Otten, *A Lycanthropy Reader* (Syracuse, NY, 1986), p. 1.
3 William Carl Eichmann, 'Catal Huyuk: The Temple City of Prehistoric Anatolia', in *Gnosis Magazine*, no. 15, special issue on 'Ancient Civilisations' (Spring 1990), pp. 52–60.
4 J. H. Moore, *The Universal Kinship* (Chicago, 1906).
5 Ralph Waldo Emerson, *Demonology* (New York, 1903).
6 Eliphas Levi, *Mysteries of Magic* (London, 1897), p. 237.
7 Otten, *A Lycanthropy Reader*, p. 1.
8 'Werewolf', *Cambridge Dictionary* online.
9 Ibid.
10 Ibid.
11 Richard Rowlands, *A Restitution of Decayed Intelligence* (Antwerp, 1605).
12 Montague Summers, *The Werewolf* (London, 1933), p. 6.
13 Geoffrey Chaucer, 'Hypermnestra', in *The Legend of Good Women*, v. 125.
14 Geoffrey Chaucer (attrib.), *Romaunt of the Rose*, v. 5695.
15 Algernon Herbert, 'Letter to Lord Cawdor', 12 March 1831, in *William and the Werewolf*, trans. Frederick Madden (London, 1832).
16 Manifesto in Douglas H. Primlott, ed., *Wolves: Proceedings of the First Working Meeting of Wolf Specialists* (Morges 1975).
17 Otten, *A Lycanthropy Reader*, p. 2.
18 Elliott O'Donnell, *Werwolves* (London, 1912), p. 6.
19 Leslie Sconduto, *Metamorphoses of the Werewolf* (Jefferson, NC, 2009), p. 1.

ONE: Of Man and Beast: *The Prehistoric Cults of Europe*

1 Frank Hamel, *Human Animals* (London, 1915), p. 1.
2 E. William Monter, *Witchcraft in France and Switzerland*, in Charlotte Otten, *A Lycanthropy Reader* (Syracuse, NY, 1986), p. 161.
3 Brenda Ralph Lewis, *Ritual Sacrifice* (Stroud, 2001), p. 19.

4 John B. Campbell, *The Upper Palaeolithic of Britain* (Oxford, 1977), p. 2.

5 Hamel, *Human Animals*, p. 28.

6 Alan Leslie Armstrong, 'Discovery of an Engraved Drawing of a Masked Human Figure', in *Proceedings of the Prehistoric Society*, VI (1929), p. 29.

7 Matthew Beresford, *Beyond the Ice* (Oxford, 2012), p. 31

8 Prentice Mulford, *The Gift of the Spirit* (London, 1904), p. 170.

9 Hamel, *Human Animals*, p. 29.

10 David Lewis-Williams, *The Mind in the Cave* (London, 2008), p. 206.

11 Roger Lewin, *Human Evolution: An Illustrated Introduction* (Washington, DC, 1993), p. 185.

12 Lewis, *Ritual Sacrifice*, p. 20.

13 Steven J. Mithen, 'The Mesolithic Age', in *The Oxford Illustrated History of Prehistoric Europe*, ed. Barry Cunliffe (Oxford, 2001), p. 126.

14 M. Oliva, *Palaeolithic and Mesolithic Moravia* (Brno, 2005), p. 68.

15 Paul Pettitt, *The Palaeolithic Origins of Human Burial* (London, 2010), p. 153.

16 Kurt W. Alt et al., 'Twenty-five thousand-year-old triple burial from Dolní Věstonice: An Ice Age Family?', in *American Journal of Physical Anthropology*, CII/1 (1997), pp. 123–31.

17 Pettitt, *The Palaeolithic Origins*, p. 192.

18 Algernon Herbert, 'Letter to Lord Cawdor', 12 March 1831, in *William and the Werewolf*, trans. Frederick Madden (London, 1832).

19 Ibid.

20 Herodotus, *Histories*, trans. George Rawlinson, Book 1, 216: classics.mit.edu/Herodotus/history.html.

21 S. K. Koslowski and E. Sachse-Koslowska, 'Maszycka Cave: A Magdalenian Site in Southern Poland', *Jahrbuch der Römisch-Germanischen Zentralmuseums Mainz*, XL (1993), p. 170.

22 See Beresford, *Beyond the Ice*, p. 71.

23 Herbert, 'Letter to Lord Cawdor'.

24 See Beresford, *Beyond the Ice*, p. 74.

25 Jean Beauvois de Chauvincourt, *Discours de la lycanthropie ou de la transmutation des hommes en loups* (Paris, 1599), pp. 3–4.

26 Campbell, *The Upper Palaeolithic of Britain*, p. 129.

27 See Beresford, *Beyond the Ice*.

28 Ibid., p. 88.

29 See A. Labunsky, *The Central Asian Hounds: The Travel Notes of a Cynologist* (Dnepropetrovsk, Ukraine, 1994).

30 Mietje Germonpré et al., 'Fossil dogs and wolves from Palaeolithic sites in Belgium, the Ukraine and Russia: osteometry, ancient DNA and stable isotopes', *Journal of Archaeological Science*, XXXVI (2009), pp. 473–90.

31 Ibid., p. 488.

32 Ibid., p. 481.

33 Steve Mithen, *After the Ice* (London, 2003), p. 174.

34 James Mellaart, *Çatal Hüyük: A Neolithic Town in Anatolia* (New York, 1967), p. 181.

35 I. Hodder, 'New Finds and New Interpretations at Çatalhöyük', *2005 Archive Report*, Çatalhöyük Research Project, Institute of Archaeology (2005).

36 Richard W. Bulliet et al., *The Earth and its Peoples: A Global History to 1550*, 4th edn (Boston, MA, 2009), p. 13.

37 William Carl Eichman, 'Ancient Civilisations', *Gnosis Magazine*, 15 (Spring 1990), pp. 52–60.

38 Bulliet et al., *The Earth and its Peoples*, p. 13.

39 Juan Schobinger, 'Argentina's Oldest Rock Art', *Dating and the Earliest Known Rock Art*, ed. M. Strecker and P. Bahn (Oxford, 1999), p. 57.

40 R. Casamiquela, *El arte rupestre de la Patagonia* (Neuquen, 1981).

41 Stephanie Meece, 'A Bird's Eye View – of a Leopard's Spots: The Çatalhöyük "Map" and the Development of Cartographic Representation in Prehistory', *Anatolian Studies*, LVI (2006), p. 4.

42 Eichmann, 'Ancient Civilisations', p. 11.

43 John Grigsby, *Beowulf and Grendel* (London, 2005), p. 32.

44 Isabella Mulhall, 'The Peat Men from Clonycavan and Oldcroghan', *British Archaeology*, 110 (January–February 2010).

45 Ibid.

46 For example, see Beresford, *From Demons to Dracula*, p. 38.

47 Mulhall, 'The Peat Men'.

48 Melanie Giles, 'Bog Bodies: Representing the Dead', paper delivered at the conference Respect for Ancient British Human Remains: Philosophy and Practice, Manchester Museum, 17 November 2006.

49 E. P. Kelly, 'Secrets of the Bog Bodies: The Enigma of the Iron Age Explained', *Archaeology Ireland*, XX/1 (Spring 2006), pp. 26–31.

TWO: The Wolves of Rome: *Classical Accounts of the Werewolf Myth*

1 Pausanias, *Description of Greece*, trans. W.H.S. Jones and H. A. Omerod (Cambridge, MA, 1918), 7, 18.7.

2 Brenda Ralph Lewis, *Ritual Sacrifice* (Stroud, 2001), p. 52.

3 Pausanias, *Description of Greece*, 3, 23.8.

4 Its date is uncertain, but an inscription says it is dedicated to 'Alcimus, steward of T. Claudius Livianus'. Livianus was commander of the Praetorian guard in *circa* 101. See Richard L. Gordon, 'The date and significance of CIMRM 593 British Museum, Townley Collection', *Journal of Mithraic Studies*, II (1978), pp. 148–74.

5 Manfred Clauss, *The Roman Cult of Mithras* (Edinburgh, 2000), p. xxi.

6 See Roger Beck, *Beck on Mithraism: Collected Works with New Essays* (London, 2004), p. 194.

7 Ibid.

8 Rodney Castleden, *The Knossos Labyrinth: A New View of the 'Palace of Minos' at Knossos* (London, 1990), p. 123.

9 Sabine Baring-Gould, *The Book of Werewolves* (London, 1865), p. 12.

10 Isaiah 31: 21.

11 Elliot O'Donnell, *Werwolves* (London, 1912), p. 9.

12 Source cited in Matthew Beresford, 'Vampires, Astrology and the Planetary Myths', *Chronicles*, II/10 (2008), p. 12.

13 See Matthew Beresford, *From Demons to Dracula* (London, 2008), p. 60.

14 Augustine, *The City of God*, ed. Philip Schaff, trans. Marcus Dods (Buffalo, NY, 1887), 18.17.

15 A. K. Michels, 'The Topography and Interpretation of the Lupercalia', in *Transactions and Proceedings of the American Philological Association*, LXXXIV (1953), pp. 35–59.

16 See Beresford, *From Demons to Dracula*, pp. 57–60.

17 Virgil, *Aeneid*, trans. John Dryden, 8.377: www.classics.mit.edu/virgil/aeneid.html.

18 Ovid, *Metamorphoses*, 1:203–242.

19 Pliny the Elder, *Historia Naturalis*, ed. John Bostock and H. T. Riley (1855), 8.32.

20 The disease is referred to in early works such as Plautus' *Amphitryon* (Prol. 1.123) and *Bacchides* (IV. iv. 1.12).

21 Pliny the Elder, *Historia Naturalis*, 8.22.

22 Plautus, *Amphitryon*, IV. iii: www.gutenberg.org.

23 Plato, *The Republic* trans. Benjamin Jowett (1991), 5.

24 See *Eph. Arch.* (London, 1904), pp. 153–214.

25 Richard Buxton, *Interpretations of Greek Mythology* (London, 1987), p. 68.

26 *The Satyricon of Petronius Arbiter*, trans. Alfred R. Allinson (New York, 1930), II, p. 62.

27 *The Epic of Gilgamesh*, trans. R. Campbell Thompson (London, 1928), Tablet VI.

28 Walter Burkert, *Homo Necans*, trans. Peter Bing, (Berkeley, CA, 1983), p. 111.

29 Herod, 4, *c* 105.

30 Pomponius Mela, 1.1. *c.* 1.

31 Quoted from Leslie Sconduto, *Metamorphoses of the Werewolf* (Jefferson, NC, 2009), p. 253.

32 Homer, *The Iliad*, trans. Samuel Butler (London, 1898), 10.

33 Ibid., 16, 156–62.

34 Plutarch, *Natural Questions*, trans. William W. Goodwin (Boston, MA, 1878), 38.

THREE: Fits of Fury: *The Wolves of Germania*

1 See Tacitus, *Germania*, trans. Alfred John Church and William Jackson Brodribb (1876): .

2   For a detailed account of such payments, see Richard Fletcher,
    Bloodfeud: Murder and Revenge in Anglo-Saxon England (London, 2002).
3   See W. H. Stevenson, ed., *Asser's Life of King Alfred* (Oxford, 1904),
    p. 62.
4   John Grigsby, *Beowulf and Grendel* (London, 2005), p. 59.
5   *Michael Wood on Beowulf*, BBC Four, broadcast 10 November 2010.
6   Actor Julian Glover narrating *Beowulf*, in *Michael Wood on Beowulf*, BBC
    Four, broadcast November 10 2010.
7   J. R. R. Tolkien, *The Monsters and the Critics and Other Essays*
    ([AQ:place of pub?],1997).
8   Tacitus, *Germania*.
9   See the Brothers Grimm, 'Iron John', www.ironjohn.net.
10 Grigsby, *Beowulf and Grendel*, pp. 56–7.
11 Ibid., p. 189.
12 Brenda Ralph Lewis, *Ritual Sacrifice* (Stroud, 2001), p. 70.
13 Matthew Beresford, *From Demons to Dracula* (London, 2008), p. 37.
14 Quoted from Barry Cunliffe, *The Ancient Celts* (London, 1997), p. 192.
15 Lucan, *Pharsalia*, trans. H. T. Riley (London, 1853), 400–425.
16 Cunliffe, *The Ancient Celts*, p. 192.
17 Grigsby, *Beowulf and Grendel*, p. 85.
18 For a more detailed account of this, see Lewis Spence's *The Mysteries of
    Britain* (London, 1905).
19 Grigsby, *Beowulf and Grendel*, p. 183.
20 R. and V. Megaw, *Celtic Art* (London, 1990), p. 174.
21 Ibid., p. 177.
22 Gale Owen-Crocker, *The Four Funerals in Beowulf* (Manchester, 2009),
    p. 100.
23 *Vatnsdaela Saga*, trans. L. M. Hollander (New York, 1949), c.xxvi.
24 *Beowulf*, 1452–54.2.
25 'Michael Wood on Beowulf'.
26 *Beowulf*, lines 1112–13.
27 Owen-Crocker, *The Four Funerals*, p. 123.
28 Ibid., p. 125, note 11.
29 Ibid., p. 117.
30 Quoted from Grigsby, *Beowulf and Grendel*, p. 190.
31 Ibid., p. 185.
32 H. R. Ellis Davidson, 'Shape-Changing in the Old Norse Sagas', in
    Charlotte Otten, *A Lycanthropy Reader* (Jefferson, NY, 1986), p. 149.
33 Sabine Baring-Gould, *The Book of Werewolves* (London, 1865), p. 15.
34 Davidson, 'Shape-Changing', p. 146.
35 *Vatnsdaela Saga*, c.xvi.
36 Baring-Gould, *The Book of Werewolves*, p. 40.
37 Ibid., pp. 16–17.
38 Davidson, 'Shape-Changing', pp. 149–50.
39 Ibid., p. 147.

40 Baring-Gould, *The Book of Werewolves*, p. 45.

41 Davidson, 'Shape-Changing', p. 147.

42 Noted in the *Holmverja Saga*, trans. Frederick York Powell (1905).

43 Translated by Henry Adams Bellows (New York, 1923), p. 93.

44 Taken from 'Project Samnordisk Runtextdatabas Svensk, 21 January
    2011: www.nordiska.uu.seforskn/samnord.htm.

45 Translation available at http://axeholdarchives.hyperboards.com.

46 Brian Bates, *The Real Middle Earth* (London, 2003), p. 230.

47 Bede, *Ecclesiastical History of the English People*, 2:15.

48 Taken from B. Thorpe, ed., *Ancient Laws and Institutes of England*
    (1840), pp. 160–61.

49 John Blair, *The Dangerous Dead in Early Medieval England* (Oxford,
    2008).

50 Ibid., pp. 6–7.

51 *Anglo-Saxon Chronicle, Peterborough Manuscript (E)*, entry AD 869.

52 From the *Life of St Edmund, Anglo-Saxon Primer*, 9th edn (Oxford,
    1961).

53 Richard Stone, *The River Trent* (Cambridge, 2005), p. 63.

54 R Bartlett, ed., *Life and Miracles of St Modwenna* (Oxford, 2002),
    pp. 196–9.

55 See Beresford, *From Demons to Dracula*.

FOUR: The Medieval Werewolf

1 R. Buxton, *Interpretations of Greek Mythology* (London, 1987), p. 74.

2 C. Lecouteux, *Witches, Werewolves and Fairies* (Rochester, VT, 2003),
   p. 8.

3 Kathryn A. Edwards, ed., *Witches, Werewolves and Wandering Spirits:
   Traditional Belief and Folklore in Early Modern Europe* (Kirksville, 2002),
   p. xviii.

4 Nicole Jacques-Lefèvre, 'Such an Impure, Cruel and Savage Beast:
   Images of the Werewolf in Demonological Works', in Edwards, *Witches,
   Werewolves and Fairies*, pp. 181–99.

5 Sonja Danielli, 'Wulf, Min Wulf: An Eclectic Analysis of the Wolf-Man',
   in *Neophilologus*, XCI (2007), pp. 505–24.

6 Ezekiel 22: 27.

7 Augustine, *De Spiritu et Anima*, cap. 26; *De civitate Dei*, lib. 18, cap. 17.

8 Augustine *The City of God*, 18. 18.

9 Patrick L. O'Madden, *Cruach Phadraig: St Patrick's Holy Mountain*
   (Dublin, 1929).

10 Ibid.

11 Quoted from Lecouteux *Witches, Werewolves and Fairies*, p. 121.

12 Algernon Herbert, 'Letter to Lord Cawdor', 12 March 1831, in *William
    and the Werewolf*, trans. Frederick Madden (London, 1832).

13 Regino de Prüm, *Libri duo de synodalibus causis et disciplinis ecclesiaisticis*,

II, 364, ed. Migne, *Pat. lat.* 132, col. 352.

14 Burchard de Worms, *Decretum*, 19., 151.

15 Sonja Danielli, 'Wulf, Min Wulf: An Eclectic Analysis of the Wolf-Man', in *Neophilologus*, XCI (2007), p. 522.

16 *Reminiscences of Vseslav Bryacislavic*, trans. Leonard A. Magnus (London, 1915), Part II, *The Tale of the Armament of Igor*, Chapter IX, 590–92.

17 Part I, lines 8–10.

18 Line 156.

19 Part III, lines 678–82.

20 'The Writings of Bishop Patrick: 1074–1084', trans. Aubrey Gwynn, *Scriptures Latini Hiberniae I* (Dublin, 1955), 96 and 109.

21 Translated by John Carey, in 'Werewolves in Medieval Ireland', *Cambrian Medieval Celtic Studies*, XXXIV (2002), pp. 37–72.

22 See Lecouteux, *Witches, Werewolves and Fairies*, pp. 80–81.

23 Kathryn L. Holten, 'Metamorphosis and Language in the Lay of Marie de France: A Twelfth-century Poet', in Chantal A. Marechal, ed., *Medieval and Renaissance Series*, X (1992), p. 195.

24 Humphrey de Bosun, trans., in *Extra Series, Early English Text Society*, I (1867).

25 Gervaise of Tilbury, *Otia Imperiala*, 1 December, I. c. 15. p. 895.

26 Rachel Kaufmann, 'Werewolves and Courtesy in Medieval Literature', Symposium: Adelphi University's *Journal of Ideas*, VII (2006–07), p. 84.

27 Ibid.

28 Quoted from Norman Hinton, 'The Werewolf as Eiron', in Nona C. Flores, *Animals in the Middle Ages* (London, 1996), pp. 133–46.

29 Étienne de Bourbon, *Septem doni spiritus sancti*, 364, ed. E. Lecoy De La Marche (Paris, 1940), p. 320.

30 Lecouteux, *Witches, Werewolves and Fairies*, p. 79.

31 V. Meyer-Matheis, *Die Vorstellung eines Alter Ego in Volkerzählungen*, dissertation (Fribourg, 1974), 67f.

32 See Matthew Beresford, *From Demons to Dracula* (London, 2008).

33 Lecouteux, *Witches, Werewolves and Fairies*, p. 84.

34 Jacob Grimm, *Deutsche Mythologie*, III, 477, no. 1121.

35 Lecouteux, *Witches, Werewolves and Fairies*, p. 95.

36 Ibid., p. 96.

37 Lee M. Hollander, *The Poetic Edda* (Austin, TX, 1928), p. 334.

38 Lecouteux, *Witches, Werewolves and Fairies*, p. 86.

39 Ibid., p. 87.

40 R. Boyer, *Le Monde du Double. La Magie chez les anciens Scandinaves* (Paris, 1986).

41 Lecouteux, *Witches, Werewolves and Fairies*, p. 87.

42 Ibid., pp. 90–91.

43 See the translation by Dom Roger Huddlestone , www.ewtn.com.

44 Barry Lopez, *Of Wolves and Men* (New York, 1979).

45 *The Chronicle of Peter of Erfurt* (1608).

46 W. W. Skeat, ed., *Pierce the Plowman's Crede* (London, 1867), line 459.
47 *Episcopus*, 36.5 in *Malleus Maleficarum*, trans. Montague Summers (London, 1928), Part I, Question x.
48 *Summa*, 5.5, in *Malleus Maleficarum*, Part I, Question x.
49 Beresford, *From Demons to Dracula*, p. 50.
50 *Malleus Maleficarum*, Part I, Question IV.
51 *Morte D'Arthure*, lib. xix. *c.* xi. ed. Southey, ii, 385.
52 Olaus Magnus, *Historia de Gentibus Septentrionalibus*, p. 711.
53 Ibid., p. 713.
54 Pierre de Rostegny de Lancre, *Tableau de l'inconstance des mauvais anges et démons*, (1613), p. 259.
55 Elliott O'Donnell, *Werwolves* (London, 1912), p. 3.
56 Jean-Jacques Boissard, *De Divinatione et Magicis Praestigiis* (1605).

FIVE: A Cruel and Savage Beast: *The Werewolf in Folklore*

1 Jean Beauvois de Chavincourt, *Discours de la lycanthropie ou de la transmutation des hommes en loups* (Paris, 1599), II.
2 Harry Senn, 'Romanian Werewolves: Seasons, Ritual, Cycles', *Folklore*, XCIII/2 (1982), p. 213.
3 Ibid.
4 Charles Robert Maturin, *The Albigensis*, II (1824).
5 J. Greenwood, 'Penny Packets of Poison', in J. Greenwood, *The Wilds of London* (London, 1874).
6 See Beresford, *From Demons to Dracula* (London, 2008).
7 Senn, 'Romanian Werewolves', p. 206.
8 See Emily Gerard, 'Transylvanian Superstitions', in *XIX Century*, XVIII (1885), pp. 130–50.
9 'Were-wolves', in *A Book of Fabulous Beasts: Old Stories Retold by A. M. Smyth* (London, 1939), p. 34.
10 Ibid.
11 Sabine Baring-Gould, *The Book of Werewolves* (London, 1865), p. 115.
12 Ibid., p. 115.
13 Senn, 'Romanian Werewolves', p. 209.
14 J. C. Lawson, *Modern Greek Folklore and Ancient Greek Religion* (New York, 1964), p. 208.
15 Beresford, *From Demons to Dracula*, p. 25.
16 D. Demetracopoulou Lee, 'Greek Accounts of the Vrykolakas', *The Journal of American Folklore*, 54 (1941).
17 Ibid.
18 *Vampire Island*, aired on the History Channel, Monday 20 September 2010.
19 Dorothy Carrington, *The Dream-Hunters of Corsica* (London, 1996), p. 36.
20 Ibid., p. 57.

21 Ibid., p. 61.
22 S. B. Casanova, *Histoire de l'Église Corse* (Ajaccio, 1931–38).
23 Carrington, *The Dream-Hunters*, p. 98.
24 Ibid., p. 67.
25 Ibid., p. 114.
26 John Rhys, *Celtic Folklore, Welsh and Manx* (London, 1901); J. G. Campbell *Witchcraft and Second Sight in the Highlands and Islands of Scotland* (Glasgow, 1902)
27 Carrington, *The Dream-Hunters*, p. 67.
28 Ibid., p. 77.
29 Ibid., p. 87.
30 Ibid., p. 127.
31 Ibid., p.158.
32 Ibid., p. 160.
32 Ibid., p. 162.
34 Baring-Gould, *The Book of Werewolves*, p. 108.
35 From Benjamin Thorpe, ed., 'The Werwolf', in *Yule Tide Stories: A Collection of Scandinavian and North German Popular Tales and Traditions* (London, 1863), p. 7.
36 Ibid., p. 11.
37 Ibid., p. 15.
38 Baring-Gould, *The Book of Werewolves*, p. 100.
39 Ibid.
40 Ibid., pp. 103–4.
41 Montague Summers, *The Werewolf* (London, 1933), p. 217.
42 Baring-Gould, *The Book of Werewolves*, p. 105.
43 Ibid., p. 106.
44 Summers, *The Werewolf*, p. 218.
45 Baring-Gould, *The Book of Werewolves*, p. 107.
46 Summers, *The Werewolf*, p. 218.
47 Ibid., p. 219.
48 Ibid., p. 223.
49 See ibid., p. 228.
50 Pierre de Rostegny de Lancre, *Tableau de l'inconstance des mauvais anges et demons* (1613), pp. 252–326.
51 See the *London Magazine* (21 December 1764).
52 For more on the 'Beast of Gévaudan', see J.D.C. Linnell et al., 'The Fear of Wolves: A Review of Wolf Attacks on Humans', *Norsk Institutt For Naturforskning*, 731 (January 2002); Michel Louis, *La Bête du Gévaudan: l'innocence des loups* (Perrin, 2001).
53 Douglas Starr, *The Killer of Little Shepherds* (London, 2011), p. 112.
54 Eugen Weber, *Peasants into Frenchmen: The Modernisation of Rural France, 1870–1914* (Stanford, CA, 1976), p. 21.
55 Quoted from Starr, *The Killer of Little Shepherds*, p. 78.

SIX: Of Wolf and Man: *Werewolf Cases from Europe*

1 For a modern interpretation of Vlad Dracula, see Chapter Five of my *From Demons to Dracula* (London, 2008). See also, M. J. Trow, *Vlad the Impaler* (London, 2003).

2 Quoted in Sabine Baring-Gould, *Book of Werewolves* (London, 1865), p. 182.

3 Ibid., p. 183.

4 Ibid., p. 186.

5 Ibid.

6 Ibid., p. 191.

7 Ibid., pp. 204–5.

8 Ibid., p. 211.

9 Ibid. p. 220–21.

10 Ibid. pp. 228–9.

11 Margaret Murray, *The Witch-Cult in Western Europe* (Oxford, 1921), Appendix IV.

12 Ibid.

13 Ibid.

14 Ibid.

15 Montague Summers, *The Werewolf* (London, 1933), p. 224.

16 Ibid., p. 224.

17 Baring-Gould, *Book of Werewolves*, p. 73.

18 Ibid., p. 75

19 Summers, *The Werewolf*, p. 227.

20 Daniel d'Auge, *Arreste contre Gilles Garnier* (Paris 1574).

21 Baring-Gould, *Book of Werewolves*, p. 78.

22 Ibid., p. 74.

23 Reprinted in full in Summers, *The Werewolf*, pp. 253–9.

24 See Henri Boguet's *Discours de Sorciers* [1610], trans. Montague Summers (New York, 2009).

25 Baring-Gould, *Book of Werewolves*, p. 78.

26 Ibid., p. 79.

27 Boguet, *Discours de Sorciers.*

28 Baring-Gould, *Book of Werewolves*, pp. 81–2.

29 Ibid., p. 84.

30 Ibid., p. 87.

31 Ibid., p. 89.

32 Ibid., p. 92.

33 Ellen Tullo, 'Duke Ferdinand: Patient or Possessed? The Reflection of Contemporary Medical Discourse in John Webster's "The Duchess of Malfi"', *Journal of Medical Ethics*, XXXVI/1 (2010), pp. 19–22.

34 John Webster, *The Duchess of Malfi*, v. ii. 8–9, in David Gunby, ed., *John Webster: Three Plays* (Harmondsworth, 1972).

35 Ibid., p. 19.

36 Ibid., I. ii.184.
37 Brett D. Hirsch, 'An Italian Werewolf in London: Lycanthropy and "The Duchess of Malfi"', *Early Modern Literary Studies*, XI/2 (September 2005), pp. 1–34.
38 Henry Holland, *A Dialogue Concerning Witches and Witchcraftes* (London, 1593).
39 Tullo, 'Duke Ferdinand: Patient or Possessed?', p. 22.
40 Gunby, ed., *John Webster: Three Plays*, p. 445.
41 Hirsch, 'An Italian Werewolf in London', p. 9.
42 Ibid., pp. 10–11.
43 Ibid., p. 13.
44 Ibid.
45 Edmund Spenser, *A View of the State of Ireland* (Dublin, 1633)
46 Bob Curran, *Werewolves: A Field Guide to Shapeshifters, Lycanthropes and Man-Beasts* (Pompton Plains, 2009).
47 Ibid.
48 *The Travels of Cosmo the Third, Grand Duke of Tuscany* [1699], ed. Lorenzo Magalotti (Memphis, TN, 2010).
49 Quoted from Ralph Montagu Scott, 'The History, Character and Description of the Irish Wolfhound', *Irish Wolfhound Association* (September 1925).
50 Étienne-Jean Géorget, *Examen médical des procès criminels* (Paris, 1825).
51 Quoted from Louise Welsh, 'Sympathy for the Devil', *The Guardian* (9 June 2007).
52 William Gray, *Robert Louis Stevenson: A Literary Life* (Basingstoke, 2004).
53 Robert Louis Stevenson, 'A Chapter on Dreams', in *Across the Plains* (London, 1892).
54 See John A. Sanford *Evil: The Shadow side of Reality,* (New York, 1981)
55 Romans 7: 20.
56 Welsh, 'Sympathy for the Devil'.
57 Stevenson, 'A Chapter on Dreams'.
58 Ibid.
59 Ibid.

SEVEN: Methods to the Madness:
Medical Explanations of the Werewolf Myth

1 Montague Summers, *The Werewolf* (London, 1933), p. 2.
2 Sabine Baring-Gould, *The Book of Werewolves* (London, 1865), pp. 153–4.
3 Ibid., p. 130.
4 'The Social Biology of the Werewolf Trials', letter from W.M.S. and C. Russell in the *Journal of the Royal Society of Medicine*, LXXXII (June 1989), p. 379.
5 Francis Adams, trans., *The Seven Books of Paulus Aegineta*, 2 (London, 1844), pp. 389–90.

6   See Charlotte Otten, *A Lycanthropy Reader* (Syracuse, NY, 1986), pp. 24–5.

7   Robert Burton, *The Anatomy of Melancholy* (1621), Subsect IV.

8   Johannes Arculanus, *In Nonum Librum Almansoris Expositio*, caput. xvi, *De Melancholia* (1557), pp. 28–33.

9   Baring-Gould, *The Book of Werewolves*, p. 145.

10 Ibid., p. 144.

11 Ibid.

12 Charles Morel, *Études cliniques* (Paris, 1852), II, p. 58.

13 Summers, *The Werewolf*, p. 51.

14 Baring-Gould, *The Book of Werewolves*, p. 144.

15 Girolamo Mercuriale, *Medicina Practica* (Frankfurt, 1601), lib. i, cap. xii, *De Lykanthropia*.

16 Adams, trans., *The Seven Books*, pp. 389–90.

17 Algernon Herbert, 'Letter to Lord Cawdor', 12 March 1831, in *William and the Werewolf*, trans. Frederick Madden (London, 1832), p. 17.

18 The source refers to Louis Pasteur (1822–1895), the French chemist and microbiologist; 'The Social Biology of the Werewolf Trials', letter from W.M.S and C. Russell.

19 Joe McNally, 'All right Nowooo!', in *Bizarre Magazine*, XXI (June 1999).

20 Ibid.

21 Ibid.

22 Elizabeth Page-Nelson, 'Explanations for Vampires and Werewolves: Real, Medical or Mental?': www.excollege.tufts.edu.

23 Matthew Beresford, *From Demons to Dracula* (London, 2008), p. 104.

24 Lee Illis, 'On Porphyria and the Aetiology of Werwolves' in *Proceedings of the Royal Society of Medicine*, 57 (1964), p. 23.

25 Ibid., p. 25.

26 Ibid., p. 26.

27 David Dolphin, 'Werewolves and Vampires', paper given at the annual meeting of the American Association for the Advancement of Science (1985).

28 Jennifer Cruver-Plaza, 'Lycanthropy: Myth and Medical: The Theoretical History of Lycanthropy': www.suite101.com.

29 'The Social Biology of the Werewolf Trials', letter from W.M.S. and C. Russell.

30 McNally, 'All right Nowooo!'.

31 H. Sidky, *Witchcraft, Lycanthropy, Drugs and Disease: An anthropological Study of the European Witch-hunts* (New York, 1997).

32 See 'Werewolf Boy', www.dailymail.co.uk, 21 December 2007.

33 R. M. Rashid and L. E. White, 'A Hairy Development in Hypertrichosis: A Brief Review of Ambras Syndrome', *Dermatology Online Journal*, XIII/ 3 (2007).

34 For a detailed discussion of Vlad Dracula and his alleged connections to Bram Stoker's creation, see chapter Five of Beresford, *From Demons to Dracula*.

35 'Solving the Mystery of the Bearded Lady', http://news.sciencemag.org.
36 Ibid.
37 See Katharine Ramsland, 'The Werewolf Syndrome: Compulsive Bestial Slaughterers.', http://www.trutv.com.
38 Richard Rowlands, *A Restitution of Decayed Intelligence* (Antwerp, 1605).
39 Reginald Scott, *A Discoverie of Witchcraft* (London, 1584), p. 276.
40 Johann Weyer *Deceptions of Demons* [1583], trans. John Shea (Binghamton, NY, 1991).
41 'The Social Biology of the Werewolf Trials', letter from W.M.S. and C. Russell.
42 Jaroslav Nemec, *Witchcraft and Medicine (1484–1793)* (Washington, DC, 1974), pp. 6–7.
43 Jean de Nynauld, *De la Lycanthropie* (Paris, 1615).
44 Sabine Baring-Gould, *The Book of Werewolves* (London, 1865), pp. 149–50.
45 Burton, *Anatomy of Melancholy*, Subsect III.
46 Ibid.
47 See John Martin, *Four Hundred Years Later: An Appreciation of Johann Weyer* (Iowa City, IA, 1993).
48 Nemec, *Witchcraft and Medicine*, p. 3.
49 See Daniel Sennert, *Practica Medicina*, Lib. I, pars ii, cap. xvi, in *Opera omnia* (Paris, 1641).
50 Ibid.
51 Nemec, *Witchcraft and Medicine*, p. 3.
52 Keith Thomas, *Religion and the Decline of Magic* (Harmondsworth, 1985), p. 560.
53 Ibid., p. 569.
54 Cited by George Lyman Kittredge, *Witchcraft in Old and New England* (Cambridge, MA, 1929), p. 135.
55 Denis Hill, 'John Darrell: Exorcist or Exhibitionist?': www.ourmansfieldsarea.org.uk.
56 E. Garner, *Hanged for Three Pennies: The Story of Capital Punishment in Derbyshire* (Derby, 2000), p. 63.
57 Ibid., p. 63.
58 Ibid., p. 63.
59 See The Devil is an Ass': http://personal.rhul.ac.uk.
60 Nemec, *Witchcraft and Medicine*, p. 5.
61 F.H.D. in Hildesheim, *Factus inde Maniacus*, spic. 2, Fol. 147.
62 Ramsland, 'The Werewolf Syndrome'.
63 Bram Stoker, *Dracula* [1897] (Harmondsworth, 1994), pp. 21–3.
64 Summers, *The Werewolf*, p. 16.
65 Ibid., p. 23.
66 King James VI and I, *Dæmonologie* (Edinburgh, 1597), II.5.
67 See Dr N. Parker, *Journal of Medical Science* (1854), p. 52.

68 Daniel Hach Tuke, *Dictionary of Psychological Medicine* (Philadelphia, 1892), II, pp. 752–5.
69 Illis *On Porphyria*, p. 24.
70 Summers, *The Werewolf*, p. 22.
71 Richard Noll, *Vampires, Werewolves and Demons: Twentieth Century Reports in the Psychiatric Literature* (London, 1992).
72 Ramsland, *The Werewolf Syndrome*.
73 Ibid.
74 Ibid.
75 *The Daily Telegraph* (14 December 2009).
76 Leonie A. Calver, Barrie J. Stokes and Geoffrey K. Isbister, 'The Dark Side of the Moon', *Medical Journal of Australia*, CXCI/ 11/12, 7/21 (December 2009), pp. 692–4.
77 Ibid., p. 693.
78 Ibid.
79 Aristotle, *De Part Animal*, II, 7: *De Sens et Sensato*, II: *De Somn. Et Virgil*, III: www.classics.mit.edu/aristotle/parts_animals.html.
80 Thomas Aquinas, *Summa Theologica*, Part I, Q.115 (1274): www.ccel/aquinas/summa.html.
81 Matthew 4: 24 and 17: 15 (Authorized Version).
82 Aquinas, *Summa Theologica*, Part I, Q.115 (1274).

EIGHT: Evolution Creates Dissolution: *The End of the Myth?*

1 Brian Regal, 'Where have all the Werewolves Gone?', in *Fortean Times* (March 2010).
2 Letter from Charles Darwin to G. R. Waterhouse, 3 December 1843, *The Life and Letters of Charles Darwin* (London, 1887), II: www.darwin-online.org.uk.
3 Michael Pitts and Mark Roberts, *Fairweather Eden* (London, 1998), p. 14.
4 Douglas Starr, *The Killer of Little Shepherds* (London, 2011).
5 Ibid.
6 Albert Sarrout, *La dépêche de Toulouse* (10 November, 1897).
7 Starr, *The Killer*, p. 192.
8 Ibid., p. 55.
9 E. Fourquet, *Vâcher: Le plus grand criminal des temps modernes par son juge d'instruction* (Besançon, 1931), pp. 30–31.
10 Starr, *The Killer*, p. 197.
11 Ibid., p. 195.
12 Ibid., p. 201.
13 Ibid., p. 221.
14 Ibid., p. 174.
15 Gustave Le Bron, in Laurent Mucchielli, 'Criminology, Hygienism and Eugenics in France, 1870–1914', in *Criminals and their Scientists: The*

History of Criminology in International Perspective, ed. P. Becker and
R. F. Wetzell (Cambridge, 2006), p. 212.
16 Maurice de Fleury, *The Criminal Mind* (1898).
17 'Le tueur de bergers' in *La dépêche de Toulouse* (7 November 1897).
18 Philippe Artières, *Le livre des vies coupables: autobiographies de criminels
(1896–1909)* (Paris, 2000), pp. 285–6: a translation by Nicole Edelmen
is at www.rh19.revues.org/269.
19 Starr, *The Killer*, p. 249.
20 Sigmund Freud, *The History of an Infantile Neurosis* [1918] (London,
1990).
21 Ibid., p. 259.
22 Ibid., p. 260.
23 Ibid., p. 261.
24 Muriel Gardner, ed., *The Wolf-Man and Sigmund Freud*
(Harmondsworth, 1973), p. 24.
25 'Letters Pertaining to Freud's History of an Infantile Neurosis',
Psychoanalytic Quarterly, XXVI (1957), p. 449.
26 Freud, *History of an Infantile Neurosis*, p. 261.
27 Stephen Greenblatt, *Renaissance Self-Fashioning: From More to
Shakespeare* (Chicago, 1980).
28 'Who was the Wolf-Man?', interview with Lawrence Johnson on *The
Philosopher's Zone*, ABC National Radio, 28 October 2006.
29 Lawrence Johnson, *The Wolf-Man's Burden* (New York, 2001).
30 Carlo Ginzburg, 'Freud, the Wolf-Man and the Werewolves', in *Clues,
Myths and the Historical Method*, trans. John and Anne C. Tedeschi
(Baltimore, MD, 1986), pp. 146–55.
31 'Declassified war papers reveal Nazi plan to spread death and fear with
poisoned food', *i Newspaper* (4 April 2011).
32 Ibid.
33 Nick Redfern, 'The Werewolves of Britain', posted 11 March 2006,
www.cryptomundo.com.
34 Ibid.
35 Ibid.
36 'Wes', comment posted 18 May 2007, in a reply to Nick Redfern's article
'There's something in the woods'.
37 F. G. Surawicz and R. Banta, Lycanthropy Revisited', *Canadian
Psychiatric Association Journal*, XX (1975), pp. 537–42.
38 T. A. Fahy, 'Lycanthropy: A Review', *Journal of the Royal Society of
Medicine*, LXXXII (January 1989), pp. 37–40.
39 R. Eisler, *Man into Wolf* (Santa Barbara, CA, 1978).
40 Carl Jung, *The Development of Personality* (London, 1954).
41 P. M. Jackson, 'Another Case of Lycanthropy', *American Journal of
Psychiatry*, 135/1 (1978), pp. 134–5.
42 H. A. Rosenstock and K. R. Vincent, 'A Case of Lycanthropy', *American
Journal of Psychiatry*, 134/10 (1977), pp. 1147–9.

43 P. A. Keck, G. P. Harrison, J. I. Hudson, et al., 'Lycanthropy: Alive and Well in the Twentieth Century', *Psychological Medicine*, XVIII/1 (1988), pp. 113–20.

44 Ibid.

45 *Daily Mirror* (4 July 1970).

46 *Fortean Times* 25:8.

47 The Mysterious case of the shadowy werewolf', www.gbhw.co.uk.

48 Ibid.

49 Ibid.

50 Ibid.

51 Don Robins, The Secret Language of Stone (London, 1988), pp. 4–9.

52 See 'The Wolves of Hexham', www.bbc.co.uk.

53 Charles Fort, *Lo!* (New York, 1931), pp. 157–8.

54 Interview with John Landis, bonus on the DVD of *An American Werewolf in London*.

55 Quoted from David Clarke, 'Cursed Stones: The Mouselow Mystery', *Peak District Magazine* (2003): www.drdavidclarke.co.uk/urban-legendary/cursed-stones.

56 Ibid.

57 Ibid.

58 Ibid.

59 Ibid.

60 Ibid.

61 'Himmelsscheibe von Nebra: Das Gold stammt aus England', *Focus Magazine* (12 May 2010): www.focus.de.

62 See http://mediumjoannebrown.webs.com._

63 Quoted from an anonymous email received by D. L. Ashlimann at the University of Pittsburgh, 16 November 1998: www.pitt.edu/~dash/werewolf.html#morbach.

64 From a posting by 'Ann', 'Broadmoor Sirens', www.bagshotvillage.org.uk.

65 See 'Werewolves', www.bbc.co.uk.

66 See www.bbc.co.uk, 6 May 2008.

67 'Wolf-like creature terrifies motorists', *Birmingham Post* (28 June 2006).

68 Ibid.

69 *Stafford Post* (26 April 2007).

70 'Werewolf sightings on Cannock Chase part of new paranormal report', *Birmingham Post* (28 September 2009).

71 Claudia Puig, 'Red Riding Hood: The better to bore you with', *USA Today*, www.usatoday.com.

SELECT BIBLIOGRAPHY

Alt, S., et al., 'Twenty-Five Thousand-Year-old Triple Burial from
    Dolní Věstonice: An Ice Age Family?', *American Journal of Physical
    Anthropology* CII/1 (1997), pp. 123–31
Aldhouse-Green, S. and P. Pettitt, 'Paviland Cave: Contextualising the Red
    Lady', *Antiquity*, LXII/278 (1998), pp. 756–72
Armstrong, A. L.,'Discovery of an Engraved Drawing of a Masked Human
    Figure', *Proceedings of the Prehistoric Society of East Anglia*, VI/1 (1929),
    pp. 27–9
Baring-Gould, S., *The Book of Werewolves* (London, 1865)
Bates, B., *The Real Middle Earth* (London, 2003)
Beauvois de Chavincourt, Jean, *Discours de la Lycanthropie ou de la
    transmutation des hommes en loups* (Paris, 1599)
Beck, R., *Beck on Mithraism: Collected Works With New Essays* (London, 2004)
Becker, P. and R. F. Wetzell , eds, *Criminals and their Scientists: The History
    of Criminology in International Perspective* (Cambridge, 2006)
Beresford, M., *From Demons to Dracula* (London, 2008)
——, *Beyond the Ice* (Oxford, 2012)
Binford, L., *Bones: Ancient Men and Modern Myths* (Michigan, 1981)
Boguet, H., *Discours de Sorciers* (1610)
Bourgault du Coudray, C., *The Curse of the Werewolf* (London, 2006)
Bulliet, R., et al., *The Earth and its Peoples: A Global History to 1550*, 4th edn
    (2009)
Burton, R., *The Anatomy of Melancholy* (1621)
Buxton, R., *Interpretations of Greek Mythology* (London, 1987)
Campbell, J. B., *The Upper Palaeolithic of Britain* (Oxford, 1977)
Campbell, J. G., *Witchcraft and Second Sight in the Highlands and Islands of
    Scotland* (Glasgow, 1902)
Carrington, D., *The Dream-Hunters of Corsica* (London, 1996)
Casamiquela, R., *El arte rupestre de la Patagonia* (Siringa, Neuquen, 1981)
Castleden, R, *The Knossos Labyrinth: A New View of the 'Palace of Minos' At
    Knossos* (London, 1990)

Clauss, M., *The Roman Cult of Mithras* (Edinburgh, 2000)

Coles, J. M. and E. S. Higgs, *The Archaeology of Early Man* (London, 1969)

Cunliffe, B., ed., *The Oxford Illustrated History of Prehistoric Europe* (Oxford, 2001)

Curran, B., *Werewolves: A Field Guide to Shapeshifters, Lycanthropes and Man-Beasts* (Morris County, NJ, 2009)

Demetracopoulou, D., 'Greek Accounts of the Vrykolakas', *The Journal of American Folklore*, 54 (1941), pp. 126–32

Diakomanolis, E., K. Stefanidis, A. Rodolakis et al., 'Vaginal intraepithelial neoplasia: report of 102 cases', European Journal of Gynaecological Oncology XXIII/5 (2002)

Eisler, R., *Man into Wolf* (Santa Barbara, CA, 1978)

Ellis, S., *The Man Who Lives With Wolves* (London, 2010)

Fourquet, E., *Vâcher: Le plus grand criminel des temps modernes par son juge d'instruction* (Besançon, 1931)

Freud, S., *The History of an Infantile Neurosis* (London, 1990)

Gardner, M., ed., *The Wolf-Man and Sigmund Freud* (Harmondsworth, 1973)

Garner, E., *Hanged for Three Pennies: The Story of Capital Punishment in Derbyshire* (Derby, 2000)

Georget, E.-J., *Examen médical des procès criminels* (Paris, 1825)

Gerard, E., 'Transylvanian Superstitions', in *XIX Century*, XVIII (1885), pp. 130–50

Germonpré, M. et al., 'DNA' *Journal of Archaeological Science*, XXXVI/2 (2009), pp. 473–90

Gray, W., *Robert Louis Stevenson: A Literary Life* (Basingstoke, 2004)

Greenblatt, S., *Renaissance Self-Fashioning: From More to Shakespeare* (Chicago, 1980)

Greenwood, J., *The Wilds of London* (London, 1874)

Grigsby, J., *Beowulf and Grendel* (London, 2005)

Gunby, D., ed., *John Webster: Three Plays* (Harmondsworth, 1972)

Hamel, F., *Human Animals* (London, 1915)

Herbert, A., 'Letter to Lord Cawdor', 12 March 1831, in *William and the Werewolf*, trans. Frederick Madden (London, 1832)

Hirsch, B. D., ''*Early Modern Literary Studies*, XI/2 (September 2005), pp. 1–34

Hodder, I., 'New Finds and New Interpretations at Çatalhöyük', *2005 Archive Report*, Çatalhöyük Research Project, Institute of Archaeology (2005)

Holland, H., *A Dialogue Concerning Witches and Witchcraftes* (London, 1593)

Illis, L., 'On Porphyria and the Aetiology of Werwolves', *Proceedings of the Royal Society of Medicine*, LVII (1964), pp. 23–6

Johnson, L., *The Wolf-Man's Burden* (New York, 2001)

Jung, C., *The Development of Personality* (London, 1954)

Kelly, E. P., 'Secrets of the Bog Bodies: The Enigma of the Iron Age

Explained', *Archaeology Ireland*, xx/1 (2006), pp. 26–30

Koslowski, S. K., and E. Sachse-Koslowska, 'Maszycka Cave: A Magdalenian Site in Southern Poland', *Jahrbuch der Römisch-Germanischen Zentralmuseums Mainz*, xL/1 (1993), pp. 115–205

Labunsky, A., *The Central Asian Hounds: The Travel Notes of a Cynologist* (Dnepropetrovsk, 1994)

Lawson, J. C., *Modern Greek Folklore and Ancient Greek Religion* (New York, 1964)

Lewin, R., *Human Evolution: An Illustrated Introduction* (Washington, DC, 1993)

Lewis, B. R., *Ritual Sacrifice* (Stroud, 2001)

Lewis-Williams, D., *The Mind in the Cave* (London, 2008)

Martin, J., *Four Hundred Years Later: An Appreciation of Johann Weyer* (1993)

Maturin, C. R., *The Albigensis*, II (1824)

Meece, S., 'A Bird's Eye View – of a Leopard's Spots: The Çatalhöyük 'Map' and the Development of Cartographic Representation in Prehistory', *Anatolian Studies*, LVI (2006), pp. 1–16

Megaw, R. and V. Megaw, *Celtic Art* (London, 1990)

Mellaart, J., *Catal Huyuk: A Neolithic Town in Anatolia* (New York, 1967)

Michels, A. K., 'The Topography and Interpretation of the Lupercalia', *Transactions and Proceedings of the American Philological Association*, LXXXIV (1953), pp. 35–59

Mithen, S., *After the Ice* (London, 2003)

Moore, J. H., *The Universal Kinship* (Chicago, 1906)

Mulford, P., *The Gift of the Spirit* (London, 1904)

Mulhall, I., Isabella Mulhall, 'The Peat Men from Clonycavan and Oldcroghan', *British Archaeology*, 110 (January / February 2010)

Murray, M., *The Witch-Cult in Western Europe* (Oxford, 1921)

de Nynauld, J, *De la Lycanthropie* (1615)

Nemec, J., *Witchcraft and Medicine (1484–1793)* (Washington, DC, 1974)

O'Donnell, E., *Werwolves* (London, 1912)

Oliva, M., *Palaeolithic and Mesolithic Moravia* (Brno, 2005)

Otten, C., *A Lycanthropy Reader* (Syracuse, NY, 1986)

Owen-Crocker, G., *The Four Funerals in Beowulf* (Manchester, 2009)

Pettitt, P., *The Palaeolithic Origins of Human Burial* (London, 2010)

Pitts, M. and M. Roberts, *Fairweather Eden* (London, 1998)

Rashid., R. M. and L. E. White, 'A Hairy Development in Hypertrichosis: A Brief Review of Ambras Syndrome', *Dermatology Online Journal*, XIII/ 3 (2007)

Rhys, J., *Celtic Folklore, Welsh and Manx* (London, 1901)

Robins, D., *The Secret Language of Stone* (London, 1988)

Rowlands, R., *A Restitution of Decayed Intelligence* (1605)

Sanford, J. A., *Evil: The Shadow side of Reality* (New York, 1981)

Sconduto, L., *Metamorphoses of the Werewolf* (Jefferson, NC, 2009)

Scott, R., *A Discoverie of Witchcraft* (1584)

Senn, H., 'Romanian Werewolves: Seasons, Ritual, Cycles', *Folklore*, XCIII/2 (1982), pp. 206–15

Sidky, H., *Witchcraft, Lycanthropy, Drugs and Disease: An Anthropological Study of the European Witch-hunts* (New York, 1997)

Spenser, E., *A View of the State of Ireland* (Dublin, 1633)

Starr, D., *The Killer of Little Shepherds* (London, 2011)

Strecker, M. and P. Bahn, *Dating and the Earliest Known Rock Art* (Oxford, 1999)

Summers, M., *The Werewolf* (London, 1933)

Thomas, K., *Religion and the Decline of Magic* (Harmondsworth, 1985)

Weber, E., *Peasants into Frenchmen: The Modernisation of Rural France, 1870–1914* (Stanford, CA, 1976)

Weyer, J., *Deceptions of Demons* (1583)

ACKNOWLEDGEMENTS

Thanks go to my publisher, Michael Leaman, at Reaktion for the initial book concept. As with *From Demons to Dracula*, my previous book, I have been aided greatly by both Michael and his team.

Special thanks must also go to those who gave advice, suggestions and clarifications. I would like to express my gratitude to Amanda Hopkins at the University of Warwick for her suggestions on the Breton Lays, Paul Screeton for his advice on the Hexham Heads case, Alison Wilson at the University of Nottingham for allowing me to reproduce the Southwell deviant skeleton photograph, and Will Bowden, also from the University of Nottingham, as well as to the many others who have helped me.

PHOTO ACKNOWLEDGEMENTS

The author and the publishers wish to express their thanks to the below sources of illustrative material and /or permission to reproduce it.

Creswell Heritage Trust: p. 21; University of Nottingham: p. 121. For all other material, Matt Beresford: pp. 62, 68, 69, 76, 90, 107, 228.

INDEX

Index